The Nature of Educational Theories

This important book offers a meta-theoretical account of educational theories and how they work. It offers a classification scheme of distinct types of educational theory in which the account developed can inform the work of educational theorists and practitioners.

Kvernbekk observes throughout how meta-theoretical knowledge of the structure of theory types will improve the understanding and representation of educational phenomena and enhance theorists' and practitioners' ability to change those phenomena for the better. She explains how philosophical accounts of scientific theories can help us understand the nature of educational theories by applying two influential but different theory conceptions – the Received View and the Semantic Conception – to the field of education. Kvernbekk argues that educational theories, like other scientific theories, are representational devices that allow us to understand, describe and explain phenomena, and, when desired, to change them. The classification scheme offered allows us to discriminate distinct types of educational theory: goal-directed, equivalence and interlevel theories. Examples of all three types are discussed, explaining their structure, what they say about the phenomena and how they say it. The book also offers a critical overview of different conceptions of practice and different understandings of the theory–practice relationship.

Encouraging a strong understanding of what theories say about the phenomena they represent, this book will be of interest to educational researchers and postgraduate students in the fields of philosophy of education, education theory and education policy, and to philosophers of science and philosophers working on 'practical' philosophical issues.

Tone Kvernbekk is Professor of philosophy of education in the Department of Education at the University of Oslo, Norway. She mainly publishes on philosophical and epistemological issues as they bear on problems in educational theorizing. She also publishes in argumentation theory and narrative theory and likes to combine perspectives and draw on multiple sources.

Routledge Research in Education

This series aims to present the latest research from right across the field of education. It is not confined to any particular area or school of thought and seeks to provide coverage of a broad range of topics, theories and issues from around the world.

Recent titles in the series include:

Towards Rational Education
A Social Framework of Moral Values and Practices
Demetris Katsikis

Schooling and Social Change Since 1760
Creating Inequalities through Education
Roy Lowe

Pioneering Perspectives in Cooperative Learning
Theory, Research, and Classroom Practice for Diverse Approaches to CL
Edited by Neil Davidson

Activity Theory and Collaborative Intervention in Education
Expanding Learning in Japanese Schools and Communities
Edited by Katsuhiro Yamazumi

Developing Trauma-Responsive Approaches to Student Discipline
A Guide to Trauma-Informed Practice in PreK-12 Schools
Kirk Eggleston, Erinn J. Green, Shawn Abel, Stephanie Poe, and Charol Shakeshaft

Interculturality and the Political within Education
Fred Dervin and Ashley Simpson

For a complete list of titles in this series, please visit www.routledge.com/Routledge-Research-in-Education/book-series/SE0393

The Nature of Educational Theories

Goal-Directed, Equivalence and Interlevel Theories

Tone Kvernbekk

Routledge
Taylor & Francis Group
LONDON AND NEW YORK

First published 2021
by Routledge
2 Park Square, Milton Park, Abingdon, Oxon OX14 4RN

and by Routledge
605 Third Avenue, New York, NY 10158

Routledge is an imprint of the Taylor & Francis Group, an informa business

British Library Cataloguing-in-Publication Data
A catalogue record for this book is available from the British Library

Library of Congress Cataloging-in-Publication Data
Names: Kvernbekk, Tone, author.
Title: The nature of educational theories : goal-directed, equivalence and interlevel theories / Tone Kvernbekk.
Description: Abingdon, Oxon ; New York, NY : Routledge, 2021. |
Series: Routledge research in education | Includes bibliographical references and index.
Identifiers: LCCN 2020055226 (print) | LCCN 2020055227 (ebook) |
ISBN 9781138488557 (hardback) | ISBN 9781351039987 (ebook)
Subjects: LCSH: Education–Philosophy.
Classification: LCC LB14.7 .K86 2021 (print) | LCC LB14.7 (ebook) |
DDC 370.1–dc23
LC record available at https://lccn.loc.gov/2020055226
LC ebook record available at https://lccn.loc.gov/2020055227

ISBN: 978-1-138-48855-7 (hbk)
ISBN: 978-1-032-01067-0 (pbk)
ISBN: 978-1-351-03998-7 (ebk)

Typeset in Galliard
by Taylor & Francis Books

Contents

Figures

Preface

For as long as I can remember I have been interested in abstract matters. When I trained as an elementary school teacher in the 1980s, I was, I presume, the only student who did not look forward to placement in schools. I much preferred theoretical studies in college to practice in schools. This may sound like a paradox for two related reasons: first because I naturally thought I was going to work as a teacher, and second, because I, like my fellow students, perceived the problems of using theory in practice. It did not work and did not fit. Nevertheless, I wanted *more* theory. Thus, after graduating from teacher education college I went on to university study, where I gradually developed an interest in meta-theory. Theory about theory – it does not get more abstract than that.

The world of education is full of theories and appeals to theory in educational scholarship are ubiquitous: education scholars of all stripes routinely construct, discuss, critique, and/or apply theories in their research. They might, however mean different things with the term, and one of the aims of this book is to provide "theory" in education with substantive content. This is a book about the nature of theories in general, and about the various types of theories we find in the field of education.

A lot of people deserve thanks. First and foremost the philosophers whose views I have studied, wrestled with, revisited, and learned so much from. I am greatly indebted to all of them. I would like to extend my general thanks and greetings to friends and colleagues in various Philosophy of Education networks around the globe, for good discussions, friendship and much fun over the years. As always, thanks are also due to the members of the Humanities in Education research group at the University of Oslo for being there, asking incisive questions and providing encouragement throughout the process. Last, but not least, special thanks go to Ola Bøe-Hansen, who has drawn up the figures.

Oslo, November 2020
Tone Kvernbekk

1 Introduction

This book is about the various types of theories we find in the field of education and their nature. The world of education is full of theories: theories of reading, upbringing, motivation, *Bildung*, instruction, and so on. Appeals to theory in education scholarship are ubiquitous: education scholars, whatever their specialties, routinely construct, critique, and/or apply theories in their research. But what is an educational theory, exactly? Different answers to that question have been proposed by different scholars over the years. The answer I provide in this book will in significant respects differ from the others. In order to identify different kinds of theories we need a meta-theoretical framework to guide our search. In that regard this book is also a meta-theoretical book: it presents and compares two major meta-theories. Armed with my preferred meta-theory – the Semantic Conception (SC) of theories – I offer a classification scheme that allows us to discriminate distinct types of educational theory, discuss a number of specific theories and their theoretical strengths and weaknesses, offer an account of how educational practice relates to theory, and provide general insights into the uses (and misuses) of theory. Thus, while the topic of this book is highly abstract, it does have important practical implications. Theorizing that is unreflective about theory itself – its nature, its good-making features, and its presumed tasks – will likely lead to many misunderstandings about what theories *say*, *how* they say it, what they can and cannot do for us, and what it is reasonable and unreasonable to critique them for. A suitable meta-theory will add to our understanding and representation of educational phenomena, and may, by improving these, enhance our ability to change those phenomena for the better.

My unpublished doctoral dissertation, *In search of the nature of educational theories* (Kvernbekk, 1994), will provide much of the backbone for this book; but updated, extended, deepened, repackaged and critically discussed. In a sense I am borrowing from myself, but it is a transformative form of borrowing, not a merely derivative one. Working on this book has given me a welcome opportunity to revisit my own dissertation and how it came about. Even at the university I could not let go of the question of theory and practice. But the question took on philosophical rather than practical overtones. Textbooks would typically define education (pedagogy) as an intentional discipline, with theories that aim at modifying and improving the world in some way. Such theories were described as "practical" or as "applied", as opposed to "theoretical" or "pure", as described by, for example Reidar Myhre (1980) and Hans Skjervheim (1992). Pure theories are supposed to be *about* some phenomenon, practical theories are supposed to be *for* it (in the sense of guiding actions). Hence, the distinction between practical educational theories and theoretical scientific theories got firmly ingrained in my mind during my student years, and clearly came to the fore in my master's thesis. My master's thesis in the philosophy of education was about the basic educational metaphors "influence" and "development" and how they played out in educational theory. For this I needed a concept of theory and I found it in Carl Hempel's writings (Hempel, 1966). I did not know then what I know now about Hempel, namely that he adhered to a certain meta-theory, the so-called Received View of theories (RV), which is the logical-empiricist view of theories. So I tried my best to adapt his view of theories to the practical theories of education, connecting Hempel's axiomatic calculus to basic views of human nature and his bridge principles to a didactical "superstructure" consisting of aims, content and methods of instruction. Human nature supposedly served as a basis from which aims, content and method were derived or deduced.

I recall being rather dissatisfied with this rendering of educational theory, for two reasons. First, I worried about the coherence of such theories, since authors with the same view of human nature demonstrably advocated different aims, content and methods. Second, most of the theories I encountered in textbooks simply could not be called "practical", despite clearly belonging to the domain of education. The intellectual restlessness thus experienced led me to my dissertation. My dissertation proposal directly attacked the notion of an educational theory, but still with the understanding that all educational theories were supposed to be *for* education; that is, practical and action-guiding in nature. I proposed to find out what characteristics and elements a theory would need to possess, on the assumption that they should not only tell you what to do but should also incorporate empirical facts and metaphysical presuppositions concerning what is possible. I had only been a doctoral student for a couple of months when I came across Frederick Suppe's writings on meta-theory (Suppe, 1989). Reading Suppe completely overturned my original proposal. His book alerted me to the centrality of meta-theory and supplied tools for me to come to grips with my general dissatisfaction with educational theory as action-guiding as well as with my own Hempelian rendering of it. Reading Suppe sent me searching not for the nature of educational *theory*, but for the nature of educational *theories*. The assumption that *all* educational theories are by their nature practical and action-guiding could be discarded. And with that assumption safely done away with, another assumption could follow suit: the assumption that there is a difference in kind between educational theories and scientific theories. There is not.

Working on this book has also given me a welcome opportunity to revisit some (by no means all) of the literature that I read for my dissertation. Some of this literature now counts as old, I suppose. In a day and age when research is supposed to be *recent*, one might well ask what the point is of rehearsing old literature, for example Carl Hempel, D. J. O'Connor, Paul Hirst and Erich Weniger – authors who figure prominently in my discussions. Revisiting old literature is a pleasure! It generally provides an opportunity to track how the viewpoints of various authors have changed or remained constant, and in this case it also provided me with an opportunity to reassess not only the literature but my own old viewpoints in the light of things I have learned since I defended my dissertation. Old texts are not invalid just because they are old – on the contrary, they provide insights and information, and, not least, they make good, clear examples of viewpoints in the extensive debates over the nature of educational theory. That is by and large how I use them in this book: as examples of viewpoints, not necessarily attributable to the authors in question *now*. And of course – philosophical problems, such as the nature of theory, do not grow old. That is one of the best things about them.

I entertained many implicit and at the time only vaguely understood assumptions concerning the nature of theory while I was working on my dissertation. Some of them have since taken explicit shape and can no longer be said to be "mere" assumptions for me but rather convictions. While I was able to formulate them only toward the end of my dissertation work, I list them here at the beginning of this book, as basic presuppositions underlying the chapters to follow. First, while Hirst, Myhre, Skjervheim and Weniger (and others) all take a certain view of the field of education as their point of departure for their discussions about the nature of educational theory, I hold that the *concept of theory* is an equally if not more adequate point of departure. The mentioned authors all assume a tight coupling between the presumed nature of a given discipline and the presumed nature of its theories. This coupling leads to the distinction between scientific/pure and educational/practical theories (an intentional discipline "must" have practical theories) and presupposes that education is a unified discipline with a single type of theory. I have already claimed that the distinction between scientific/pure and educational/practical theories is unfortunate and should not be upheld. A meta-theoretical approach, given a sound meta-theory, will regard the unity of the domain as an open question, and a plurality of theories can be identified. I share the meta-theoretical approach with O'Connor. He too took his point of departure in the concept of theory, but – as will become apparent in chapters to come – we employ different meta-theories.

Second, I think that *all* articulated theories, regardless of which discipline or domain they belong to, share certain central features. Third, and following from the two previous assumptions, these shared features straddle the distinction between scientific/pure and educational/practical theories. Education does not have a unique type of theory. Fourth, I assume that there are bodies of knowledge that beyond doubt can be called "educational theories". In passing, it is worth noting that the field is also full of borderline cases: bodies of knowledge that are theoretical in character, invoke theoretical (unobservable) entities, are structured to some degree and in some way, and yet their status as *theory* is unclear or ambiguous, as seen from a meta-theoretical point of view. Didactic models, for example – theories or not? Regrettably, I have not found space in this book to inquire into such cases, so for now they remain uncharted territory. All these presuppositions are substantiated throughout the book, especially in Chapters 4, 5 and 6, where I analyze different types of educational theory.

Fifth, I simply presuppose that education as a discipline, and so its theories, answers to the same kind of criteria for evaluation as do other disciplines: consistency, argument, evidential support, clarity, and so on. This presupposition underlies my discussion about the good-making features of theories in Chapter 7, and for my overall concern with the tenability of educational beliefs in general. All people form beliefs about the world and its many aspects, and in some cases tenability is of no great concern. But when educational researchers and professional practitioners construct theories and form beliefs, their theories and beliefs are potentially of great significance to a wide audience, and tenability becomes a major concern.

Finally, some comments about meta-theories are in order. First, a terminological remark. I use the term "meta-theory" to mean "theory about theory" – a second-order theory, if you like, that takes the nature of scientific theories as its object. Others use the term to mean something like "overall perspectives on science", for example Philip Higgs, editor of the volume *Metatheories in the Philosophy of Education*, takes meta-theory to address issues of what is and is not scientifically possible (Higgs, 1995). Thus, in Higgs' edited volume, empiricism, constructivism, hermeneutics, and so on, are presented as meta-theories. Second, both meta-theories that I discuss and employ in this book have received much attention by philosophers of science in the years since I submitted my dissertation. The literature now is burgeoning and it has been a delight to catch up and, again, reassess my own old viewpoints and revise them (e.g. concerning the role of language in theory individuation and counterfactuality as the nature of the relation between theory and phenomena, see Chapter 3). Third, importantly, both meta-theories to be discussed here originally grew out of the natural sciences. That requires caution and care in their application to a different field. Nevertheless, I shall argue that my meta-theory of choice, the SC, is eminently generalizable – one just has to proceed cautiously. As said above, I have come to hold that theories from all disciplines share certain features. That does not mean that the phenomena treated by those theories share the same nature – social and natural phenomena have distinctive features to be represented. Fourth, different features of the SC might come into play when it is applied to the natural sciences than when it is applied to education. For example, mathematical substructures and formalization might be more apt in, say, biology and physics than in education. I envision a feedback loop here. On the one hand, the SC, as I shall show in subsequent chapters, helps identify theories in education, their constituent elements and the various relations between those elements, and draws out the thoroughgoing effects of theory structure on issues of truth and application. On the other hand, education provides a challenge for the SC and may contribute to its development and expansion in ways not anticipated by its developers. Fifth, there is a trade-off to be made between the *discussion* of meta-theories and their *employment*. Paradoxically, given my interest in abstract entities and things, I tip the scales in favor of the applied aspect. Perhaps this is a legacy from my years in teacher training.

It means that I am leaving out a number of details and finer points concerning the two meta-theories in the interest of applying them to the field of education to see what we find there. However, I also think that showing what a meta-theory can *do* is important when it comes to judging its adequacy. After all, just like theories are supposed to do a job for us, meta-theories are also supposed to do a job for us. Roughly, I suggest, the job of meta-theories is to help us understand better *what* theories say about their phenomena and *how* they say it, as well as help us understand better what we should consider when *constructing*, *evaluating* and *using* theories.

The chapters

Chapter 2 attempts to describe and circumscribe the field of education. It will serve as a background to the types of theory that I discuss in subsequent chapters: the field is such that it has theories of this kind. A *definition* of education will not suffice for this purpose. A better approach is to look at what research in and on education looks like. The picture I draw will hardly come as a surprise, I presume: education nowadays is a pluralistic, hybrid domain with rather fluid boundaries and an unstable and contested nature. This picture does not separate education from other disciplines or domains. All scientific disciplines have grown immensely in recent years (e.g. Keiner, 2002, Terhart, 2016). The professionally oriented part of education is, to be sure, a part of the domain, but does by no means constitute the entire domain – hence, it is reasonable that such a field should have some theories that are practical and action-guiding, but it is not reasonable that all theories should be so. The state of the domain by itself strongly suggests that education encompasses a plurality of theory types. This chapter also includes a discussion of the traditional view of educational theory. The philosophy of education has witnessed longstanding discussions about the nature of educational theories. A good many authors argue that scientific and educational theories need to be firmly separated, being fundamentally different in kind (e.g. Carr, 1986, Hirst, 1966, Weniger, 1990). Typically, these writings take educational *practice* (or assumptions about its nature) as their point of departure, practice supposedly being *the* object of educational theory. They all seem to rely on the tacit premise that educational theories are of the same kind and that we are justified in talking about *the* nature of educational theory. I discussed these views in my dissertation, and here I revisit, update and expand on my selection of sources, but I by no means assume I have exhausted all possible sources. It transpires that the view of educational theory as practical is remarkably similar across the Anglo-American and the Nordic-Continental traditions. Basically, the traditional view has it that educational theories are theories *for* education, that they are normative in character and largely prescriptive, aiming to tell an educator how to proceed and act so that aims can be achieved. This understanding of the nature of theory naturally is connected to a certain understanding of the nature of the domain. This, I shall argue, unduly narrows the scope of educational theorizing.

My own preferred approach to the problem of the nature of educational theory is meta-theoretical. Thus, in Chapter 3 I look to the philosophy of science to find a suitable analytical toolkit. There are several different meta-theories to choose from. I will confine discussion to two of them: the Received View of theories (RV) and the Semantic Conception of theories (SC). RV is the logical-empiricist conception of theories, and SC is in many ways its successor. While SC is my meta-theory of choice, it is important to include a discussion of RV, for two reasons. First, it was highly influential in its day and remnants of it can still be discerned in various utterances about theory (e.g. that a theory consists of sentences and their logical connections). Second, later meta-theories tend to take their point of departure in what they view as inadequate and untenable in RV, which naturally influences what characteristics one believes an adequate meta-theory should have. SC, I shall argue, is philosophically superior to RV, and it is also the conception most able to shed light on this book's target, *educational* theories. SC is my chief analytical tool, the lens through which I view the domain of education, and I lay out its basic tenets in some detail using as my main sources (albeit supplemented by others) Bas van Fraassen (1970, 1976, 1980, 1989), Ronald Giere (1979, 1988, 2004, 2010) and Frederick Suppe (1972, 1977, 1989, 2000). SC is a rich and detailed conception that offers many resources for the identification and analysis of theories. In particular, it allows the identification of different *types* of theory, which I exploit in the next three chapters.

Chapter 4 is an analysis of *goal-directed theories* – the kind of theory that traditionally is thought to be *the* kind of theory that education has: theory *for* practice, normative and action-guiding in character. Goal-directed theories come in different sizes and shapes and I analyze a handful in some detail. I also briefly compare goal-directed theories to means-end reasoning, to tease out significant similarities and equally significant differences.

Chapter 5 examines *equivalence theories*. This is the first of two counterexamples to the traditionally conceived nature of educational theories. Unlike goal-directed theories, equivalence theories do not have built into them temporality, development or sequencing. They rather determine which *different* states we should regard as *equivalent*, as being of equal worth. The best examples are probably various forms of evaluation theories, most notably criterion-referenced evaluation, which will be familiar to all actors in the educational system. But as I discuss in this chapter, there are other examples of such theories in the field of education. In fact, it is my hypothesis that we reason much more in terms of equivalence than we are aware of.

Chapter 6 examines *interlevel theories*. This is the second counterexample; another type of theory that does not conform to the traditional idea of educational theories. "Interlevel" straightforwardly means "between levels" and points to different entities of aggregation serving in the same theory. Any field of inquiry that deals with, for instance, the relation between individuals and institutions incorporates interlevel conditions. Education is full of entities at different levels of aggregation: in addition to individuals we have families, groups, classes, schools, organizations of all kinds, culture and society. It stands to reason that interlevel theories exhibit a highly complex structure. This chapter introduces the vocabulary of grand theories and middle range theories as well as sources of inspiration from the philosophy of biology, where SC is used to analyze the structure of evolutionary theory. Since interlevel theories also bring up the issue of theoretical integration, I include a section on that.

Chapter 7 is devoted to a discussion about the good-making features of educational theories. What makes an educational theory *good*? The first part of this chapter is concerned with evaluative considerations that flow directly from employing the SSC. The second part discusses the question of whether a theory has to be true to be good, and the third part discusses the question of whether a theory has to be useful to be good. Deliberations on truth and usefulness lead straight into deep philosophical problems, and this chapter briefly introduces realism and antirealism as the two major philosophical perspectives on how to account for the success of science.

Chapter 8 is about conceptions of practice. This chapter represents a break with the general logic of this book, since no meta-theory entails a specific view of practice. All the same, practice looms large in educational contexts. It is a multi-faceted term, used in different ways by different people for different purposes. I examine three approaches to the understanding of practice. The first equates practice with the actions of the educator – a view which, incidentally, sits very well with the traditional view of educational theories. The second considers Alasdair MacIntyre's much cited and highly influential definition of practice (MacIntyre, 1996). The basic problem with both these approaches, I argue, is that they include the pedagogue but not the *educands* (students, learners) in the definition. That makes them inadequate as definitions of educational practice. The third approach is therefore an account developed to explicitly include students (or any other relevant "client" category) in the concept of educational practice. It is of vital importance, I argue, that we keep a holistic, complex and abstract conception of practice, to serve as an inoculation against unduly narrow focuses that mistake one part of practice for the whole enterprise.

Chapter 9 addresses the theory–practice relationship and how it should be conceived. The discussion requires a bird's eye view, as it were, so in this chapter both "theory" and "practice" are treated as large, undifferentiated entities. This chapter has allowed me to revisit some of my own writings on theory and practice, and I find myself in agreement with myself: the best way to understand the relationship between theory and practice, at least for some theory (but not all), is a gap. This leaves (some) theory at a distance from practice, from which it can provide surprising angles and insightful perspectives. The chapter also includes a brief examination of (practical) experience, which now and again is launched as an alternative to theory.

Chapter 10 is a continuation of Chapter 9, but also of topics introduced in previous chapters; all centered on the *use* of theory. The first section of the chapter investigates in some detail the consequences of SC for the application or use of theory; the SC version of the theory–practice relation. SC requires the separation of a theory from its method of application, and I argue that this leaves the user of the theory with much flexibility – but also requires much thought – because both abstract theoretical and contextually particular considerations can enter into decisions about what to do. I discuss this issue at length to bring out the contrasts between this way of thinking and the practice-orientation associated with the traditional view of educational theory. The second section of the chapter deals with other uses of theory. Usefulness as a good-making feature of theories, discussed in Chapter 7, is thus brought up again, but this time discussed on a much broader basis: the use of theory for the purposes of description, explanation and prediction. The third section is a short discussion of possible negative side effects of using theory.

In the Conclusion, Chapter 11, I offer some conclusions concerning what can, might and should be said about educational theories from a meta-theoretical point of view. I also offer some conclusions concerning the adequacy of meta-theories and concerning what the SC can do for the field of education. Abstract things such as meta-theories can be quite practical after all, I conclude.

2 Education

Field and theory

About one hundred years ago, in 1911, an attempt was made to establish *the* science of the child; called *pedology* (Hofstetter, 2012). This new science was supposed to treat both the origin and the future of humankind. The founders had great hopes for it, thinking it would unify all knowledge about children and education. What happened to it? Today, Hofstetter states, neither the word, nor the thing, nor the ambition exists anymore. The question is what we have instead.

What we have, I suggest, is a field that studies complex, developing and changing individual, social and institutional processes, interactions and effects; from normative, empirical, conceptual, comparative, philosophical, historical and contemporary perspectives. How young children learn to read, the historical development of curricula, educational policy, formulation of competencies, conceptions of childhood, admission to higher education, grading of exams, feedback strategies, the integration of new technology in teaching and the nature of upbringing are all hugely complex phenomena, both compositionally and dynamically. They involve multiple levels of organization, multiple actors, multiple beliefs, multiple intentions, multiple causal components and multiple effects. There are multiple levels of analysis (change, value, function, relation, cause, intention) that can be brought to bear on educational policy, processes and products. The field thus shows up a plurality of perspectives, models, approaches and explanations, all aiming to illuminate some aspect of some educational phenomenon.

Is it a science? Ellen Lagemann (2000), writing from an American point of view, thinks that the question of whether "there is or can be a 'science' of education remains controversial to this day" (p.ix). Rita Hofstetter (2012), on the other hand, writing from a Continental point of view, does not hesitate to use the term "educational sciences" and concludes that the educational sciences "have been recognized as a legitimate discipline, in fact, as a pluridisciplinary field" (p.324). How one answers the question of course depends on what one takes "science" to be, how broadly or narrowly one defines it. I am simply going to side-step this whole issue – for the purposes of this book it does not matter whether education falls under the concept of science or not. Unless, of course, an argument is mounted somewhere that only "genuine" sciences and disciplines have theories. In that case, this book provides evidence that education indeed is a science. It does have proper theories, and these theories deal with different kinds of phenomena and exhibit different structures.

I shall take plurality in education, as described above, to be a fact. What we are after here is a broadly painted picture. What does a pluridisciplinary field look like? Obviously, several pictures are possible. Ewald Terhart (2016) provides a simple and useful "map" of the present-day predicament of education as an academic endeavor. He portrays education as a fluid landscape, fragmented and without unity, with an interior in constant flux and outer boundaries constantly shifting. His "map" of this unwieldy field involves three dimensions, all depicted as continua and admitting of degrees; so that many middle positions are possible (p.11). The first dimension runs between a mono-disciplinary form at one extreme and a multi- or non-disciplinary form at the other. The second dimension concerns the degree to which education is involved in the qualifying of pedagogical practitioners (most notably teacher education). Terhart's third dimension has education as an academic and autonomous, not applied, field at one extreme and education as closely tied to challenges and stakeholders defined by government or market (or both). Together these three dimensions make up a systematic space to characterize and compare institutional forms of education studies and research, and to map their changes in time by tracking their wanderings through the space provided. Terhart's conclusion about the field of education and its disciplines is as follows:

> Visions of homogeneity or the idea that in the end a certain encompassing and unifying theory for the whole academic endeavor devoted to education … will probably never be realized. The absence of such a grand theory and unifying methodology should not be regarded as a deficit, and its creation should not be proclaimed as the visionary aim of all work. In highly specialized, fluid knowledge and science systems with specialized and also constantly changing and competing expert cultures that deal with constantly changing societal realms and challenges, you have to get used to pluralistic, heterogeneous, fluid, inconsistent and incompatible landscapes of theory and research. There will be no other.
>
> (2016, p.12)

While this may sound like a bleak picture to some, I am going to adopt *something like* this view of the field of education, including Terhart's assertion that disciplinary unity is a lost cause and that there is no reason to mourn it. But we need to cover some more ground before we can come to such a conclusion.

Education: Characterizing its "interior"

Terhart's three-dimensional space is a useful "map". It effectively communicates the enormous complexity of the field of education as well as the complexity of the context education finds itself in. I shall use Terhart's map as my guiding light in my exploration of the field, but not stick faithfully to it all the way. Furthermore, I shall employ the notion of "boundary work" (Gieryn, 1983), which I judge to be a highly productive notion. Even fluid landscapes need some kind of boundaries. The term "boundary work" mainly refers to demarcation of science from non-science; not as a matter of principle, but as a matter of practice: the various strategies employed by practicing scientists to distinguish their own work from other intellectual activities. The term serves equally well for demarcation of disciplines and specialties *within* science or *within* a given field, as a way of coming to grips with the fluidity and the dynamics of the field.

When I was a student, one of my professors at the university used to say that education is not a discipline; it is a field of study. It is not clear exactly what he took a discipline to be, but the intimation was clear, as I recall it: it is better, more academically respectable, to be a discipline than a mere field. I suspect that my old professor had time-honored epistemological criteria in mind: clear disciplinary boundaries, order, unity, coherence, and a high degree of consistency across the different perspectives employed in the discipline. That is to say, I suspect he had adopted what Paul Trowler (2014) calls a "strong essentialist position". In fact, Trowler thinks that much of the literature about the nature of disciplines and fields has adopted such a position. This is unfortunate, Trowler argues, because it "closes down an appreciation of the complexity of disciplines as a whole and of individual examples of them" (p.1720). Strong essentialist views involve at least two things: the claim that a phenomenon has a definable and necessary character, and the claim that these characteristics have the power to affect other phenomena around them. It is the first one of these that interests us in this context; the demand that a discipline should possess a unique set of characteristics, a specialized vocabulary, a systematic research strategy and perhaps specialized criteria for validity – all identifying characteristics to mark a discipline as being *itself*. Being education and not, say, psychology. Trowler argues that strong essentialist accounts of disciplines flatten out internal differences, occlude complexity, and are conceptually limiting and reductionist. They take a part for the whole, we might say.

So – is there something that marks education as being itself? Is there a phenomenon with a definable and necessary character? Classical definitions of education tend to name the phenomena (supposedly) falling under its scope; typically teaching and upbringing, these days also perhaps learning. Definitions invariably narrow the field and focus on what is (now) just a small part of it. Even Hofstetter, despite her description of education as a pluridisciplinary field, identifies educational action as *the* subject to be studied (2012, p.330). Definitions suffer from the same problem as essentialist accounts; they occlude complexity and are conceptually limiting and reductionist. Pluralistic, heterogeneous, fluid, inconsistent and incompatible landscapes of theory and research are hardly captured in any definition, I suggest. So we move from definitions to the question of disciplinary identity.

In the English-speaking world, education is commonly perceived as an interdisciplinaryfield; the most prominent constituent disciplines being psychology, sociology, history and philosophy. This viewpoint has instigated many discussions about whether or not education is an autonomous discipline and what its necessary characteristics are – what makes its theories distinctively *educational* rather than being "merely" applied psychology or applied sociology. Thus, for example, Paul Hirst (1966), in the first of a now classical series of articles, claims that educational theory is not and *cannot* be an autonomous academic discipline. *Educational* theory does not add anything to the understandings of educational phenomena that are created by the fundamental disciplines. Hirst's main reason for this view is that since educational principles are informed by the constituent or foundational disciplines, they must be evaluated by the relevant criteria of the discipline in question. Educational principles, Hirst states,

> ...are justified entirely by direct appeal to the knowledge from a variety of forms, scientific, philosophical, historical, etc. Beyond these forms of knowledge it requires no theoretical synthesis.
>
> (p.55)

Hirst later modifies this view somewhat (Hirst, 1993). While educational theory still is viewed as drawing on all theoretical knowledge available in the social sciences, and other significant sources as well, it also has to stand up to the test of practice. "It is therefore", he now says,

> as mistaken to think of the practical principles of educational theory being justified by appeal to the disciplines as it is to think that a theory in physics is justified by appeal to the validity of the mathematical system it employs.
>
> (p.157)

I shall return to Hirst's views later in this chapter as well as in the chapters to follow. In the meantime, let me briefly notice that Charles Clark (1976) most emphatically shares Hirst's view that education is not an academic discipline, for slightly different albeit related reasons. Clark might qualify as an essentialist in Trowler's sense of the term. He insists that education *must* be studied with practical concerns in view, and that it cannot be studied by academics in their reflective academic fashion: "...indeed I shall attack the assumption that there is any 'it', in the sense required, that such people could meditate upon" (p.11). There are two strong essentialist tendencies in Clark's position. The first is that he defines practice as the sole object of educational study and thus seriously limits the field and what can be studied. The second is that he thinks that any serious study of education happens from the inside, by the practitioners. Or so I read him. He says:

> One cannot identify a practice, then, unless one already knows the principle being practiced, since one cannot characterize the practice except by reference to the principle. Our theoreticians, from their theoretical standpoint could, then, knowing the principle, see whether practitioners really practiced what they preached; indeed this is regularly done by sociologists 'studying education' .... But this, for us is not sufficient, for is it *educational* practice which

> our observers are observing? ... To see *education* one must embrace the principles or values constitutive of the concept.
>
> (p.15, emphasis in original)

We shall have ample opportunity to return to Clark's views (and related views) in Chapter 3. Suffice it here to note that the boundaries he draws around a "core" of education is rather limiting, as Trowler suggests. People who do sociology of education or philosophy of education are involved in academic disciplines, Clark argues, and therefore cannot claim to be grappling with *educational* problems. Thus, the traditional foundational disciplines of education fall outside the boundary.

While the Anglo-American tradition largely perceives education as consisting of foundational disciplines and questions its status as autonomous, the Nordic-Continental tradition treats education as a discipline in its own right (German: Pädagogik, Nordic: pedagogik). Gert Biesta (2011) provides an interesting comparison of the two traditions. He takes the most striking difference between them to concern the role and status of educational theory: "From a Continental perspective it is remarkable that the idea of education as a discipline in its own right with its own forms of theory and theorising is almost entirely absent in the Anglo-American construction of the field", he says (p.189). There is certainly a point of contention here. It could be that Clark would have agreed with the Nordic-Continental perspective had he investigated it – as Biesta points out, from this angle it makes perfect sense to ask *educational* questions about education, questions that are different from psychological, sociological, philosophical and historical questions about education. Whereas, as Clark laments, from the Anglo-American perspective the foundational disciplines can study educational phenomena from their own angles, they do not have the theoretical and methodological resources to study the phenomena of education as precisely *educational*. Biesta concludes that the Anglo-American and Nordic-Continental traditions are to a certain degree incommensurable paradigms. My own take on this in subsequent chapters will be rather pragmatic; for the purposes of this book nothing much hangs on these two traditions. The conception of theory I shall employ straddles them. Yes, there are indeed educational theories. No, they are not of some special kind; they are like theories found in other fields.

Growth and hybridization

On Trowler's view, individual disciplines have no essential core characteristics, all present and identifiable at all times (Trowler, 2014). This is clearly so if we take these characteristics to consist of certain phenomena or knowledge structures, as I suspect my old professor did. But the standard criteria for identifying disciplines are more lax than the essentialist view on Trowler's construal of it. Indeed, if we apply the standard criteria, education qualifies as a discipline in its own right: the existence of specific objects of knowledge or phenomena for study, even if these are shared by other disciplines; the existence of a more or less specialized knowledge base concerning these phenomena, generated over time; the existence of theories and concepts that organize the knowledge base; the existence of specific vocabularies and discourses; the existence of research methods and inferential rules (shared by other disciplines); the existence of research journals in the field; the discipline belongs institutionally at a university or college and can be studied by students and researchers (see Bridges, 2006, Lawn & Furlong, 2009). Trowler prefers what he calls a moderately essentialist position, modeled on Wittgenstein's notion of family resemblances: "it argues that phenomena have objective defining features but does not require them all to be present in every instance" (p.1723). This avoids the rigidity of the essentialist position, but still maintains a fairly tight grip on the discipline. It may take new forms, but retain some familial resemblance to other forms. The characteristics may change over time but yet retain recognizability, he suggests. This, as we can see, is nowhere near Terhart's description of the field of education as fragmented, hybrid and fluid. On the other hand, Trowler's perspective might provide a take on the problem of an outer boundary: if new forms are viewed as *sub-disciplines*, we automatically assume the existence of an overarching discipline. But what, then, keeps it together as a discipline? If there is no essence to be found, Trowler could argue that sub-disciplines are kept together by family resemblances. However, it is not clear how far we can stretch this metaphor. Suffice it to say that herein lies one boundary issue: how to keep various (sub)components as parts of the field and how to understand the nature of the whole and what (if anything) keeps it together.

Education as a field has grown immensely in the past decades. We have seen an enormous proliferation of topics, themes, perspectives and orientations. This is one of the main driving forces behind the fragmentation and hybridization of the field. Terhart's three dimensions point at pressure for diversification from inside the discipline as well as pressure from the outside in the form of massification of education, structural changes and professionalization issues. Concerning internal diversification let me invoke Rudolf Stichweh (1996). He describes how the problem spaces of sciences and disciplines are progressively decomposing into smaller, more fragmented and more specialized areas. This suggests that even if we could draw a waterproof boundary around education as an academic discipline and insist on an essentialist understanding of its core, we would still face a growing heterogeneity inside the discipline. One implication of this is that any clear-cut epistemological structures of the discipline become invalid and cannot be upheld. Another implication is that it may lead to identity problems for the discipline, unless, as Trowler suggests, the development takes the shape of new forms which retain family resemblance with older forms. On the other hand, of course this fragmentation may also lead to renewal, with new problems and new perspectives emerging. Moreover, Stichweh argues that this internal differentiation is the most important cause of the globalization of science. The "incessant proliferation of ever-new communities of scientists with progressively restricted jurisdictions" serves to shape the social and cognitive space of science in a way that is incompatible with national scientific communities: "The decomposition of the problem space of science makes it progressively improbable that relevant and necessary collegial relationships should accidentally be coextensive with national contexts", he says. (p.332). This should be recognizable for all of us: our closest colleagues tend to live in other countries. It also suggests that the landscape of education, education studies and education research goes well beyond the internal epistemological structures of the traditional academic disciplines.

Hofstetter (2012) cashes out her concept of pluridisciplinarity in terms of disciplinarity, multidisciplinarity, interdisciplinarity and transdisciplinarity. This is because educational action, which she defines as the very subject of education, is a topic that crosses, transcends or subsumes several other disciplines (p.330). Multidisciplinarity denotes the combination of several disciplinary perspectives, whereas inter- and transdisciplinarity integrate and transcend disciplines and thus serve to constitute new specific fields or topics as common objects. This is a topic I shall discuss at length in Chapter 6. Here I would also like to draw attention to postdisciplinarity, a term that suggests that both inner and outer boundaries have been dissolved and there is nothing anymore that a discipline is in itself. Some might find such a situation rich in opportunities; others might find it worrying, like David Bridges (2006, p.263):

> The notion of post-disciplinarity in educational research worries me in so far as it suggests that educational research cannot any longer be thought of as having any discipline. It is worrying because the loss of 'discipline' has two huge consequences. The first is that it undermines the basis of the special claim of educational research on our or anyone else's attention; the second is that it renders meaningful conversation within communities of arguers impossible.

One thing is the proliferation of topics, problems, questions and perspectives, which makes education more diverse and heterogeneous. Another is the hybridization of issues, hinted at by Hofstetter in her description of interdisciplinary topics: different disciplines integrate and make new specific fields or common objects. The growth of (and in) subject didactics is a case in point. Traditionally, didactics is a core educational subject, taking center stage in the discipline of education (at least in the Nordic-Continental construction of the field). Didactics offers a general vocabulary that can be applied to all or most school subjects. But things changed when research in didactics was taken up by school subject specialists and teacher education researchers. They were concerned that education (pedagogy) be integrated into the subjects; that is, into languages, literature, mathematics, geology, home economics, etc. These subjects, as school subjects, have internal epistemological structures that place restrictions on how they should be taught; hence, didactics move "into" the subjects to interact with their nature. We get little communities of subject-didactics specialists: mathematics didactics, religion didactics, geology didactics, etc. Subject didactical topics are hybrid in that they are neither pure subject nor pure didactics, but both. This development poses a challenge for *general* didactics, which risks losing its status as common and overarching. We find this sort of hybridization in the entire field of education. For example, general didactics and political science meet in issues concerning governance and policy; education and law meet in issues concerning the juridification of education; sociology and education meet in issues concerning e.g. admission procedures to secondary education and their possible consequences for social equality. Such issues, I submit, are not framed as being pure and belonging to *one* discipline; they are framed as hybrids. This suggests that the disciplinary boundaries are porous, as Terhart claims.

At this point it is pertinent to bring back into the picture the Anglo-American view of education and its foundational disciplines. Let us bring back up Hirst's old argument that educational principles are justified entirely by direct appeal to the foundational disciplines that constitute them (Hirst, 1966): sociology, philosophy, history and psychology (for a recent discussion, see Biesta, 2011). I take this to imply that Hirst would reject the kind of hybridization I have described above. The sociology of education asks *sociological* questions about education, psychology of education asks *psychological* questions about education, etc. None of them ask *educational* questions about education. Clearly this implies that the boundaries between education and its foundational disciplines are presumed to be waterproof; not porous, as I have suggested. But I think that questions about, say, admission to higher education constitute a hybrid topic; it is both educational and sociological and one would be hard put to disentangle the educational from the sociological. Such questions fall equally to education as to sociology. Biesta (2011), it will be recalled, says of the Nordic-Continental view of education that it is in a position to ask *educational* questions about education, questions that are different from psychological, philosophical, historical and sociological questions about education. I leave it open whether this means that Biesta also would uphold fairly waterproof boundaries between education and other disciplines and not allow for hybrid topics, questions and perspectives. To me it seems that the international landscape of education, as it is found in universities and professional fields, has long since outgrown narrow maps of the field which insist on clear-cut non-porous boundaries. Thus, what we have is a diverse, fluid field which keeps growing and diversifying. It stands to reason that such a diverse field can have theories of different types – all of them *educational*, in the sense that they find themselves in the large landscape we call *education*.

Professional field and social/political demands

While there is great pressure for diversification of topics from inside the discipline or field itself, there is also great pressure from the outside, concerning structural changes, issues of funding, and professionalization issues. This is partly because research has become globalized, but also because education is an academic field that is built in reference to practices and professions that pre-exist it. These practices and professions have also grown and diversified, and education finds itself between specialization for a certain professional field – teaching – on the one hand, and differentiation on the other hand, to make itself relevant to as broad a spectrum of society as possible, and thereby to a number of other fields and professions. In this context, Hofstetter's claim that education has been pluridisciplinary from its very inception makes good sense. I can also locate my own preference for the term "field" over the term "discipline" here: I simply think it is a truer description of the landscape of education. "Field" indicates something more disorderly, fragmented, pluralistic, heterogeneous, fluid and hybrid, with porous boundaries; something that is bigger than a discipline because it encompasses different perspectives on different phenomena which sit more or less well together and sometimes not at all – hence my reservation concerning the applicability of Trowler's family resemblances. There simply might not be any.

Education as research and study was established to meet the need for qualifying teachers. This is where we find Terhart's second dimension, a continuum "between a heavy integration of education-as-a-discipline or field in the preparation of teachers and other education professions *versus* qualifying for these professions being done outside university and heavily regarded as a process of inculcating practical capacities" (2016, p.11). This is a recurring tension in education, being an academic discipline on the one hand and being a relevant professional knowledge base on the other. We thus find an important boundary issue here: the boundary and the connections between academic field and professional field. As Edwin Keiner (2002) puts it, "a relationship between forms of knowledge specific to education as an academic discipline and those specific to education as a profession" (p.87). But it is by no means clear where this boundary is, and in any case it is highly porous. The professional field, which once made up the context for a university-based academic discipline, has more or less merged with the academic field. Education research today is dominated by professional topics and questions that originated in professional contexts, most notably in teacher education, where among other things the developments in subject didactics come from. The old foundational disciplines still exist, but occupy a very modest space, even in the universities. Thus, even the outer boundaries of education are fuzzy and unstable.

We need to look at one last kind of boundary: that between education and its social/governmental surroundings. This is Terhart's third dimension (2016, p.11):

> The third dimension is where educational expertise is regarded and institutionalized as a purely academic, not applied, field and is following its own problems and rules *versus* education's expertise being tightly connected to educational and societal reform movements or to state- or administration- or market-defined challenges and stakeholders. There are also several possible positions in between.

In other words, education as autonomous and self-steering at one extreme of the continuum and education as dependent on state and/or market at the other extreme. Even here the boundaries are porous. It would appear that more and more education research is commissioned by government or other agencies, thus becoming more "applied" in nature. And thus, Terhart concludes, not only do we not *have* a unifying grand theory for the entire field, we *cannot* have one, and we *should not* want one. And I agree, with some caveats.

The landscape of education

I take it to be a fact that the landscape of education today is heterogeneous, hybrid and pluralistic and that it therefore accommodates different types of theory. The field has grown immensely in the past decades, in terms of topics, questions, perspectives and approaches, and in terms of the number of people doing educational research. The boundary around the traditional "interior" of education, with attempts to identify *the* objects of education – upbringing, teaching, education as Bildung, educational action – cannot be upheld in the face of the myriad of new topics. Thus, there is pressure from within as well as pressure from without. The net result is a great proliferation of topics and approaches and porous, shifty boundaries. This state of affairs is a double-edged sword. On the one hand, the more fragmented and specialized the field becomes, the less structure and integration can be expected from general educational issues, general concepts and perspectives. Without overarching concepts or principles, it is hard to provide a unifying structure for the highly specialized sub-disciplines or sub-domains. On the other hand, it makes the field of education a very *rich* one. And, I shall argue in subsequent chapters, theoretical integration can be "local" and take place without unification. Theorizing is one way of integrating parts of a pluralistic field.

I have at several places indicated that a part-whole understanding of education is an attractive picture. That would allow for a huge number of sub-fields, topics and perspectives to be viewed as parts of the whole. It leaves us with the problem of keeping the whole together and, not least, defining what, if anything, it is that keeps it together, once we have given up on the traditional core of education. As Trowler says, to insist on an essentialist conception of education makes for a narrow and limiting view. An alternative figure is that of typicality: some topics and perspectives might be viewed as more typical of education (e.g. upbringing, teaching, Bildung) whereas others are more untypical (e.g. admission procedures, effects of granting students various rights, conceptions of educational theory) but still perceived as belonging to the educational field. But what would be so untypical that it falls outside even this boundary? I have no answers to these questions. However, some form of outer boundary is needed, because this is where the autonomy problem is located. This is not autonomy understood as internal epistemological structures which makes a field *itself*, but as the relation between the field on the one hand and politics and consumption of knowledge on the other. If we do not uphold some form of outer boundary, we risk that it is drawn for us by external forces without any internal, conceptual or content considerations by those active in the field.

Educational theory

The philosophy of education witnesses longstanding discussions about the nature of educational theories. That of course presupposes that the interlocutors think that there *are* such things as educational theories. Occasionally people voice doubts about this; perhaps the best-known skeptical view is that of D. J. O'Connor (1957). In a now classical formulation he says,

> ...the word 'theory' as it is used in educational contexts is generally a courtesy title. It is justified only where we are applying well-established experimental findings in psychology and sociology to the practice of education.
>
> (p.110)

More recently, Wilfred Carr (2006) has argued that the educational theory project simply should be abandoned. Educational theory, he states, has run its course and should be brought to a dignified end. His chief reason for this dramatic conclusion is that educational theory has failed to achieve its stated goal, namely to govern practice "from the neutral perspective of an abiding general rationality" (p.147). In further detail, this is set out as follows:

> From this [post-foundationalist] perspective, educational theory cannot *inform* practice because it is itself a *form* of practice. Educational theorists cannot abstract themselves from the contingent norms, values and beliefs inherent in this practice since it is only within them that educational theorizing can take place.
>
> (p.147)

In fact, Carr says, educational theory's way of understanding educational realities should not be seen as theoretical, but as an extension of a community's practical common sense (p.153). I shall come back to Carr's views shortly. Suffice it here to establish that there are skeptical voices concerning the existence of educational theory, and that the reasons for their skepticism differ widely.

One important (assumed) trait of educational theory is hinted at in the quotes above, namely the relation to practice. As pointed out above, "education" encompasses a huge and diverse professional field and this professional field (including practice) pre-exists education as an academic field. It seems only natural that educational theory should be discussed, defined and determined in relation to practice. And by the same token, educational theory seems inextricably connected to what Trowler calls a form of essentialistic understanding of the field of education. Traditionally, practice, in its various forms, makes up the core of the field and this is clearly reflected in the debates about the nature of educational theories. If the field is practical in nature, its theory should cater to this.

Before we explore this matter any further, it might be instructive to name a couple of theories that are often put forward as examples of educational theories. We have, for example, the great education classics, whose views are referred to as Dewey's educational theory, Rousseau's educational theory, Pestalozzi's educational theory, Key's educational theory, and so on – all comprehensive bodies of knowledge connected to a certain thinker. Piaget's theory is also considered to be an educational theory. That is something of an irony, according to Rita Hofstetter – in

Piaget's time as professor of psychology at the University of Geneva, education was reduced to a mere terrain of application, a laboratory for psychological experiments. Under Piaget's direction, psychology did not integrate educational phenomena at all, Hofstetter says; it was rather the case that psychology and pedagogy ignored and despised each other. Piaget's psychology was interested in "the genetic construction of intelligence as a natural functional process of assimilation and accommodation" (Hofstetter, 2012, p.323); assimilation and accommodation supposedly being natural, biological mechanisms. Yet, as history shows, Piaget's theory has been appropriated to the field of education and is often referred to in educational reform documents. The boundary has shifted, or it became porous enough to let Piaget's theory move into education.

At the other end of the spectrum, Wilfred Carr (2006) argues that extracting passages from Plato or Rousseau and calling them Plato's educational theory or Rousseau's educational theory amounts to a gross historical misrepresentation, since neither writer saw himself as contributing to "that twentieth-century academic specialism we now call 'educational theory'" (p.138). But while Carr thinks there is no such thing as Rousseau's educational theory, Jürgen Oelkers (1994) clearly thinks there is. Oelkers uses Rousseau to exemplify one of the basic paradigms of Western educational theory, namely *development*. The second basic paradigm he calls *influence*, with Locke as the main example. These theories are at a very high level of abstraction indeed, turning directly on ontological conceptions of the nature of children. The former says that "Nature is a self-acting force *in* man, it develops *itself*, and the art of education consists in following its track" (p.98, emphasis in original). The latter says that "'educational' is something happening between *persons* that constructs *inner* (mental) states from the *outside*. ... the child becomes the object of an external construction, the educator becomes the designer, who is no longer required to show consideration for 'psychic' *preconditions*" (p.96). Oelkers finds both theories wanting and proposes a third kind, a theory of education (*Erziehung*, upbringing), which he calls "moral communication" and which focuses on participation in processes dealing with "morality" – the normative demarcations within the framework of social groups (p.103). Moral communication is inevitable, but its impact is uncertain, Oelkers says. His proposed alternative theory is designed to overcome the perceived one-sidedness of the other two. All three of them are presented as educational *theories* and will be returned to in subsequent chapters.

There are several definitions of educational theory and I shall in the following discuss a selection of them. For convenience I organize them in two big samples: an Anglo-American one and a Nordic-Continental one.

Definitions of educational theory: An Anglo-American sample

There are, naturally, different views as to the nature of educational theories. Despite their differences they also exhibit striking similarities: most definitions relate to the perceived core of the field, namely educational action or practice, and most seek to distinguish between educational theories and scientific theories. These two traits are intimately connected.

It seems to be quite common to envision a sharp and non-porous boundary between science and education. To set the stage for the discussion, let me briefly cite the Norwegian philosopher Hans Skjervheim (1992). He proposes to categorize scientific disciplines according to their *raison d'être*. This yields two large categories, which he calls theoretical and practical, respectively. The theoretical sciences are the traditional disciplines, whose inner core is constituted by the connections in its topical domain – the map is constituted by the features of the landscape, so to speak. Paradigmatic examples are physics, history and biology. The practical sciences have some form of *change* as their *raison d'être*, an interest in being able to intervene and modify the phenomenon of interest. Paradigmatic examples are medicine and education (pedagogy). This distinction, between theoretical and practical sciences, is co-extensive with another distinction: that between different types of theories. The theories of the theoretical sciences aim at explanation and understanding of phenomena; the theories of the practical sciences aim to guide practice. As Paul Hirst puts it, the function of theoretical knowledge is primarily explanation; the function of practical theory is primarily the determination of practice (1993, p.149). A few short comments are in order. First, there is much agreement in the literature about this distinction and the concomitant categorization of educational theory as practical theory, but there is room for differing views as to what this really entails, as we shall see. Second, the distinction presupposes very sharp boundaries between the two types of sciences. Third, there seems to be an assumption here that theories belonging to different categories of sciences do different jobs; in other words that the function of the theory is determined by the *raison d'être* of the science, discipline or field. This is an assumption I shall dispute – I shall argue that theorizing is not fundamentally different across the two domains. Moreover, I doubt that the boundary is as clear-cut and sharp as the theoretical/practical science distinction would have it.

Let us begin with O'Connor, who in many ways is the odd one out here. The term "theory" played a crucial role in the debates between Hirst (1966, 1973) and O'Connor (1957, 1973) on the nature of educational theories. These exchanges are well worth looking at; they have been influential in the philosophy of education and people still keep coming back to them – people such as myself, for example. Aiming to clarify the function of educational theories, O'Connor begins by delineating four different uses of the term theory found in science. Two of these are judged to be important in educational contexts. In the first sense of the word, theory is contrasted with practice and refers to "a set or system of rules or a collection of precepts which guide or control actions of various kinds" (1957, p.75). This, he says, is a vague sense of the word theory and amounts to no more than a general conceptual background to some practical activity. In the second sense of the word, "theory" is used as it occurs in the natural sciences: as a logically interconnected set of hypotheses confirmable by observation. This is O'Connor's preferred sense, since it "gives us standards by which we can assess the value and use of any claimant to the title of 'theory'" (p.76).

Now, O'Connor asks, how far should educational theories properly be called theories? He attacks the problem by providing a description of the basis for educational practice, commonly designated educational theories. This basis embodies three distinct kinds of statements: metaphysical statements, empirical statements and judgments of value. Collections of such statements underlying established educational practices must be viewed as rationalizations of practice rather than as genuine reasons for practice, O'Connor argues. The statements are different in kind and their logical distinctiveness prevents them from comprising a theory which would conform to the proposed standard. Roughly, this sketch suffices to establish that "theories in education do not, in general, conform to the models that we find in a well-developed natural science" (p.104). On the other hand, we cannot deny that education has a theoretical basis, so the question of the function of educational theories must be reformulated somewhat, into "what job these educational theories do if they do not have the logical status of standard scientific theories" (p.104). And thus his conclusion, already cited above but worth citing again, "the word 'theory' as it is used in educational contexts is generally a courtesy title" (p.110).

According to Hirst (1966), O'Connor fails to do what he set out to do: to clarify the function of educational theories and pinpoint the job they do for us. Still according to Hirst, this failure is largely due to O'Connor's obsession with scientific theory as a paradigm for all theories, since this leads him to misjudge "the importance of the non-scientific elements that he himself diagnoses in educational discussions" (p.39). Hirst thus finds O'Connor's treatment of metaphysical statements and value judgments far too dismissive. For Hirst, statements of these kinds fundamentally characterize education as a field of discourse. And hence, we surmise, these elements must be represented also in educational theories.

Unlike O'Connor, Hirst maintains that it is the *first* of O'Connor's two main senses of "theory" that is meaningful for education, not the second as O'Connor suggests. As Hirst sees the matter, "Educational theory is in the first place to be understood as the essential background to rational educational practice, not as a limited would-be scientific pursuit" (1966, p.40). Hirst thus subscribes to the distinction between theoretical and practical sciences and their concomitant theories. He was very clear about this in 1966 and deserves to be quoted at length:

> Yet the theories of science and the theories of practical activities are radically different in character because they perform quite different functions; they are constructed to do different jobs. In the case of the empirical sciences, a theory is a body of statements that have been subjected to empirical tests and which express our understanding of the physical world. Such tested theories are the objects, the end products, of scientific investigation, they are the conclusions of the pursuit of knowledge. Where, however, a practical activity like education is concerned, the place of the theory is totally different. It is not the end product of the pursuit, but rather it is constructed to determine and guide the

> activity. *The function of the theory is to determine precisely what shall and what shall not be done, say in education.*
>
> (p.40, emphasis added)

I have italicized Hirst's description of the function of educational theory. This is a striking formulation, and as I see it, completely wrong. No theory can do this. But much ground has to be covered before we can return to Hirst's claim and analyze it in more detail in Chapter 9. Suffice it here to say that Hirst actually employs two conceptions of educational theory: the one cited above and then a wider one that covers the "whole enterprise of building a body of rational principles for educational practice" (p.41). In this sense, "educational theory" is to be understood as the label for a domain, which in addition to educational theory in the first sense also draws on many other sources in the formation of practical principles. Ultimately, Hirst says, the difference between scientific and educational theories is a logical one, expressed in terms of judgments of what *is* and judgments of what *ought to be* (p.42).

So what does a concrete educational theory look like on Hirst's view? Unfortunately, Hirst has not provided us with any examples. Some years after his debates with O'Connor, Hirst remains convinced that educational theory is a form of practical theory and the domain that seeks to develop rational principles for practice (Hirst, 1993). It will be recalled that he (1966) sees the field of education as being constituted by the foundational disciplines of psychology, philosophy, history and sociology and that educational theory has no independent contribution to make. In 1993 he espouses the same view. The constituent disciplines can only tackle questions that can be raised within their own conceptual apparatus, he states, and these questions are not practical (p.151). Furthermore, the disciplines tackle no common questions of any kind, something which leads to an inevitable gap between the conceptual frameworks of the disciplines and the framework of practice. So how should we understand the relation between the foundational disciplines and education theory? It is not derivative – the knowledge provided by the disciplines is not sufficient for practical principles. The is-ought relation is truly an unbridgeable gap for Hirst. Educational theory is thought to *mediate* between foundational disciplines and practice, but it is hard to envision how a theory which is constituted by foundational disciplines can mediate between the same disciplines and practice. Hirst (1993) says that the disciplines provide *reasons* for the practical principles (p.151). Are practical principles here identical to educational theory? Hirst is often unclear on the relation between educational theory and practical principles. Sometimes he talks of educational theory as if it amounts to practical principles, as above. Sometimes he states that it is the job of educational theory to determine rational practical principles (p.158), which suggests two different entities. Hirst does not provide any concrete examples of rational practical principles either, so it is equally hard to judge their epistemological status. They are not sociological, nor psychological, philosophical or historical in nature, so what are they, if education contributes nothing and is nothing in itself? Whereas Hirst (1966) argues that the validity of the principles of education theory should be judged by the criteria of the foundational contributing disciplines, the Hirst of 1993 argues that the validity of practical principles must stem from their being abstracted from practice (p.153). It is a mistake, he now says, to think of practical principles as being justified by appeal to the disciplines. They must also pass the test of practice. Hirst does not go into detail about how such tests are conducted or how their results are to be judged, but the change of view seems profound.

Next up is British philosopher of education Wilfred Carr. Many of his publications about the nature of educational theories center on the relation between theory and practice, commonly identified as a "gap". In all his publications, Carr places himself firmly on the side of practice and subscribes to a clear-cut, impenetrable boundary between theoretical reason and practical reason. Education, he says (1980, p.63) is not a theoretical activity but a practical activity, concerned with developing students' minds. He thus assumes a fairly narrow conception of education, perhaps what Trowler would term essentialist. All educationists already possess some theory in virtue of which practices are conducted and assessed, Carr argues. In other words, practice is theory-laden. The gap between theory and practice arises because it is assumed that "educational theory" refers to theories other than those that already guide educational pursuits. But the conception of educational theory as it is discussed by philosophers of education – and here he refers to both O'Connor and Hirst – fails to recognize the theory that exists in practice. It is the theory that guides practitioners that constitutes the source of their educational principles, not theory which is constituted by foundational disciplines. The only entity that "educational theory" can coherently refer to is the theory that *actually* guides practice, he says (p.66). Educational theory can only arise for and be resolved by educational practitioners, Carr concludes. Not researchers, not philosophers. This claim, we should note, is premised on a non-porous boundary between commonsense theory and academic theory. But as Pamela Moore (1981) pointed out in a critical response to Carr, commonsense theory is permeated by academic theory.

Carr's view is dramatically different from Hirst's, despite their shared practical orientation, and one of their chief disagreements concerns the *source* of educational theory. Hirst locates it in the foundational disciplines; Carr locates it in the practical experience of teachers. Carr's view is reminiscent of Clark's view, referred to in a previous section. Academic disciplines such as sociology and philosophy are theoretical and therefore have no bearing on people's action, Clark claims; they are reduced to studying education from the outside (1976, p.13) and do not really grapple with *educational* problems (p.14). Educational theory, Clark concludes, belongs exclusively to the practitioner:

> I have, of course, been arguing all along that an educator is guided by principles. ... I am happy to have this called the 'educational theory' of the practitioner in question. ... I have also been arguing, however, that a practitioner must himself fashion his own 'theory' in answer to problems arising for him at the coal-face and that, since he will be the only person

> with specifically *educational* problems, he will be the only person who can do *educational* theory.
>
> (1976, p.16, emphasis in original)

Again, this is what Trowler presumably would call an essentialist conception of the field of education. It also amounts to a strong variety of "insiderism" – in reality, only practitioners have access to education, and as a result only practitioners can develop educational theory. Clark attacks the notion that educational theory can be a stable substantive body of subject matter that anyone can meditate upon. While Richard Peters, a well-known British philosopher of education, is Clark's primary target, his arguments equally apply to Hirst's understanding of educational theory, despite the fact that Hirst agrees with Clark that education is not and cannot be an autonomous discipline. Hirst's educational theories are constituted by knowledge from the foundational disciplines, what Carr calls theories other than those that already guide educational pursuits. What place, Clark asks, could any such theory have in an educator's life? Given his undeniable gift for apposite formulations, he is worth quoting at length:

> ...the usual picture conjured up is that it is, at least in prospect, a kind of *Code Napoléon*, all nicely 'integrated' and 'synthesized' which an educator consults before he starts (to tell him what to do), as he goes along (to tell him how he is doing) and after he has finished (to tell him how he has done). If that is what is intended, then it is an *ignis fatuus* which we should abandon immediately.
>
> (p.16)

In the article *Theories of Theory and Practice* (1986), Carr takes a somewhat different view. The premise for his discussion is that questions about educational theory tend to cluster into two areas of concern. On the one hand, there are philosophical issues concerning the logical structure of educational theory and its relation to foundational disciplines; on the other hand, there are problems concerning how educational theory should be used in relation to educational practice. This separation mirrors the separation between education as an academic discipline and education as a professional field – a distinction, Carr argues, that is highly unfortunate and only serves to distort and impair our understanding of educational theory. Questions about the nature of educational theory and questions about how this theory relates to practice are not separate questions at all, Carr says. I agree with this viewpoint in so far as it can be understood to mean the nature of theory, whether educational or other, has implications for its use in practice. I am, however, not sure that that is how Carr himself would interpret his own viewpoint. Carr's reason for his view is that

> ideas about the nature of educational theory are always ideas about the nature of practice and always incorporate a latent conception of how, in practice, theory should be used. ... There are not, therefore, theories of

> theory and theories of practice and yet other theories about the relationship between the two. All educational theories are theories of theory and practice.
>
> (1986, p.177)

Hence, Carr argues, rival views of educational theory incorporate rival views of how theory relates to practice. But at least there are such things as educational theories.

That brings us back to the beginning of this section, with Carr's suggestion that the educational theory project should be brought to a dignified end (Carr, 2006). Carr's views concerning educational theory have thus been on a remarkable journey, from belonging to practitioners, to theories of theory and practice and finally to the claim that education would do better without theory. What does he take theory to be that it should be brought to a dignified end? Educational theory, he now says, is a foundationalist project, inspired by Enlightenment values and ideals. Thus, the project "was predicated on the assumption that educational institutions and practices should be governed by theoretical knowledge that rests on rational foundations that are invariable across contexts and cultures..." (p.144). The purpose of the whole project, Carr says, was to accomplish two tasks:

> The first was essentially philosophical: to identify epistemological foundations for educational theory that would enable educational practice to be erected on rational principles that are more objective and rational than mere belief of unexamined practice. The second was essentially practical: to replace the contextually dependent, subjective beliefs of practitioners with the context-free, objective knowledge generated by theory.
>
> (p.144)

This is an astoundingly sweeping statement which simply assumes that educational theory is everywhere the same, sharing the same presuppositions. As an alternative Carr puts forward a post-foundationalist view, out of which emerges a handful of equally sweeping claims:

> ...far from being a special activity that is conducted from outside of practice, educational theory is itself a historically formed practice inextricable from the local and parochial contexts within which it is produced and always embedded in...
>
> ...far from being 'universal' or 'general' such theoretical generalisations are always abstractions from the malleable world of practice and thus always shaped by the very features of practice ...[which] educational theory claims to transcend.
>
> From this perspective, educational theory cannot *inform* practice because it is itself a *form* of practice.
>
> (p.147)

Hence Carr's conclusion that educational theory, understood as theories other than those that emanate from practice, is a self-defeating foundationalist project that should be abandoned. Both education and its theories are for practitioners only (university teachers apparently not being among them).

Finally, let us look briefly at the view propounded by American philosopher Ernest Nagel (1969). It is interesting in itself that Nagel wrote about educational theory. He ranks among the best-known analytic philosophers of science and wrote mainly about logic and the intricacies of scientific method, and he freely admits that his familiarity with discussions about educational theory is limited. He singles out three components in educational theory: a theory of human nature (p.12), a component "which deals with a variety of social and institutional questions pertinent to the understanding the educational process" (p.13), and educational ideals, whether general or specific (p.15). Educational theory is understood mainly as an attempt to formulate and justify educational ideals, not to provide any principles as to *how* things should be done. Nagel expresses various doubts about educational theory and its assumed components:

> And I would like to ask, in the first place, can educational aims be derived from any descriptive theory of human nature? And I want to maintain that this is not, in point of fact, possible despite the attempt to supply a foundation for educational goals by a consideration of physical, biological, psychological or, perhaps, even social and anthropological facts.
>
> (p.19)

Nagel thus subscribes to the same view as Hirst: statements about what *ought* to be are not deducible from statements of what *is*. In Chapter 10 I shall come back to the issue of incorporating of a view of human nature into the educational theory itself, and I shall argue that we are better off viewing it as extrinsic to the theory, as a background assumption, rather than an integrated part of the theory.

Definitions of educational theory: A Nordic-Continental sample

First, let me briefly remind us of the second dimension in Terhart's field map: a continuum "between a heavy integration of education-as-a-discipline or field in the preparation of teachers and other education professions *versus* qualifying for these professions being done outside university and heavily regarded as a process of inculcating practical capacities" (2016, p.11). Terhart here makes a distinction between (teacher) education programs inside and outside the university, strongly suggesting that the programs at the university keeps features of the discipline – theory, for example – whereas education programs outside the university are practice-based and mostly a matter of teaching practical skills. Be that as it may. The point here is to keep in mind education as situated between discipline and profession, and as encompassing them both. The first example of a definition of educational theory fits Terhart's second dimension well: that of Leo Friedrich

(1987). He argues that since the process of education (broadly conceived) invariably contains normative elements, this should be reflected in our scientific theorizing about education. The resulting conception of educational theory is one which depicts such theories as moving back and forth on an axis like Terhart's dimension, between factual and normative considerations, mediating between the two, coupling the *is* and the *ought* together. It is hard to say what such a theory might look like, and Friedrich provides no examples.

It will be recalled that Skjervheim (1992), briefly mentioned in the previous sub-section, makes *practical interest* play a substantial role in his conceptualization of educational theory. The interest informing educational as well as medical theories is one of modification of some aspect of the world, and the theory will guide your intervention. Skjervheim does not dig into this in any detail, but he does make one point which speaks to the epistemic status of educational theory. It will be recalled that he categorizes education as a *science*. Practical, action-oriented theories, Skjervheim argues, stand in danger of degenerating into some mysterious entity, like some individualized form of art that can neither be described nor explained. This must be prevented. I infer from this that he assumes that educational theories essentially belong to the practitioner. But they should not be understood as private and tacit or impossible to articulate. Rather, I surmise, educational theories should have a public character, making them accessible for evaluation and critique. How is this to be achieved? The practical sciences, Skjervheim argues, must make use of insights produced by the theoretical sciences to prevent practical theories from degenerating into some mysterious, inarticulate entities. This is so, he says, because theoretical insight is needed to understand *why* things happen. We see here that Skjervheim agrees with both Hirst and Carr that educational theories are practical in nature. But he differs from Carr in thinking that theoretical sciences have an important role to play, and he differs from Hirst in thinking that educational theory is not constituted by other sciences, but draws on them when pertinent. Epistemic status arises as an issue because Skjervheim seems to make the practical sciences dependent on the theoretical sciences for the insights they need into the *why* of things; an insight the practical sciences seemingly do not produce themselves.

Reidar Myhre, Norwegian philosopher of education, expresses the same view: whereas "pure", scientific theories have prediction and explanation as their ultimate aim, educational theories are practical in nature and have attainment of specified goals as their ultimate aim (Myhre, 1980). Such practical theories, Myhre claims, contain three basic elements. The first is a view of human nature, an anthropology. This is the fundamental element of a theory and the other elements are based on this one, even derived from it. The second and third elements are aims and process – the *what* and the *how*. Interestingly, Myhre constructed the same basic view of educational theory as did Nagel – the two authors being unfamiliar with each other's work and coming from wildly different traditions (Nagel was an analytic philosopher of science and Myhre was a Continentally oriented philosopher of education). But there are differences as well: Myhre's educational theories tell us *how* the aims are to be attained, whereas Nagel's educational theories center on the justification of ideals. Myhre understands the view of human nature as the foundation of the educational theory, and sees no problems in deriving aims, content and process (the main didactical categories) from this foundation, and in that order – aims are closer to the foundation than the other two. Nagel, as we have seen, thinks we cannot derive an *ought* from an *is*. For Myhre the three elements hang tightly together, such that different views of human nature give rise to different aims and different didactical considerations toward the aim.

Let us move to Erich Weniger's conception of educational theory (Weniger, 1990). This conception is complex, something quite unto itself, and merits a more detailed analysis. Weniger distinguishes between three different *degrees* of theory. The first is described as "das weltanschauliche Apriori, das ein etisches Apriori in sich schließt" [an a priori outlook on the world, containing an ethical a priori, my translation] (p.38). A theory of the first degree belongs to the practitioner, making up his or her fundamental ethical attitude and responsibility. A theory of the second degree is that which the practitioner can articulate, expressed in "Lehrsätzen, in Erfahrungssätzen, in Lebensregeln, in Schlagworten und Sprichwörtern und was es so gibt" [doctrines, experiences, rules of life, slogans, proverbs, and the like] (p.39). These are beliefs which belong to the practitioners and which they use in their practice.

These two forms of theory are, however, not enough. At the point of intersection between theories of first and second degree arises one of the fundamental problems of educational theory: the question of the relation between "Wirklichkeit und Theorie, Begriff und Leben, Sein und Sollen in der Pädagogik" [reality and theory, concept and life, what is and what should be in pedagogy or education] (p.39). This relation is of vital importance to Weniger, because a true, genuine theory turns on the internal consistency of the practitioners' theories of first and second degree. Their explicitly expressed beliefs must be in agreement with their fundamental attitudes. If there is a discrepancy between the two, the resulting practice will be "unwahrhaft" – untrue, not genuine.

This is where the theory of the third degree enters the picture, to have the relation between theory and practice *in* practice as its object. A theory of the third degree thus presupposes an already theory-laden practice. It is only valid, Weniger suggests, to the extent it makes practice more conscious and rational. As distinct from theories of first and second degree, a theory of the third degree is a *theoretical* theory, a "Theorie des Theoretikers" (p.43). For Weniger, a theoretical theory serves as a kind of meta-theory, the function of which is to monitor the relation between first and second-degree theories and ensure agreement between practitioners' fundamental values and their espoused values and knowledge claims. This constant monitoring is required in order to promote a better practice. As Weniger puts it (p.42),

> Bewußter und systematischer will die Theorie die Praxis machen, Rationalität und klare Einsicht vermitteln, die Zufälligkeit des Handelns ausschalten [theory will make practice more conscious and systematic; it will

> contribute rationality and insight and eradicate the randomness of action (my translation)].

A few observations are in order. First, I think Weniger's theory conception should be understood as three theories in one, since they evidently are meant to be intimately connected. Second, his conception is practitioner-centered; the theories all belong to the practitioner. Third, it is unclear where the theory of the third degree comes from. There is nothing to suggest it originates in educational research, even if Weniger calls it a "Theorie des Theoretikers". To judge by its function, it simply amounts to reflection: practitioners reflecting on what they do in their practice and how they conceive of what they are doing. Thus, there is built into the three degrees of theory a deep dynamic between performance and understanding. Fourth, since it is the job of the theoretical theory to monitor this dynamic, it follows that even such theories are deeply rooted in concrete situations, in the context of practice. Not even the theoretical theories take you out of practice. In that respect, Weniger's view is reminiscent of Carr and Clark, but not of Skjervheim.

A comparison between Hirst and Weniger on the function of educational theories is most instructive. It will be recalled that Hirst takes the function of the theory to be "to determine precisely what shall and what shall not be done, say in education" (1966, p.40). Weniger (1990, p.32) takes a radically different view:

> …daß es ein grundsätzliches Mißverständnis der Funktion der Theorie durch den Praktiker ist, wenn er glaubt, die Theorie könne und wolle ihm die Entscheidung in dem konkreten Fall vorschreiben oder abnehmen [the practitioner fundamentally misunderstands the function of theory if he thinks it can prescribe his concrete decisions or absolve him from them (my translation)].

Weniger reaches his view because he thinks that practice is characterized by great diversity, which means that no theory can prescribe what a practitioner should do in a given situation; and because he is at pains to endow the practitioner with the responsibility for his own actions, which means that the practitioner cannot "hide" behind theory or blame theory if something goes wrong. For the record, practitioners cannot "hide" behind experience either.

I shall round off this sub-section by looking very briefly at Jürgen Oelkers's conceptualization of theories of upbringing (*Erziehung*). There are clearly many ways of bringing up children and theories of upbringing naturally express different viewpoints concerning aims, content, processes, interactions and ways of doing things in general (Oelkers, 2001). But, Oelkers suggests, all theories of upbringing presuppose the idea that certain ways of doing things will bring about certain effects. All theories of upbringing therefore share at least three characteristics: they all focus on morality, they all presuppose interaction between people, since children do not bring themselves up, and the fundamental pedagogical relationship is asymmetrical, most commonly between children and adults. Thus, Oelkers argues (p.263), all theories of upbringing should include a statement of the aims of upbringing, an account of the process(es) involved, and a description of the object.

Summary

Edwin Keiner (2002), in his analysis of the field of education as it looks in Germany, describes it as "characterised by differences, contradictions and ambivalences between programmatic self-concepts and the daily practice of research and teaching" (p.83). He lists several examples of such contradictions. For example, educational theory is determined by a practically oriented self-concept, yet those who define education as a practical science increasingly have no practical pedagogical experience. As another example, education is defined as a field characterized by plurality, yet it manifests an astonishing "continuity and uniformity of a traditional, practical-oriented kind of thinking" (p.84). This latter characteristic, to be sure, does not apply to Germany only. When we look at what different theorists say about educational theory, the continuity and uniformity of a traditional, practice-oriented kind of thinking is striking. Keiner is absolutely right, and not only about the German case. There are, of course, striking differences as well. There is, in general, not much agreement about the field of education, what it contains, what it should contain, where its boundaries go and where they should go. There is no agreement about the sources of educational theory: some say it is the foundational disciplines; others say it is educational action and practice. There is no agreement about the academic status of education: some say it is a discipline it its own right; others say it is not. Most writers make a distinction between scientific and educational theories, implying that these are different not only in content but also in epistemic aims. Gert Biesta (2011) takes the most striking difference between the Anglo-American tradition and the Nordic-Continental tradition to concern educational theory: its nature, role and status. This is a point that may have to be modified. Yes, as we have seen, there are obvious differences. These differences seem to concern mainly two aspects: one is the autonomy of the field of education and by implication the academic status of educational theory; the other is the is-ought issue. Concerning the latter, Anglo-American authors (e.g. Hirst) seem preoccupied with this logical difference between scientific and educational theories; the former describing what *is* and the latter stating what *ought to be*. As far as I can see, this issue does not seem to be a problem for the Nordic-Continental authors – Myhre, for example, does not seem to think it in any way problematic to derive aims and didactical considerations from the basic view of human nature that is said to underlie them.

But when we come to the perceived function of educational theories, we see a striking similarity: there is widespread agreement that educational theories are normative; their function is to guide practice, solve problems – that is, *one* type of theory is depicted for the entire field of education. The understanding of the nature of the field of education is intimately connected to the understanding of the nature of educational theory. *One* type of theory suggests a narrow understanding of the field and Keiner's description merits repetition: the continuity and uniformity of a traditional, practical-oriented kind of thinking is indeed astounding. The exception, of course, is O'Connor. The common view is that he got it wrong. I shall return to his views in both Chapters 3 and 10.

In the meta-theoretical vernacular of this book, I shall call theories that contain aims, are normative, action-guiding and practice-oriented *goal-directed* theories. I shall analyze them in great detail in Chapter 4. But this is only one of the types of theories we find in the field. With a heterogeneous field such as education, it stands to reason that many types of theory are possible.

3 What theories are

Researchers have at their disposal many different forms of representation, such as photos, paintings, models, formulas, equations, narratives, calculi, computer-generated images, histograms and graphs. The most common form of representation, however, surely is *theory*. The world of science is full of "things" we call theories, and so is the world of education.

In education the concept of theory is used in a bewildering variety of ways. This fact might tell us different things. It might tell us that the concept completely lacks a definition and has no clear meaning at all; it may suggest that there are different forms of theory; and it certainly might suggest that the term is thought to have a role to play. Gary Thomas (1997) finds the allure of theory in education puzzling, given its vagueness and lack of utility in education. Theory, he argues, has been successful in other fields, but that itself is no good reason to think that theory is useful in education. In education, he claims, "any kind of theory is a force for conservatism, for stabilizing the status quo through the circumscription of thought within a hermetic set of rules, procedures, and methods" (p.76). Theory is therefore neither emancipatory nor a vehicle for thinking otherwise – it is an instrument for reinforcing existing practices. It thus comes as no surprise that he in the end wishes to make a case for "ad hocery" rather than theory: progress is seldom the fruit of theory, Thomas concludes. This conclusion is of course a challenge to all educationists who claim that theory is somehow essential, and also to this book, since I wish to make the case that there are theories in education, that we can pinpoint them, evaluate them and use them. I shall therefore have occasion to revisit Thomas' views in subsequent chapters.

He does have some important points. While there are many debates about theory in education, Thomas argues, there is little consensus about the meaning of the term. What exactly does the term refer to? The field of education must appear very confusing to students, since it sports a range of different kinds of theory: attribution theory, learning theory, critical theory, etc. Students are also encouraged to develop their own personal or practical theories – difficult for anybody, but especially so if one has no idea what a theory is. Thomas takes the reader through a number of proposed definitions of theory found in textbooks on educational research and points out that while they are as different as "chalk and cheese" they all provide a description of ways in which "theory" is sometimes used in education. This is a serious problem, he argues:

> "Theory" as a word must be one thing or another. It cannot – if it is to be used seriously to describe a particular kind of intellectual construction in education – have two or more meanings, unless the context in which it is used can universally and unequivocally distinguish those meanings. If we are to understand what "pipe" means, the word must refer only to the class of objects normally thought of as pipes; it must not also refer to dogs, vacuum cleaners, and trees.
>
> (p.79)

Thomas here touches on the problem of reference, which I shall come back to shortly. But first let us look briefly at uses of the term theory – Thomas is correct that it is used in a multitude of ways. John Chambers (1992) distinguishes nine meanings for "theory". These he organizes into nine clusters with slight variations in each cluster. In cluster one, theory is contrasted with fact and is used to mean hunch or speculation. There is commonly a denigratory connotation to this, Chambers suggests; something is *only* a theory, not a fact. In cluster two, theory is contrasted to practice; "theory" denotes thought, "practice" denotes action. In this cluster Chambers also places theory as a collation of instructions and principles to be applied. Cluster three is theory as evolving explanation. This is a rather diffuse form of theory and hard to distinguish from the field out of which it grows. In cluster four, we have practical theory, the function of which is to determine practice. This form of theory is of great interest to us and is easily recognized from Chapter 2 – Chambers indeed includes Hirst's conception of educational theory in this cluster. A practical theory is a composite and its unity is provided by the consistency of the set of principles underpinning the *what* and *how* of the theory. Pedagogical theory understood as practical theory is continually being developed; it learns from its own activities as results are fed back into it. In characterizing practical theory, Chambers says,

> Its present form would seem to be a mixture of facts, rules, precepts, pedagogical traditions, professional wisdom, assumptions about the nature of learning, psychological and sociological claims, beliefs about the nature of persons, social norms and values, philosophical argument, general principles, socio-political assumptions, and so on. Despite its conglomeration of different disciplines and logical kinds its point is to *help teachers and administrators decide what ought to be done in their classrooms and how it should be done.*
>
> (pp.13–14, emphasis in original)

In cluster five we find theories as hypotheses. This cluster includes an important variety. First, theories as models; so called because they extrapolate particular aspects from one domain and apply them in another, with an eye to what insights this might suggest about the second domain. Second, theories as heuristics or, as

Chambers puts it, hopeful hypothetical ideas (p.15). This is to be distinguished from theory as hypothesis, which, unlike hopeful hypotheses, is prompted by scientists' deep understanding of their material. Cluster six concerns theory as ontological presupposition. Here we find ontological assumptions underlying experiments – I suggest causal models as a candidate – and we also find epistemological presuppositions – theory in the form of beliefs, knowledge, orienting principles, which we not only bring to our experiences, but which make our experiences possible. Cluster seven is normative theory, with or without a rational basis. Cluster eight Chambers calls empiricist theory. Empiricist research in education is Chambers' main target of criticism. Empiricist theory is established inductively by trial and error, based on observation and experience, and consists in generalizations, rules of thumb, procedures and traditions. While empiricist theory might be useful, it is to be distinguished from the ninth cluster, which is scientific theory.

Before Chambers presents his ninth and last cluster, he interjects a chapter on scientific research. "Science" has become an honorific and hortatory term, Chambers says (p.28), and some deliberate restriction on the term is necessary to prevent it from becoming so vague it is useless in philosophical discussions. All his examples of scientific research come from the natural sciences; the reason being that "the approach and status to which *social scientists and pedagogical researchers themselves aspire* is that of natural science" (p.29). Scientific theory is not the same as the generalizations of empiricist theory, Chambers says. He defines scientific theory as follows:

> *So Scientific Theory consists of interrelated sets of propositions, of rational connections between the rational abstract concepts, and of abstractive connections between abstract concepts and the corresponding empiricist features, the observables of the empirical world.*
>
> (p.71, emphasis in original)

Chambers does not tell us where he gets his definition from, but as we shall see it is easily recognizable as the syntactical conception of theories. Now what should we think of these clusters? Gary Thomas queries several of Chambers' categories, proposes to conflate some and add a new one, and ends up with the following four broad uses of theory in education (1997, p.82): (1) Theory as the opposite of practice, (2) Theory as hypothesis, (3) Theory as developing explanation, and (4) Scientific theory. These four types or uses can be expressed in two continua, one between theory and practice, and one between theory as plural and theory as singular or unitary. The problem is that "theory" strays along and between them. The concept is simply too open-ended to be of any value, Thomas argues; it escapes scrutiny because it constantly shifts shape. Hence, his assertion that "theory" should not have more than one meaning.

If I understand Chambers correctly, he thinks that the variety in usage in itself is not necessarily a problem, but it becomes a problem if researchers do not understand the multiple roles played by theory and ignore or worse, muddle up, the different types of theory. On the other hand, he implies that scientific theories and educational theories are non-contiguous – pedagogical theories are classed as practical. It will be recalled that we find the same view in Hirst. Thomas puts it even stronger and speaks of the impossibility of emulating scientific theory in education (p.84). I would say that depends both on what we take scientific theory to be, and of course what we take educational theory to be. We therefore need some definition of theory.

Meta-theories

As said above, Gary Thomas (1997) consults textbooks on educational research to find a definition of "theory", and the ones he finds are as different as chalk and cheese (p.78). One definition says that theories are sets of interrelated constructs, propositions and definitions, aiming at explanation and prediction. Another says that theory is a convenience, a way of organizing facts, laws and concepts into meaningful wholes; being, as Thomas puts it, "a toolshed view: theory is a repository, a way of tidying the various bodies of knowledge and analytical instruments found in education" (p.78). Both describe a way in which "theory" is sometimes used in education, and Thomas takes this to show that talk about theory in education is pretty confused.

What we need to do, I propose, is to enlist the aid of a meta-theory – a theory about theories. That will give us a far better grip on the nature of theory than a mere definition will do. We construct theories to do various jobs for us. The traditional view is that the function of theory is to describe, explain and predict – as we have seen in Chapter 2, many writers of education hold that the job of theory is to guide or even determine practice. Obviously, there are many other jobs that theory can do as well; for example, understanding of situations or behavior, observation and interpretation of complex phenomena and justification of actions. But what should we expect a meta-theory to do for us? Basically, I would suggest, a meta-theory should help us get a better understanding of *how* theories do their job, what they actually *say* about the phenomena they represent and *how* they say it. To this end I propose the following desiderata for a meta-theory:

- It should tell us what kind of "elements" theories contain; that is, what sort of "things" we find if we unpack a theory
- It should tell us how these "elements" hang together
- It should tell us how the theory is related to the phenomenon within its scope

I should say here that my proposed desiderata are tentative and reflect what I think might be useful for the field of education. As we shall see, the leading meta-theorists have different views on what they think the vital criteria should be for judging the adequacy of a meta-theory.

I have selected two major meta-theories for treatment here. Before we dive into them there is an initial distinction I wish to make concerning the term theory, one not captured by Chambers, to make clear what sort of theories we are going to deal with here. Sylvain Bromberger (1963) identifies two main uses of the term theory in science. First, there are theories like the electromagnetic theory of light, which can be "accepted, rejected, believed, remembered, stated, granted, confirmed, refuted, have authors" (p.83). Then there are theories which can "include contributions from many sources; they have founders and perhaps foundations; they are academic subjects" (p.83). This distinction is important. Bromberger's theories of the second sort are supra-theoretical entities, such as areas, domains or fields. They do not take any specific phenomenon as their object but rather denote a whole field of inquiry. This is a common usage of the term theory in the sciences; for example, "social theory", "psychological theory" or "educational theory" are sometimes used with the understanding that what we have in mind is not a specific theory (such as Piaget's theory of cognitive development or neo-behaviorist learning theory) but rather the domain we call psychology or education. Paul Hirst makes the same distinction. Educational theory, he says, can denote,

> ...the body of scientific knowledge on which rational educational judgments rest. It is, however, also used for the whole enterprise of building a body of rational principles for educational practice. In this second sense it is the label for a domain of theory that not only draws on educational theory in the first, scientific sense, but draws on much else besides...
>
> (1966, p.41)

The field denoted "educational theory" contains many different theories of Bromberger's first sort, some of which we shall meet in subsequent chapters – my analysis will be confined to specific theories that have some defined phenomenon within their scope.

There are several meta-theories from which to choose. I shall look into the two major ones, commonly known in the literature as the Received View of theories (RV) and the Semantic Conception of theories (SC). Ironically, the labels have become rather unfitting – by all accounts, the SC has now become the received view, in the sense that this view, in its various versions and with its unsolved philosophical problems, now rules the meta-theoretical stage. The RV has become the Once Received View, as Carl Craver puts it (Craver, 2002). For convenience, I am going to keep the old labels, shortened to RV and SC, respectively. Both of them concern theory structure.

The Received View

RV is the logico-positivist conception of scientific theories and mainly came out of the work of the Vienna Circle. The name was coined by Hilary Putnam in 1962 (Putnam, 1962), but the view itself existed prior to getting its name and dates back at least to the 1920s (Winther, 2015). Throughout its history it has enjoyed other names as well; for example, the Syntactic View, the Standard Conception, the Orthodox View and the Axiomatic Approach. One of the textbook definitions of theory cited by Gary Thomas (1997) is easily recognized as being reminiscent of RV: theories as sets of interrelated constructs, definitions, and propositions. It is, in fact, still not uncommon to come across definitions of theory in terms of interrelated sentences – something which testifies to the wide circulation of RV.

My presentation of RV concentrates primarily on Rudolf Carnap's (1936/1937, 1956) and Carl G. Hempel's (1952, 1958, 1965, 1966, 1977) formulations, since they together were the main authors of RV in its final form. "Final" does not mean that this is the last version of RV to be held, but rather involves the idea that this is the version for which the strongest case can be made (see Suppe, 1977). Other versions have been developed by a number of other philosophers, including Pierre Duhem (1954), Abraham Kaplan (1964), Ernest Nagel (1961) and Hans Reichenbach (1962). These will not require separate consideration since their distinctive features can be subjected to the same criticisms made against the Carnap and Hempel version.

The short story is that RV defines theories as partially interpreted axiomatic systems, commonly designated TC. T is the set of theoretical sentences making up the axioms, theorems and laws of the theory; all expressed in a theoretical language, the theoretical vocabulary V_T. The axioms are primitive (i.e. basic); the theorems are derivative (Hempel, 1958), and together they form a tight, deductive inferential pattern and a systematization of the phenomenon. C is the set of correspondence rules that provide the axiomatic structure with a partial empirical interpretation. C connects T with testable consequences; these are formulated in an observational language, the observational vocabulary V_O. Thus, theories are linguistic structures composed of the conjunction of TC, expressed using three kinds of vocabularies contained in scientific language: theoretical, logical and observational.

This characterization is strikingly schematic and formalistic in nature. Patrick Suppes once made the comment that "Concerning ... the logical calculus, it is unheard of to find a substantive example of a theory actually worked out as a logical calculus in the writings of most philosophers of science" (1967, p.56). If this is true for the natural sciences, it is certainly also true for "softer" sciences such as education. The RV has big limitations when it comes to describing theories as they are in their fields; that is, as they are presented, learned, taught or remembered. But as Craver (2002) points out, RV was not typically defended as an accurate description of theories; rather "it is a regimented reconstruction of their shared inferential structure" (p.58). RV thus had to accommodate all genuine examples of good theories and exclude all examples of bad theories. This meant, Frederick Suppe argues, that advocates of RV "adjusted their analyses to accommodate the best physics had to offer, but deployed them normatively in evaluation of the social sciences" (2000, p.S104). In passing, this is exactly what O'Connor did – deployed RV normatively in evaluation of educational theories and found them wanting. Let us explore some of the features of RV in greater detail.

Bifurcation of objects and terms

The divide between theory and observation is central to the RV, as suggested by the two vocabularies V_T and V_O. The terms in V_O are thought to refer to directly observable objects, entities and attributes, and are defined directly in terms of these. Advocates of RV have devoted remarkably little attention to the notion of being directly observable; it has typically been taken as unproblematic. It probably got its fullest treatment in Carnap (1936/1937), where he, "for the sake of simplicity", draws a sharp line between observable and nonobservable predicates – although admitting that the line is arbitrary. What is crucial, however, is his requirement that observational terms refer to *directly* observables. In later writings, adherents to RV seem to have assumed that the notion of being directly observable is generally understood, and were content to give examples to characterize it. Carnap himself writes that

> The terms of V_O are predicates designating observable properties of events or things (for example, 'blue', 'hot', 'large', and so on) or observable relations between them (for example, 'x is warmer than y', 'x is contiguous to y', and so on).
>
> (1956, p.41)

Theoretical terms are thought to refer to nonobservable entities and attributes, and hence must be defined in a different way. Standard examples are "atom", "electron" or "protein". The field of education is very rich in theoretical terms; in fact, it could be argued that most educational phenomena of interest are theoretical in this sense; for example, "learning", "intelligence", "motivation", "Bildung", "professional responsibility" and "classroom atmosphere".

This bifurcation of properties, entities or objects, and the relations between them, is based on whether they are directly perceived by the human senses or not. Carnap's distinction between observational and theoretical terms (hereafter O-terms and T-terms, respectively) is in reality a double dichotomy. First, the bifurcation of the entities of the world and their attributes; second, the division of the nonlogical vocabulary of the theory into O-terms and T-terms. That is to say, the bifurcation of terms is drawn on the basis of the bifurcation of objects and properties into the directly observable and the nondirectly observable. By 1970 Hempel had come to reject the double dichotomy:

> The distinction I have suggested between theoretical and antecedent vocabularies hinges on no such assumption [i.e. that phenomena describable by an observational vocabulary should be accessible to direct observation]. The terms of the antecedent vocabulary need not … generally be conceived as observational in the narrow sense just adumbrated.
>
> (1970, pp.143–144)

It seems reasonable to suspect that at least part of the underlying motivation for the O/T distinction is the assumption that assertions containing empirical terms only from V_O are intersubjectively unproblematic with regard to truth (Newton-Smith, 1981). That is, any two observers will be able to agree upon the truth of V_O assertions, regardless of their theoretical backgrounds. This is because the meaning of O-terms was thought to be defined directly through their connection with experience.

Correspondence rules

Correspondence rules are variously referred to as coordinating definitions, operational definitions, rules of interpretation and explicit definitions. Importantly, they are conceived of as an integral part of the theory and serve at least two functions in RV: they define the T-terms and they specify the admissible procedures for applying theory to phenomena.

The notion of correspondence rules has undergone considerable development. Initially, they were explicit definitions thought to provide necessary and sufficient conditions for the applicability of T-terms. This was an important point since T-terms were thought to be cognitively significant only if they were explicitly defined in terms of the V_O. It will be recalled that correspondence sentences string together theoretical, observational and logical terms; thus, when they were thought of as explicit definitions, it followed that theoretical assertions were guaranteed to refer to observable reality in TC's scope (Suppe, 2000, p.S104).

In the final version of RV, correspondence rules are construed as a finite set C of admissible experimental procedures for applying a theory to observable phenomena (Suppe, 1977). On this construal, correspondence rules and theoretical postulates together supply the T-terms with a partial observational interpretation. I will not continue this discussion here, but point out that this construal of correspondence rules will be important in the chapters to follow, as will the procedure for specifying the meaning of T-terms. Figure 3.1 is an illustration of the structure of RV (Feigl, 1970). The figure has become known as the "fishnet".

Remnants of RV can be found in textbook definitions of theory, and we should, perhaps, be cautious in declaring it dead. There is disagreement among

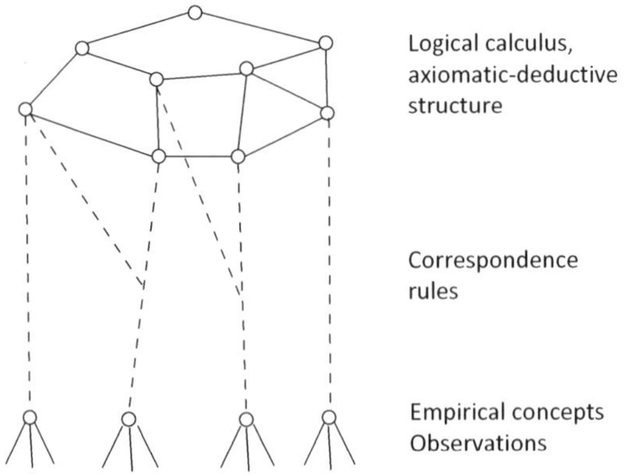

Figure 3.1 The Received View of theories
Adapted from Feigl (1970, p.6)

philosophers about the interpretation and relative merit of the various features of RV. Hans Halvorson (2016) argues that some of the criticisms leveled against RV simply miss the mark, for example, that RV confuses theory with theory formulations (p.588). In fairness it should also be said that RV is not without its defenders today; see e.g. Sebastian Lutz (Lutz, 2012).

So how does RV fare with respect to my proposed desiderata? Concerning "elements", RV tells us roughly that what we find in scientific theories are two parts: a logical calculus T (axioms, laws, terms) and correspondence rules C. Concerning how elements hang together, RV tells us that elements in T hang together by deductive and other appropriate non-ampliative inference rules pertinent to theoretical sentences. The correspondence rules are mixed sentences which contain terms from V_T and V_O, assign empirical content to the calculus by providing partial interpretations of T-terms, and embody admissible experimental procedures for applying the laws of the theory directly to phenomena. Concerning the relation of theory to phenomena, RV tells us that the theory itself thus specifies how it is to be applied to phenomena. According to Patrick Suppes (1967), this view is not necessarily wrong, but it is far too simple. And now we turn our attention to SC.

The Semantic Conception of theories

There is general agreement among philosophers of science that RV is inadequate and untenable. On the other hand, there is considerable disagreement as to why it is inadequate and untenable. The alternatives to RV are largely developed as criticisms of RV; hence it is important to have knowledge of RV, as accounts of alternative views will at least to some extent have to focus on the differences between the two. What is viewed as the source of the alleged inadequacy naturally influences what one believes is an adequate account of scientific theories. I am not concerned with theory structure *simpliciter*, but with theories in the field of education, and my analyses and judgments will naturally be colored by this contextual constraint.

Let us begin by looking at what philosophers think is wrong with RV. According to Frederick Suppe (2000), RV died in 1969 when Carl Hempel – one of the main developers of RV – declared that he was abandoning RV and its focus on axiomatization (as I suggested above, the death of RV may be an exaggeration). Summing up three decades of debate about theory structure, Suppe identifies the following central points of criticism of RV (2000, p. S103):

1 its observational-theoretical distinction was untenable;
2 correspondence rules were a heterogeneous confusion of meaning relationships, experimental design, measurement, and causal relationships, some of which are not properly parts of theories;
3 the notion of partial interpretation associated with more liberal correspondence rules was incoherent;
4 theories are not axiomatic systems;

5 symbolic logic is an inappropriate formalism;
6 theories are not linguistic entities and thus theories are individuated incorrectly.

Rasmus Grønfeldt Winther compiles a slightly different but evidently related list of grievances against RV, also discussed at length by advocates of the SC (2015, p.4):

1 *First-Order Predicate Logic Objection.* Theoretical structure is intrinsically and invariably tied to the specific choice of a language, L_T, expressed in first-order predicate logic. This places heavy explanatory and representational responsibility on relatively inflexible and limited languages.
2 *Theory Individuation Objection.* Since theories are individuated by their linguistic formulations, every change in high-level syntactic formulations will bring forth a distinct theory. …
3 *Theoretical/Observational Languages Objection.* Drawing the theoretical/observational distinction in terms of language is inappropriate, as observability pertains to entities rather than to concepts.
4 *Unintended Models Objection.* There is no clear way of distinguishing between intended and unintended models for syntactically characterized theories …
5 *Confused Correspondence Rules Objection.* Correspondence rules are a confused medley of direct meaning relationships between terms and world, means of inter-theoretic reduction, causal relationship claims, and manners of theoretical concept testing.
6 *Trivially True yet Non-Useful Objection.* Presenting scientific theory in a limited axiomatic system, while clearly syntactically correct, is neither useful nor honest, since scientific theories are mathematical structures.
7 *Practice and History Ignored Objection.* Syntactic approaches do not pay sufficient attention to the actual practice and history of scientific theorizing and experimenting.

What, then, Winther asks, does the SC propose to put in RV's place? In the remainder of this chapter I shall develop a version of SC that will hopefully be of use for the field of education. Like the developers of RV, the developers of SC all seem to take the natural sciences as their paradigm cases; practically all examples come from physics or biology. I shall cut a delicate balance here: I do *not* wish to deploy SC normatively and evaluate educational theories according to it, but I *do* wish to use it as a tool to identify theories (of Bromberger's first, concrete sort) in the field of education. That means that I shall defend the adequacy of SC as a meta-theory, but in a version of SC that fits the field of education. Given the different versions of SC that already exist, it is legitimate to make adjustments to SC so that it becomes applicable and useful as a tool for analyses of educational theories.

According to SC, a theory is a family of models. This definition itself is rather unhelpful, much the same as with RV's definition. My point of departure is Frederick Suppe's version of SC, which I by and large, but not completely, am going to adopt. I shall substantiate my choice as we go along. It is appropriate, then, that I cite his definition of theory: in 1989 he defined theory as follows:

> ...theories [should] be construed as propounded abstract *structures* serving as models for sets of interpreted sentences.
>
> (p.82, emphasis in original)

In 2000 he defines theory in the following way:

> Scientific theories are causally possible collections of state-transition models of data for which there is a representation theorem.
>
> (p. S111)

It should be noted that while Suppe's wording of the definition of theory has changed, his substantive views on what a theory *is* are basically the same. These two definitions, *qua* definitions, are skeletal and definitely need fleshing out. It is hard, on the basis of such definitions, to picture what a "real" theory might look like. I shall begin to flesh out a workable definition by describing what I take to be the heart of any theory, adopted from Suppe (1972, 1977, 1989): theories do not describe phenomena in all of their complexity; they rather characterize the phenomena within their scope in terms of a few selected *parameters*. Suppe's favorite example is classical particle mechanics: a theory which characterizes falling bodies. This theory represents its phenomenon using three parameters: mass, velocity and distance traveled over time. As an example from a field closer to home, we can look at classical behaviorism, as first described by John Watson (1930). This theory takes the learning of behavior as its object, and characterizes this learning as a function of two basic parameters, stimulus and response. These parameters together make up an abstract and idealized replica of the phenomenon. This replica is variously called a "model", a "physical system" or an "abstract system". The theory in fact is about this model or system and only indirectly about the actual phenomenon. This may sound paradoxical, but it makes eminently good sense – albeit of course bringing with it a number of intriguing philosophical problems. In addition, theories contain postulates and theoretical laws, which I shall come back to below.

Language

RV seems preoccupied with language, terms and sentences neatly divided into V_T and V_O (and correspondence sentences which contain both types of terms). It may be surprising that the issue of language has become so prominent. At some point the idea got foothold that RV views theories as linguistic entities and, furthermore, views theories as identical to their formulations. This would have the effect that any changes in linguistic characteristics, for example, a different formulation of the axioms or even a translation of the theory into a foreign language, will yield a new entity. That is, changes in theory formulation lead to changes in the theory itself. I am going to make short shrift of this issue – it seems trivially true to any educationist, I assume, that a theory originally formulated in Norwegian and then translated into English remains the same theory. Nevertheless, the point is important to Frederick Suppe, mostly because he takes the individuation of theories to be the most significant desideratum for the adequacy of meta-theories, and RV's take on individuation is incorrect, he argues, since every linguistic change leads to a new theory (2000, p.S103). As suggested above, Halvorson thinks this is a misunderstanding of RV, and that "no advocate of RV ever claimed that the language of formulation was an essential characteristic of a theory" (2016, p.588). Anjan Chakravartty (2001) claims that the independence of theory from language is an essential issue for SC and that one of its primary motivations has been to escape dealing in sentences (p.331). I am not sure that that is really the case – there seem to be many other equally if not more important motivations behind SC. However that may be, I propose to adopt the commonsensical view that theories surely can be given multiple linguistic formulations, but that they are not to be *identified* with them.

Models

The notion of a model plays a central role in SC. But this is tricky ground – not only does the term "model" have a multitude of different meanings and uses, like the term "theory", but the proponents of SC differ among themselves in what they take models to be and what their functions should be. We have to pick our way delicately here.

Bas van Fraassen, one of the main authors of SC, describes the core of SC in the following way:

> The semantic approach ... focuses on models rather than on the linguistic formulation of theories ... Its difference from other approaches is largely one of attitude, orientation, and tactics rather than in doctrines or theses. The conviction involved is that concepts relating to models will be the more fruitful in the philosophical analysis of science.
>
> (1989, p.217)

Margaret Morrison (2007), who is not an advocate of SC, claims that all the semanticists use the notion of a model as it was once formulated by the Polish logician Alfred Tarski: a model of theory T is a realization in which all the valid sentences of T are satisfied. This observation is clearly true of van Fraassen and Suppe's versions of SC – they both use "model" as it is used in formal semantics, as an entity satisfying a semantic structure, thus providing an interpretation for that structure. Van Fraassen defines a model as any structure in which the sentences of the theory are true, and Suppe (1989) argues that the abstract structures of a theory are meta-mathematical models of their linguistic formulations. In his definition of theory from 2000, Suppe employs the notion of a representation theorem – such theorems are necessary but not sufficient conditions for collections of models to qualify as scientific structures. It is not at all clear how useful this is for the purposes of understanding theories in education. I would like to register the view here that this kind of terminology and its concomitant views introduce a degree of formalism and technicality into meta-theoretical discussions that I do not think will further our quest for understanding theories and theorizing in education. Educational theories are neither mathematical nor meta-mathematical structures. But I would like to extend this comment into a general point: in all analyses of science, its products and practices, we have to consider just how serviceable formalisms are should we wish to make use of them. Education, I submit, is by and large a low-tech field and the need for formalism is not high.

I am looking for a simpler, more intuitive sense of model and I find it in Ronald Giere's work (Giere, 1979, 1988, 2004). Giere is also one of the big names in SC; his is the most readily understandable version of SC, and his use of the term "model" is in accordance with common usage – something which sometimes is a virtue. What Giere calls "model" is what Suppe (1989) calls "physical system". Giere conceives of models as a representational device. Theoretical models, Giere says, "are intended to be models *of* something; ... Theoretical models are the means by which scientists represent the world" (1988, p.80). That is to say, models are vehicles for scientific knowledge, not mere heuristics for exploration or creation of hypotheses. I shall bring together Giere's notion of a model with Suppe's idea of selection of parameters. A theory characterizes the phenomenon within its scope in terms of a few selected parameters selected or abstracted from the phenomenon. These parameters together make up an abstract *model* of the phenomenon.

Parameters are roughly the same as variables, but as I understand it "parameter" has a wider use. The term also encompasses constants, some parameters are not measurable quantities, and, finally, some parameters are normative entities. The parameters are the building blocks of the model and therefore of the theory. I would characterize parameters as the heart of the theory and a good place to start if one wants to understand what a theory says about a phenomenon and how it says it. Classical behaviorism (Watson, 1930) characterizes the learning of behavior in terms of two selected parameters: stimulus and response. Neo-behaviorism (Skinner, 1938) characterizes the learning of behavior in terms of three parameters: discriminatory stimulus, operant (behavior) and reinforcement. In passing, it is worth mentioning that Skinner's theory illustrates that counting parameters is sometimes not straightforward. Reinforcement comes in two varieties, positive and negative – so does his theory have three or four parameters? I actually do not think it matters much whether we count three or four. It is much more important to ask how many parameters a learning theory should have to be deemed satisfactory. There is obviously no absolutely right or wrong answer to that question. Which parameters should it be? There is no absolutely right or wrong answer to that question, either. But these are vital questions to consider in evaluating theories and I shall come back to them in Chapter 7.

Figure 3.2 is an illustration of what this might look like: abstraction of parameters from a concrete phenomenon, a model of the phenomenon, and the

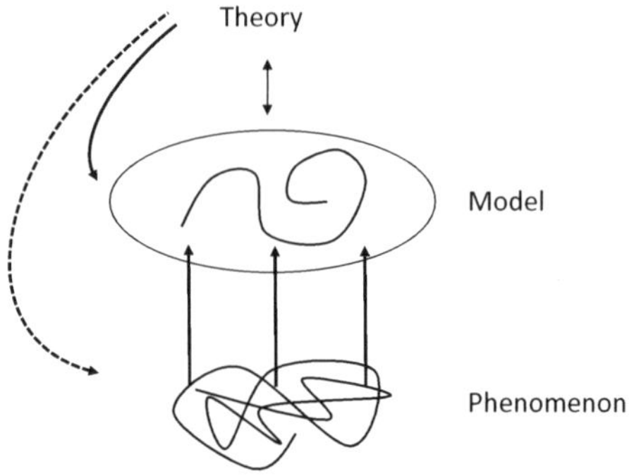

Figure 3.2 The Semantic Conception of theories: Phenomenon, model, theory

theory, which also contains theoretical postulates and theoretical laws. The theory deals *directly* with the model and *indirectly* with the phenomenon.

Selection of parameters means that a great deal of factors, attributes and causes that are characteristic of the phenomenon in fact fall outside the scope of the theory. All theories in essence amount to a simplification of the phenomena. This seems to be a necessary feature of theories which are presumed to cover a number of individual cases – the parameters selected should ideally be those common to the individual cases. In turn, selection or abstraction lead to problems concerning truth (to be discussed in Chapter 7) and in general how we tie theories to reality (to be disussed below and in Chapter 10). For now, let me just note that while simplification is unavoidable and perfectly legitimate, oversimplification is not. But there is no absolutely right or wrong answer as to where we should draw that line.

Models, modeling, theoretical postulates and state spaces

There is more to theories than models. But what, exactly? If theory is defined as a family of models, does not SC do away with theory altogether? Models can stand on their own as a representational device, so why do we need something called theory in addition? This is a contentious and in recent years much debated point. Nancy Cartwright (1999) is skeptical of SC and argues that in virtue of their abstractness, theories simply do not represent anything. Another critic of SC, Margaret Morrison, is deeply skeptical of the theory–model relationship in SC but in contrast to Cartwright she thinks that both theories and models represent, and furthermore that there is a role for theory not captured by models (Morrison, 2007). Morrison's argument at least partly turns on differing degrees of abstractness. Using the theory of superconductivity as her example, she says that theories can represent by, for example, isolating underlying causal mechanisms. Representation of such fundamental characteristics of phenomena "can be captured only in virtue of the generality that theories embody", Morrison argues (p.216). For theory to extend beyond collections of models it is required "that we be able to capture certain 'general' features used to classify physical systems, features that aren't always obvious or easily extractable from collections of models", she claims. One might think here that Morrison thus employs a ladder of abstractness and places theories near the top and sees (interpretive) models as more concrete. But this is not the case: she also states that representative models may be both highly idealized and unrealistic, and that the basic representation theory can give us is not necessarily less realistic than representation by models. "Theories just lack the kinds of details specific to how the cause operates in particular types of situations", Morrison argues (p.217). Suppe, not surprisingly, denies that SC erases the distinction between theories and models – no version of SC claims that it accommodates *all* scientific models (Suppe, 2000). This is an important point: many models are developed independently of theories, and are often advanced in areas where theoretical understanding is scant. This we might call *modeling* – the process of identifying parameters, trying them out, as it were, shuffling and reshuffling them, making assumptions explicit, hypothesizing about the relationships between the parameters, etc.

Still the relation between model and theory is tricky. Morrison's suggestion that theories provide a general representation of the entire class of phenomena is akin to what I see the model as providing. Morrison distinguishes between theory and model by separating the basic structure of theory from its many models, whereas I find it simpler to think of this basic structure as the model (model in the sense delineated above). Suppe holds that the model (which he calls physical system) is a replica of the phenomenon. The theory is *directly* about this model, its behavior, its changes over time, and only *indirectly* about the phenomenon (Suppe, 1989). Again, this is a view I shall adopt, but it is not without its problems, as we shall see.

For one thing it does not quite solve the problem of what models contain besides parameters. If models in education are going to represent dynamic educational phenomena, clearly something more is required besides parameters. This is where my second desideratum comes in: how the "elements" of the theory are connected. I would like to call assumptions concerning relationships between parameters *theoretical postulates.* I would also like to suggest that many such postulates often arise out of the modeling of the phenomenon. I furthermore venture the hypothesis that the most common theoretical postulate in educational theory is *causation*, although of course relationships can be of many kinds, such as correlational, logical, inferential, part/whole, etc. Causation is involved in much educational thinking, but it is hard to think of it as a parameter. As a theoretical postulate, however, it makes good sense. To take behaviorist learning theory, we evidently want to know how the selected parameters hang together. Many educationists have interpreted the relation between stimulus S and response R in Watson's theory as causal – even as causal sufficiency, which is a strong causal interpretation: S always leads to R. The relationship between discriminatory stimulus S_D and operant O in Skinner's theory is rather different, since Skinner's focus is the relationship between operant O and reinforcement R – reinforcement is missing from Watson's theory.

So should we think of theoretical postulates as belonging to the basic model, or as resources outside the model which can be brought into play? I do not know. For practical purposes in theory formulation it probably does not matter. The important thing is to keep an open mind about the connections between parameters – the connections can be understood in different ways. For example, causation comes in different forms: sufficient, necessary, probabilistic, strong, weak, etc. Different postulates give rise to different understandings of the relationship between parameters, and hence to different understandings of the phenomenon in question.

One more thing needs to be dealt with in this sub-section, namely *state spaces*. Winther (2015), in his account of SC, distinguishes between two main versions: the state-space approach and the model-theoretic approach. The model-theoretic approach has among its advocates Patrick Suppes (1957, 1962), Joseph Sneed (1971) and Wolfgang Stegmüller (1976). This version derives from Tarski's work, is largely based on set theory and shares RV's aim of reconstructive axiomatization (Winther, 2015). It is highly technical and I leave this version of SC on the sideline and focus instead on the state-space approach.

The state-space approach can be traced back to the works of the Dutch logician Evert Beth and his formal semantics, originally developed to analyze the formal structure of physical theories (Beth, 1949). Among philosophers who belong this approach we find both Suppe and Giere, and also John Beatty (1981) and Paul Thompson (1989). But primarily the state-space approach is connected to Bas van Fraassen – I believe it was he who coined the term state space, or phase space as it is sometimes called:

> A physical theory then typically uses a mathematical model to represent the behavior of a certain kind of physical system. A physical system is conceived of as capable of a certain set of *states*, and these states are represented by a certain mathematical space, the *state-space*.
>
> (van Fraassen, 1970, p.328, emphasis in original)

Again, we have to make allowances and adjustments to make the notion of state space suitable for the field of education. The state of the model – which van Fraassen, like Suppe, calls a physical system – is determined by the values of its parameters. As these values change over time, so the state of the model changes. But for our purposes here we will not conceive of the state space as mathematical. Specification of state spaces, van Fraassen explains, involves the specification of a certain "topological" structure. We might get a firmer grip on this by seeing the concept of a state space as roughly analogous to the more familiar statistical concept of a sample space. Within the context of stochastic trials, e.g. dice throws, a sample space denotes the set of all possible outcomes – six in total, if you only have one die. The set can be infinite, or it can be finite. Concerning the changes of the model – commonly described as its *behavior* – van Fraassen says that this is given by specifying its state at each instant of time; by a mapping of time into a state space. The admissible histories of state transitions are determined by the laws of the theory and will involve both possibilities and constraints.

Theoretical laws

The notion of a "law" is traditionally viewed with suspicion in education, on the grounds that educational phenomena hardly can be said to be lawlike in nature. What then is a law? On RV the axioms of a scientific theory are construed as laws. Laws are understood as universal empirical generalizations. According to Hempel, a scientific law is a "statement to the effect that whenever and wherever conditions of a specified kind F occur, then so will, always and without exception, certain conditions of another kind, G" (1966, p.54). The educational suspicions are well founded – educational phenomena tend to exhibit great diversity and do not lend themselves (easily) to this kind of generalization.

However, Hempel says, not all statements of this universal form qualify as laws. This depends partly on the scientific theories accepted at the time. It will qualify as a law if it is implied by an accepted theory, but not if it rules out "certain hypothetical occurrences ... which an accepted theory qualifies as possible" (p.58). Hempel's viewpoint here, making laws dependent on accepted theories and thus in a sense relative, may not be what we expect from RV, but it should be remembered here that RV was constantly adjusted to the best that physics, the model science, had to offer. For present purposes the feature of RV's notion of law which is most important to keep in mind is the requirement of universality. Universal laws are supposed to express uniform empirical connections; the requirement being that they hold true always and everywhere. For Hempel, laws are central to a theory's capacity to explain and predict by providing the link by which certain circumstances are connected to the occurrence of an event. Laws, in other words, are manifested directly in the phenomena.

Neither Suppe nor Winther lists laws among the main grievances against RV – perhaps strangely, since laws are conceived of very differently in RV and SC. On SC, the concept of a law is used with reference to entities *within* theories; hence the term "theoretical" laws. A theoretical law determines which possible sequences of states a model may assume. The state of the model is given by the values of its parameters. If these values change, the state of the model changes. The law thus determines the behavior of the model. The term "behavior" is Suppe's. It is a metaphor in this context and is to be understood in terms of preceding and subsequent states of a model. Van Fraassen prefers the term "history" to "behavior", but it is the same idea. Each point in the state space represents a possible state of the model and the law governs the sequence. For instance, S and R may co-develop such that S_a is followed by R_a, S_b is followed by R_b, etc. There are three different kinds of laws at play, each of which may be deterministic or statistical (Craver, 2002). There are laws of succession, which specify possible trajectories through the state space and thus how models or systems will change over time – co-development of S and R will be an example of a law of succession. Then there are laws of coexistence, well known in the natural sciences, where they specify possible positions in the state space by describing equations that fix the overall states of the model and thereby determining which states are equivalent. Finally, there are laws of interaction, which tell us how two (or more) models or theories interact and what the results might be.

A couple of comments are in order. First, as suggested above, laws in education are traditionally treated with suspicion. This suspicion applies to the RV conception of laws as universal empirical generalizations and it encompasses educational criticism usually leveled against S-R theory: the relation between S and R is commonly interpreted as causally sufficient and universal, which if true would mean that people's behavior can be shaped by those with the requisite knowledge of S-R relations. But on SC, laws do not govern the behavior of the phenomenon: they govern the behavior of the model which is a replica, a simplification, of the concrete phenomenon. This is a different ballgame altogether. Second, on SC, theoretical laws are integral parts of a theory, in addition to models and postulates. Yet I propose to understand them mainly as a heuristic. This is to avoid the usual connotations of the term "law" and also because the three different kinds of laws are intimately connected to theory structure. The laws of a theory serve to bring dynamics to theories in a way that models do not do on their own. Theoretical laws are a powerful lens indeed when one analyzes a field to see what can be found. The next chapters illustrate the analytical power of theoretical laws: laws of succession will be explored in Chapter 4, laws of coexistence in Chapter 5, and laws of interaction in Chapter 6. Third, theoretical laws are different from theoretical postulates. Postulates concern the relations between parameters, how we see the parameters as hanging together. They therefore do their work essentially in the model. I am inclined to understand them as not being integral parts of the model, but rather belonging to the theory, since that will leave us flexibility in shifting the postulates and thereby adjusting the model. The theoretical laws concern the behavior in the state space of the entire model and thus provide the overall structure of the theory, something postulates do not. But admittedly, it might be hard to keep laws and postulates separate on occasions, especially when postulates influence parameter value.

Relation between theory and phenomenon

Thus far we have seen that a theory is concerned with a certain kind of phenomenon only insofar as its behavior is characteristic of a small number of parameters abstracted from this phenomenon. This feature, which applies to all theories, makes theories *abstract*. It follows from this feature that many factors, attributes, causes and relations characteristic of the phenomenon fall outside the theory; the assumption being that these impact only negligibly on the behavior of the model (Suppe, 1989). Theories are *idealized* if it is physically (or otherwise) impossible for the phenomenon to take on the allowable values of the parameters. The favorite example of this is frictionless planes. It would seem that idealizations are quite common in research. This may seem odd, since idealizations by definition are false and inferences to both confirmation and disconfirmation are blocked (Laymon, 1998). But if we look at S-R theory again, it could be argued that this theory too contains idealizations. This is best seen by looking at what has been selected *away* from the model, which is everything that concerns what happens between observed S and observed R. In effect S-R theory treats humans as black boxes, and this amounts to an idealization – it is not possible for humans to be a black box. If anything, this suggests that S-R theory is an oversimplification: it has no parameters concerning stimulus processing. I shall inquire into this issue in greater detail in Chapter 7.

Abstractness leads to intricate philosophical problems concerning the relation of a model or theory to phenomenon. In what way does a simplified, perhaps idealized model represent a real phenomenon? What can S-R theory tell us about the behavior of real people? Semanticists differ on the issue of whether theories express empirical commitments, and if so how they do it. Suppe (1989) proposes we understand the relationship between theory and phenomenon as *counterfactual*. This is a logical consequence of the idea that theories characterize phenomena only in terms of a few selected parameters, since it means that theories do not characterize *actual* phenomena but rather describe what the phenomena would have been *if* the selected parameters were the only ones exerting any influence on them. Theories describe the behavior of models, and only indirectly the phenomena; theories, Suppe argues, describe what phenomena *would have* been *if* no other parameters were influencing them. Hence, theories provide counterfactual descriptions of phenomena and are counterfactually true of them; the mapping relation is counterfactual. In many ways I like Suppe's version of the mapping relation – he has certainly faced up to the consequences of conceiving theories as simplifications providing indirect descriptions of actual phenomena. Suppe himself has steadfastly held on to the counterfactuality interpretation (Suppe, 1972, 1989, 2000). But surely this view is not without its weaknesses. As Chakravartty (2001, p.333) points out, counterfactuality as the mapping relation would render any theory true. No matter how far-fetched a theory is, it would correctly describe what the phenomenon would have been if the phenomenon satisfied the selected parameters. So counterfactuality, Chakravartty argues, cannot do the job of separating true from false theories. And as suggested above, in cases of idealization it would (likely) be wrong to say that a theory is true in any realist sense, since the phenomenon necessarily is not like that described by the theory. Idealized parameters have no counterparts in reality, and idealized theories have a scope of zero, as Craver puts it (p.66). Counterfactuality and idealization sanction theories which by their nature are causally *impossible*, Chakravartty claims. This is a problem for Suppe, who is a realist and thinks that theories *represent* their phenomena.

Van Fraassen (1980) suggests we understand the mapping relation as one of *isomorphism*. A theory, he says, is empirically adequate if it has "some model such that all appearances (i.e. structures described in measurement or experimental reports) are isomorphic to empirical sub-structures of that model" (p.64). Isomorphism is a very strong requirement indeed, denoting a perfect one-to-one, bijective mapping between two structures or sets. This is tricky ground. Suffice it here to make a few comments. First, it should be recalled that van Fraassen defines models as any structure that satisfies the axioms of a theory. Second, on the face of it, isomorphism is a strange choice, since van Fraassen recognizes that theories are simplifications – a fact which by itself indicates that isomorphism does not and cannot obtain. Rather, it is common to point out the respects in which theories are not isomorphic to the phenomenon. But then, third, van Fraassen is not after empirical truth; he is after empirical adequacy, and his focus is on appearances and observable phenomena. He argues, importantly, that we do not have to commit ontologically to all state parameters or variables. I do not wish to get embroiled in technicalities concerning mapping functions, logical space and ontological commitments, but simply convey van Fraassen's conclusion that not everything referred to in theories engenders ontological commitment. Models might contain structures for which there is no correlate in the real world. Fourth, isomorphism seems to be deeply associated with SC. For example, Morrison (2007, p.214) asserts that abandonment of SC will liberate us from reliance on isomorphism as the way of representing phenomena. This is an exaggeration. As we have seen, counterfactuality is a possibility in SC, and so is *similarity*.

The most avid supporter of the similarity thesis is Ronald Giere (1979, 1988). I have already adopted Giere's understanding of models, which I find be both intuitive and serviceable. Here is how he understands theory:

> [W]e understand a theory as comprising two elements; (1) a population of models, and (2) various hypotheses linking those models with systems in the real world.
>
> (Giere, 1988, p.85)

The model is abstract and extralinguistic and therefore cannot have truth values. The theoretical hypothesis, on the other hand, is a linguistic entity, asserting that a certain relationship holds between model and phenomenon. Such hypotheses can therefore be true or false, and the relationship asserted is one of similarity. Models thus represent phenomena in virtue of some similarity relationship. Elements of the model can be identified with features of the real world, Giere argues, and it is this that makes it possible for models to represent the world. A couple of comments are in order. First, the notion of similarity accommodates the fact that models are simplifications and that they contain some degree of inaccuracy. "Similarity" is thus faithful to working scientists' own presentations of their work and Giere notes that "the texts often explicitly rule out claims of isomorphism" (1988, p.81). Second, as it stands, similarity is crucially vague and hard to pinpoint. How do we judge that model and phenomenon have a similar structure? According to which criteria are elements and relations in model and phenomenon selected, when their structures are compared? Chakravartty (2001, p.335) observes that similarity does nothing more than affirm that the model in question generates predictions that make sense of our experiences. But this is not enough for a realist view, he argues, and Giere adheres to scientific realism. Third, Giere has in recent years further developed and refined his views on models and taken them in the direction of pragmatics, but he retains the basic idea of similarity (Giere, 2004, 2010). His account remains realist: models represent, and the claimed similarities between model and world are restricted to observable aspects.

This restriction may sound empiricist to some, but Giere does not think that the distinction between observable and nonobservable is in any way fundamental to science – it suffices that we can observe enough to practice science, he says (2004, p.750). This pragmatic turn introduces other entities into the game, such as intentionality, context and scientific practice. Thus, the representational relationship is defined as "S uses X to represent W for purposes P" (2004, p.743). Model X can be any one of a variety of models, e.g. words, equations, diagrams, graphs, photos, computer-generated images (but they are abstract entities and not to be identified with linguistic formulations). Judgments of similarity thus turn on purpose. As Giere puts it,

> Note that I am not saying that the model itself represents an aspect of the world because it is similar to that aspect. ... Anything is similar to anything else in countless respects, but not anything represents anything else. It is not the model that is doing the representing; it is the scientist using the model that is doing the representing.
>
> (2004, p.747)

Giere here brings a contextual and individual dimension into representation. This dimension may not aid our understanding of representation, but it will be important in my discussion of theory *use* in Chapter 10.

One thing remains to be discussed in this sub-section: a brief comparison with RV. In my judgment the most important differences are the following: first, RV does not incorporate anything like a model. Second, SC does not embody the O/T distinction and does not incorporate anything like correspondence rules. The O/T distinction is one of the most heavily criticized features of RV. While it actually may be useful for many purposes, there is philosophical agreement that it cannot be drawn in principle (although it may be drawn contextually). Third, RV makes the O/T distinction central to its conception of theories, and therefore also central to how the relation between theory and phenomenon is depicted. SC does not need an O/T distinction because theories are not directly about phenomena, but rather about the model. The relation between theory and phenomenon is indirect and therefore allows much flexibility, for better or for worse. Fourth, in RV the theory–phenomenon connection is the job of the set of correspondence rules that correlates observation statements with theoretical statements. This has the effect of making the relation between theory and phenomenon a one-step relation, with the correspondence rules specifying how the laws of the theory manifest themselves directly in the behavior of the (directly observable) phenomena. This, as we shall see, is a highly problematic feature when it comes to theory use, which is so important in education. Because of the O/T distinction there is no room in RV for any kind of intermediary entity. And finally, the O/T distinction also forces RV's correspondence rules to lump together a variety of different epistemological and other aspects of research and theorizing; for example, design of experiment, the nature and use of empirical data, interpretation, calibration, etc.

Theory construction and theory development

What do scientists do when they develop their theories? RV does not have much to offer on this issue. That is partly due to its insistence on axiomatic reformulation: the idea that every scientific theory can be reformulated as an axiomatic system TC. Even if such reformulation should be possible, it presupposes a theory that already is highly developed and organized. And, as mentioned above, the logical empiricists had little interest in providing (descriptive) accounts of how science works.

In contrast, it is not difficult to extract an overall understanding of theory construction from SC. Suppe (1989) describes it as a two-step process: from phenomenon to model and from model to theoretical postulates and laws (these are thus not parts of the model). Suppe thinks the steps are qualitatively very different. While that may be right, we should not necessarily think of them as happening in chronological order – in scientific practice they might be hard to discern. Theories characterize phenomena in terms of some selected parameters, and an obvious job of the researcher is to select the parameters. Giere usefully invokes *maps* to make two related points. First, that abstraction does take place and that many features and details are left out when we represent a landscape on a map. Second, that this simplification is a necessary feature to make the map useful – if all details were to be represented, the map would be the same size as the landscape and, hence, of no use to us. In Suppe's framework this move in theorizing, the replicating relation between phenomenon and model, is counterfactual. We treat the phenomenon *as if* it involved only the selected parameters. All theory construction, Suppe argues, assumes the fiction that no other parameters exert an influence on the phenomenon. As he puts it,

> If P were an isolated phenomenal system in which all other parameters exerted a negligible influence, then the physical quantities characteristic of those parameters abstracted from P would be identical to those values characteristic of the state at t of the physical system S corresponding to P.
>
> (1989, p.95)

Typically, Suppe says, this move involves collection of data, and various procedures for converting "raw" empirical data into "hard" data about the model. We may add that theory constructors employ their prior knowledge of the phenomenon, they may draw on analogies from more or less remote scientific domains, they may toy with possible parameters, etc. – all to make justified decisions as to which parameters to select in order to represent the phenomenon.

The second step in theory construction, from model to theoretical postulates, statements and laws, is qualitatively different, Suppe states. Here we find, for example, predictions concerning the behavior of the model, calculated on the basis of hard data, theoretical postulates and theoretical laws. This step does not involve any counterfactual operations. On the other hand, it seems reasonable to suppose that selection of parameters, postulates and laws actually go hand in hand – and furthermore, that they develop in tandem with ideas about the "big picture". Many postulates are assumptions about connections such as causal mechanisms; these assumptions will be built into the model, perhaps even influence the selections of parameters. Morrison (2007, p.203) suggests that is may be difficult to disentangle truly empirical aspects from stylized descriptions, which are produced via the abstractions. The steps of theory construction might thus be harder to separate than Suppe thinks, but he surely is right that different operations are involved.

In recent years, Suppe (2000) has come of think of theory individuation as the most significant objection to RV. He here assumes that RV identifies a theory with its linguistic formulations, such that changes in formulation yield a different theory. And how do theories change according to SC? The obvious answer is that they change if their parameters change, for example if we add more parameters or replace some; if we entertain different postulates, for example perceive causal connections as probabilistic rather than deterministic; or decide to employ a different theoretical law, for example thinking in terms of succession rather than interaction. Such developments can come in response to new evidence, different concepts, systematic reviews or hunches. Intriguing questions arise as to when a revised theory should be viewed as a *new* theory: is addition of one parameter enough? This is the issue of theory individuation.

Summary

RV and SC, the two major meta-theories, present very different pictures of theories: what they are, what we find when we unpack them, and how they relate to the phenomena within their scope. Most aspects of RV have been heavily criticized, but critics differ on which criticisms they find telling, and RV still has its defenders. I wish to make the following points.

The idea of a two-step relation between theory and phenomenon makes eminently good sense to me. All research relies on and incorporates some form of simplification, already in the gathering of data. Abstraction is an inescapable feature of science and research, and hence of theories. If you look for parameters you will find them. They might not be termed parameters by the researchers, but instead something like "central concepts" or "basic principles". Identification of parameters takes you straight into the heart of any given theory – it tells you much about how a proposed theory purports to represent the phenomenon, something which of course is central to theory evaluation. The SC is easy to apply compared to the RV, and this is a big point in its favor.

That does not mean that SC has solved all outstanding philosophical problems concerning theory, models, representation, truth, experiments, data, confirmation and disconfirmation, etc. This is hardly to be expected of a meta-theory. As we have seen, while simplification is unavoidable and legitimate, it leads to intriguing problems concerning the relation between theory and phenomenon. This is particularly challenging for a field such as education, which in large part is oriented toward practice and to application of theories and models. Perhaps paradoxically, I shall argue that the two-step, indirect relation between theory and phenomenon, theory and practice, introduces a great flexibility in theory use, something that RV does not allow. This will be explored in Chapter 10.

The three theoretical laws mentioned can of course be used independently of SC. In SC they are intimately connected to theory structure, to the dynamics of the theory in how it characterizes the behavior of the model. Theoretical laws are highly powerful analytical tools – one can think of them as heuristics if the term "law" sounds too foreign. The power of theoretical laws will be demonstrated in Chapters 4, 5 and 6, where we shall inquire into different types of educational theory, each with different structures provided by different theoretical laws. Theory structure and theory types are intimately connected. Together they will hopefully substantiate one of my favorite hypotheses: that there is no difference in kind between scientific theories and educational theories. Chambers, Nagel and Thomas all think there is a clear boundary – there are scientific theories, and then there are educational theories. I do not wish to uphold that boundary, and the SC will be central to my argument.

4 Goal-directed theories

This chapter aims at analyzing the structure of goal-directed theories. The short story about goal-directed theories is that they supply a goal and an account of how to reach it. The topic of this chapter is the long story about goal-directed theories. I shall unpack the salient features of such theories using the Semantic Conception of theories (SC) as a lens.

In so far as writers on this topic acknowledge that the field of education has theories, this is the kind of theory they claim it is: theory that is practical in nature and serves to determine or guide practice. This view of the nature of educational theory holds for both Anglo-American and Nordic-Continental writers. While they differ on whether they take education to be an autonomous discipline or not, their understanding of the nature of educational theory is remarkably similar: educational theories are not scientific; they are practical – designed to guide action. This view of educational theories arises from a view of education as a large family of intentional, or purposeful, activities related to child rearing, teaching, training and learning. Terhart's professional dimension looms large in (traditional) perceptions of the field of education (see Chapter 2). And indeed – the field of education does have practical, action-oriented theories, and this chapter is devoted to their analysis. I shall call them goal-directed theories.

It will be recalled from Chapter 2 that D. J. O'Connor (1957) concluded that the word "theory" in educational contexts is little more than a courtesy title. He defines theory as a logically interconnected set of hypotheses confirmable by observation – this definition should now be easily recognizable as the Received View (RV): the logical-positivist view of theories. O'Connor does not spell it out in any detail, but it does not take much spelling out to conclude as O'Connor does: the thing we call theory in education does not fit this scheme. Educational theories are not logically interconnected sets of empirically confirmable sentences or hypotheses. O'Connor assumes, like so many other philosophers of education, that the theories of a discipline or field should suit the nature or object of the discipline. If you think that the nature of the field is deeply connected to practice, you think the theories should be practical or action-guiding. In O'Connor's view, what we tend to call theory in education is in reality a collection of different kinds of statements: metaphysical statements, empirical statements, and value judgments. Of course, practical normative theories do not fit RV with its logical calculus, axioms, V_T, V_O and correspondence rules. But as argued in Chapter 3, RV does not provide what O'Connor assumed it provided; namely "standards by which we can assess the value and use of any claimant to the title of 'theory'" (1957, p.76). So RV cannot accommodate or shed any light on the nature of practical educational theories. In this chapter, I shall explore what SC can contribute on the matter.

Examples of goal-directed theories in education: A small introductory bouquet

It is useful to have a selection of examples of goal-directed educational theories to draw on as the analysis unfolds. The examples will be treated more fully as we proceed, although to different degrees. What follows below is a preliminary sketch.

Goal-directed theories come in different sizes and shapes, as it were. Some are rather loosely organized bodies of knowledge that come in more or less different versions (but still count as the same theory); others are highly systematized. Some, perhaps most, are clearly normative; others are not or are at least ambiguous in that regard. Some goal-directed theories are general in character and have wide scope, such as the classical theories of upbringing of Jean-Jacques Rousseau (1712–1778) or Ellen Key (1849–1926). Others have narrow scope and treat specific topics, such as theories of reading instruction. All goal-directed theories involve change over time, but differ as to the duration envisioned and as to the mechanisms driving the change.

One variety of goal-directed theories is *Bildung* theory, or self-formation theory. Broadly conceived, a Bildung theory encapsulates an image of the ideal human being, which is perceived as the ultimate goal of education, and descriptions of the route toward this goal. Not surprisingly the history of educational thought witnesses considerable disagreement as to what characterizes "der gebildete Mensch" or "the educated man", to use Richard Peters' phrase (e.g. Peters, 1972). Bildung theories tend to be vague both when it comes to the goal and to what drives the change. At the other end of the scale we have, for example, programmed learning theory. This is a theory of instruction and learning, commonly assumed to be based on B. F. Skinner's behavioral psychology. In education the theory often goes by the name educational technology (ET for short). It comes in slightly different versions which all basically say the same: learning a desired behavior, usually precisely described, is accomplished through small steps and successive reinforcement (e.g. Percival & Ellington, 1988, Romiszowski, 1984, Rowntree, 1974). Theories in subject didactics are goal-directed in so far as they are about teaching, imparting knowledge of various phenomena. An example is Rosalind Driver's science education theory (Driver, 1989, 1995, Driver & Oldman, 1986), which is a well-developed and sophisticated goal-directed theory.

As the last flower in this little bouquet, I would like to mention Piaget's theory. As we saw in Chapter 2, he himself did not classify his theory as educational, but a good many educationalists refer to his theory as an example of a theory found in the field of education. Piaget's is a theory of cognitive development (Piaget,

1970). It is a stage theory, which sets it apart from the other theories mentioned here, but is of course not the only stage theory referred to and employed by educationalists – such authors as Erik Homburger Erikson and Lawrence Kohlberg also organize their developmental theories in terms of stages (see Phillips & Kelly, 1975, for a critical discussion). But while theories of development clearly involve change over time and exhibit a goal-directed structure, they are not necessarily normative. Other fields besides education have goal-directed theories, most notably biology. Evolutionary theory can be thought of as a goal-directed theory that incorporates change over time, but it is not a normative theory – it does not say that the change in question is desirable, only that it happens. Piaget's theory is non-normative in the same way – that is something I shall come back to subsequently.

Normativity

Normativity, Stephen Turner (2010) argues, is everywhere. We constantly and necessarily rely on and employ normative concepts and terms, such as standards, norms, obligations, responsibility, values, right and wrong, good and bad, valid and invalid. Turner defines "the normative" as "a special realm of fact that validates, justifies, makes possible, and regulates normative talk, as well as rules, meanings, the symbolic and reasoning" (p.1). The normative realm ramifies into linguistic normativity, semantic, legal, epistemic, social... and, I presume, educational. Normativity is thus a huge and complex field in itself and I shall confine myself to a few comments. But since most goal-directed educational theories are normative, a few words are warranted.

Let us return to Hirst's views on educational theory, discussed in Chapter 2 (Hirst, 1966). It will be recalled that Hirst distinguishes scientific theories from educational theories, such that "scientific theory and educational theory are as different logically as judgments of what is the case are different from judgments of what ought to be the case" (p.42). Hirst makes much of the logical distinction between *is* and *ought*. I take him to mean that scientific theories are factual whereas educational theories are fundamentally normative in that they contain an "ought". In keeping with this Hirst states that the function of an educational theory is to determine precisely what shall be done (p.40) – a phrase which contains not an *ought* but an even stronger *shall*. Furthermore, he also states that "the function of educational theory is the determination of these [i.e. in education] aims" (p.32), so that the job of educational theory is determination of both the *what* and the *how* of education. In Chapter 2 I problematized the relationship between the foundational disciplines, educational theory and rational practical principles for practice. It is unclear whether an educational theory consists of rational practical principles or whether the theory determines the principles. What are the constituents of an educational theory, which makes it capable of determining rational practical principles? If educational theory and rational principles amount to one and the same thing, it is unclear how the foundational disciplines together can make up rational practical principles for education since education, on Hirst's view, contributes nothing. If the rational principles constitute the *ought*, then how do we get to the principles from the foundational disciplines, assuming that they represent the *is*? Hirst says that educational theory acts as a mediator between foundational disciplines and practice. The relation between the foundational disciplines and educational practice is *indirect*:

> ...unless philosophical beliefs are to influence educational practice in a distorting manner, they must influence it indirectly through the medium of educational theory, before any particular principles for educational practice are explicitly formulated.
>
> (1966, p.33)

That suggests that educational theory and practical principles are different things. However we conceive of the role of educational theory in relation to rational principles and foundational disciplines, Hirst insists that there is an insurmountable logical difference between *is* and *ought*, such that we cannot derive an *ought* from an *is*. As Gert Biesta (2011) points out, this move ensures the independence of educational theory in that they are not to be understood as simply derivative of factual knowledge, since "factual knowledge in itself can never provide a sufficient justification for what ought to be done" (p.182). There is a delightful irony in Hirst's views – education is not an autonomous discipline, but educational *theory* is independent. What is clear is that a lot hangs on the *ought*; that which apparently carries the normativity of educational theories.

The is-ought problem is an old philosophical problem, also known as the naturalistic fallacy: normative and/or evaluative statements cannot be derived from factual statements alone. There is thus an unbridgeable gap between is and ought, fact and value. This view is quite widespread among philosophers of education; Hirst is by no means the only one to subscribe to it. A full-fledged discussion of the is-ought relation falls outside the scope of this book, but a couple of things are worth pointing out, especially concerning what we shall make of the *ought*.

First, let us note that *ought* is a modal auxiliary verb, alongside *must (shall)*, *can* and the copula *is*. We associate *must (shall)* with necessity, *can* with possibility, and *is* with actuality. These are linked, such that what is actual is possible; what is not possible is necessarily not actual; what is not necessary is possible, and what is necessary is (or will be) actual. But what about *ought*? *Ought* is used interchangeably with *should* when *should* is not the present tense of *shall*, and seems generally to be placed somewhere between *must* and *can*, weaker than the former and stronger than the latter. It does not tell you what you must do, but rather conveys recommendations, more or less strongly. *Ought* thus implies *can* – your recommended course of action should be possible.

Second, if Turner is right and normativity is everywhere, *is* and *ought* may be more closely intertwined than the naturalistic fallacy would have it. In that case, the *ought* may not be so exclusively tied to moral/ethical dimensions as Hirst seemingly assumes. I have no doubt that any number of norms, normative considerations and judgments are involved in research, in methodology, in theorizing and in practice, and therefore make up part of the background of any belief formation, including meta-theory. Whether a given set of data supports a hypothesis to a sufficient degree is not an empirical question – it is a question belonging to the realm of epistemic normativity, concerning what we should think or believe. The *is* of the is-ought relation is permeated with normative considerations. Research methodology is normative in character, not empirical. Thus, the is-ought distinction might not be as clear a marker of the distinction between scientific and educational theories as Hirst thinks. Both in science and in daily communication we use *ought* in non-normative ways, or better – given Turner's view – in ways which are not straightforwardly normative in the ethical/moral sense that Hirst (and others) seem to presuppose. Take for example such everyday claims as (1) "these eggs have boiled for six minutes, they ought to be done by now" or (2) "the bus should have been here by now". Also in science *ought* can be found in a large variety of sentences, for example (3) "this theorem ought to be derivable from these axioms" or (4) "this medical procedure should cure your illness". What does *ought* mean in such cases? Interestingly, even in such cases some form of norm is involved. Hirst and other philosophers preserve the *ought* for the guiding of actions, for example (5) "you ought to treat your students with respect" or (6) "to teach students the basic ideas of democracy, you should…". The *ought* of (5) and (6) can perhaps be described as prospective, as forward-looking; it recommends particular courses of actions, which you *can* adopt. The *ought* (should) of (4) suggests that there is a good probability that your illness will be cured, and is also prospective as it is formulated. The other examples are different, but still in some sense invoke a norm. Why do we think that eggs should be boiled after six minutes? Because, Daniel Kahneman and Dale Miller (1986) suggest, we compare the particular issue to a belief that has arisen out of many experiences with boiling eggs, namely that after six minutes they are done. If they are not, we wonder why they are not – they ought to be. The *ought* in this case reflects a norm based on experience. We compare the reality of the bus delay to the alternative, which in this case is the schedule. The schedule serves as a norm, and we conclude that the bus should have been here. Reality, as Kahneman and Miller put it, is compared to an alternative and the alternative functions as a norm. Thus, *ought* is heavily involved in counterfactual reasoning, for example when we assess results by comparing reality to its alternatives. Why didn't the students perform better on this test? They should have done. Why am I not able to derive this theorem from the axioms? It ought to be derivable. Such uses of *ought* are found everywhere, including logics, the empirical sciences and everyday life. The is-ought relation as standardly discussed and employed by Hirst (and others) does not capture this important use of *ought* in educational reasoning. Framing the overall normativity issue of educational theory in terms of the is-ought relation neglects several important normative dimensions, ways of reasoning and linguistically entrenched uses of *ought*, I suggest. I would also like to suggest that the presence of an *ought* is not the chief factor in making educational theories normative in the moral/ethical sense; that surely cannot depend exclusively on a versatile modal auxiliary verb. Let us view it as a fallible sign.

Third, let us return briefly to the naturalistic fallacy and the claim that normative and/or evaluative conclusions cannot be derived from factual premises alone. If you wish to draw (certain) normative conclusions from factual premises, you have to add a (certain) value premise. Here we meet a different problem. One thing is to have an action-guiding *ought*. Another thing is where its normative force comes from and how strong it is. How is it that a theory containing (or being constituted by) an *ought* can incur obligations in practitioners so strong that the theory not only recommends but determines what shall be done? I do not know, and Hirst does not say. It is probably just taken for granted.

Normativity is an issue with all sorts of intricacies. I shall argue below (and in subsequent chapters) that I do not think the distinction between scientific theory and educational theory, expressed in terms of *is* and *ought*, holds up to scrutiny. The mixture of normative and empirical constituents and dimensions in goal-directed theories is intricate and the is-ought relation does not do justice to it. However, normativity obviously has a place in the theory–practice relation, and I will come back to it in Chapter 10.

The structure of goal-directed educational theories

Goal-directed theories, like any other theories, have parameters, theoretical postulates and theoretical laws. They also have additional features which make them precisely goal-directed and normative (when they are normative).

Modifying people in some more or less specified way is the point of teaching and the traditional *raison d'être* of educational activities. All the examples of goal-directed theories sketched above presuppose that the "entity" that needs to be changed is an *individual*. For the most part this individual is a child, a student, but can of course also be an adult. We should note, however, that goal-directed theories need not concern individuals only; the entity in question may be of a supra-individual kind, such as couples, groups, classroom climates, organizations or even nations. I shall follow Suppe (1989) and analyze goal-directed theories as theories with teleological laws. The entities that are supposed to change I propose to call "teleological entities" (Suppe calls them "teleological systems") and they are, unsurprisingly, the main focus of goal-directed theories; that which our interest centers on. On the SC, then, goal-directed theories provide an account of how teleological entities move toward the goal; namely partly as a function of their interaction with the environment. The behavior of a teleological entity is thus governed by teleological laws: laws of succession that specify a pattern of change in the entity in question. The environment may fall outside the control of the teleological entity; it may fall partly under its control, or it may be influenced by the entity but not controlled by it. Typically, most – but not necessarily all – goal-directed theories presuppose that the change is occasioned by deliberate intervention (Norris & Kvernbekk, 1997). And to be sure, parents, teachers, supervisors, counselors, therapists, leaders and others can and do intervene in order to direct student behaviors, attitudes, skills, beliefs, knowledge or competence in a direction considered to be desirable. That is to say, in education the goal is imposed intentionally by some agent outside the teleological entity. More often than not it is also the case that some outside agent manipulates the environment to facilitate the desired change. I shall assume in the following that what makes goal-directed theories normative is the imposition of goals that designate the desired outcomes of educational processes. Such theories therefore contain parameters in the form of normative elements. Normative goal-directed educational theories provide accounts of how to achieve *desired* goals. The account of *how*, on the other hand, is empirical. Goal-directed theories employ a delicate mixture of normative and empirical elements.

Before we continue, two conceptual clarifications are in order. First, it should be noted that the notion of teleology, as it is used in SC, is not to be understood in terms of purposes or final causes as is the traditional view of teleology. A teleological law is to be understood as a law of succession which typically specifies patterns of change leading to some specified goal state. As described in Chapter 3, such laws can be deterministic or statistical. A teleological entity, like any model, is capable of a certain set of values. Its state at any given time is determined by the values of its parameters. The behavior of a teleological entity, in terms of its changes over time, is mapped into and represented by the state space. A deterministic law of succession means that the current state of the teleological entity determines unique subsequent states; that is, there is only one state transition path, one possible trajectory through the state space that the entity in question can take. A statistical (or probabilistic) law of succession allows that for a given current state, the teleological entity may assume a number of different subsequent states. There are several possible state transition paths or trajectories through the state space. The law involved may deem one of them more likely to obtain than others, it may assign different probabilities to all trajectories, or may refrain from assigning probabilities altogether. Second, it should be noted that the notion of manipulation (of environment) is to be understood as a neutral technical term. It does not carry any of its usual negative connotations, e.g. indoctrination. To manipulate an environment is to change it: add or subtract elements, reorganize them, etc., in order to facilitate the teleological entity's interaction with it and development toward the desired goal. This is parallel to how the term is used in manipulationist theories of causation where it denotes the changing of (the value of) input variables in order to change (the value of) some output variable.

The structure of normative goal-directed educational theories depicts state transitions as departing from a state which necessarily is conceived to be at some distance from the goal state, and ending in (or at least moving in the direction of) the specified goal state. Such theories thus consist of the following elements and structures; my description is adapted after Norris and Kvernbekk (1997, p.983):

1 A desired goal state, G. This is a normative parameter and serves to make the theory normative and practice-oriented.
2 Laws of succession defining a sequence of states of the teleological entity that moves in the direction of G. S_1 is the state at the point of departure, S_t is the

state of the entity at time *t*, and S_G represents the arrival of the entity at G. As noted above, the sequence may be determined or probable.

3 Parameters describing the teleological entity. The point of a goal-directed theory is that the values of these parameters change (or should change) in the desired direction. Depending on the measurability of the parameter in question, the values can be mapped and judgments as to progress can be made. The state of the entity at time *t* is made up of the values of all the parameters at time *t*. If parameters are idealized, their value will be constant for all states.
4 Parameters describing the environment. It stands to reason that the values of these parameters will change in tandem with the values of the entity parameters. The state of the environment at time *t* is defined by the values of the environmental parameters at time *t*.

Below is an illustration of the basic structure of normative goal-directed theories. Again, it is adapted after Norris and Kvernbekk (1997, p.984), but is simpler than the original and makes no use of technical notation. It is important to note that the *model* we are dealing with here is not just the teleological entity, even though that is where our main interest lies. The model consists of the teleological entity, the environment, the change toward the goal state, and the goal state itself. It is also important to keep in mind that the fundamental idea of such theories is that the entity changes partly as a function of its interaction with the environment.

As suggested above, this structure may represent a good many different goal-directed theories. Teleological entities may be individual students, groups, institutions or nations, and the parameters describing them may be anything the theorist deems pertinent. The environment may be classrooms, schools, curricula, policy or global student achievement test programs, and the parameters may be anything the theorist deems pertinent. Goals range from simple, narrow and specific to complex, broad, general and vague. They can encompass knowledge, understanding, skills, abilities, traits and general competencies. The change in question, undergone by the teleological entity, can be variously described as development, learning, socialization or self-formation. The law of succession involved represents *time* in this process and presses upon us the dynamic character of goal-directed theories. Whichever concrete manifestation of this theoretical structure we are dealing with, it seems clear that even normative goal-directed theories have an empirical heart: the interaction of entity and environment, illustrated in Figure 4.1 by double-headed arrows.

Goal states

The normative character of goal-directed theories, I suggest, as a rule comes from goal states. Goal states carry a purposeful interest in making some impact or other on some portion of reality, and are unequivocally normative and value-laden entities. My treatment of goal states here will be rather step-motherly, since I shall discuss goal states at length in Chapter 5, albeit from a different perspective. Suffice it here to draw attention to a couple of things.

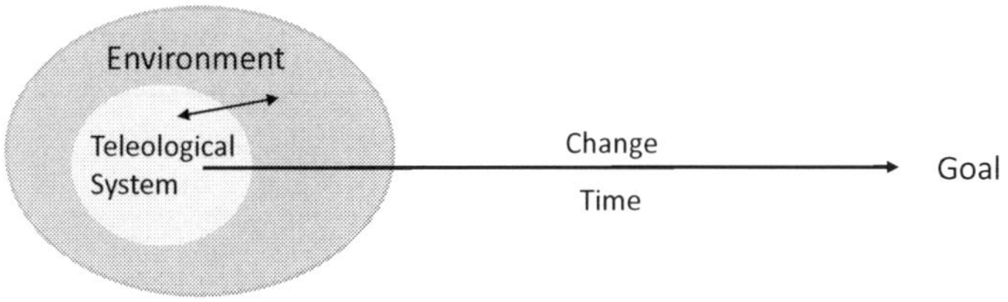

Figure 4.1 Goal-directed theory
Adapted from Norris & Kvernbekk (1997, p.984)

First, goals come in all sizes and shapes and can be categorized in different ways. Some goals are in the form of superordinate aims, such as "the educated man", tolerance or open-mindedness. Others are specific and precise, such as understanding the principles of multiplication (or memorizing the multiplication table, as the case was when I went to school). Whether narrow or broad, goals are value-laden and considered to be desired – although not necessarily by all. Aims and goals vary with context and epoch but may become more similar as an effect of the international assessment programs, which make student achievement comparable across the globe (or purport to do so). Today we tend to call goals "learning outcomes" and the current ideology is that they should be so precisely formulated that they are easily measurable. I would like to introduce here an example that I also shall discuss in Chapter 5, namely the desired goal state of Rosalind Driver's science education theory (Driver, 1989, 1995). Driver's theory is a detailed and well-articulated normative goal-directed theory which concerns the modification of students' nonscientific understandings of various natural phenomena so that they become more scientific, modification of their views about what science is so that they become more accurate, and modification of their attitudes toward science so that they become more positive and science can play a bigger role in their lives. This is a complex goal state and in Chapter 5 I shall decompose it further. For now, let me just comment that it provides a nice contrast to today's highly specific learning outcomes.

Second, where do the aims come from? As we have seen, Paul Hirst (1966) claims that it is the job of an educational theory to – among other things – determine the goals. No doubt goals have many sources. Educational theory may be one of them, but in the case of specific competencies it is more reasonable to think that the goals originate in the subject in question. It does not seem reasonable to say that Driver's theory has determined the specific goals of that theory; for example, that students should understand the concept of density. In many countries including my own the curriculum, which is national, is passed by the Parliament, and schools and teachers have limited freedom to choose goals. The aim of Bildung, on the other hand, is not passed by any institution. Rather, Ingerid Straume (2013, p.17) suggests, self-formation or Bildung ideals grow out of the larger social context. Bildung ideals therefore reflect time, place, society, social order, norms and customs. They change as the context changes;

influenced by material, political and ideological dimensions as well as tensions that exist within a society. Perhaps we can say that the Bildung ideal is everywhere yet nowhere in particular, that it can make its presence felt by normative expectations we all pick up on. If so, it has considerable normative force, despite its vagueness. It is worth mentioning here that the idea of Bildung takes its point of departure in what I above referred to as an "alternative" – the possibility that we can become something other than what we currently are; something better than our first, natural selves.

Third, there is the question of goal states that are not normative, but that rather simply mark the end point of a development. Jean Piaget's developmental theory is a case in point, assuming that it can count as an educational theory. The theory describes the development of cognitive functions through four stages, and the fourth stage – the formal operational stage which is reached around age 11 to 12 – represents the end stage. Here the individual has developed the ability to reason deductively, systematically and counterfactually, and to evaluate potential solutions to problems. But first and foremost, the individual has acquired the ability to think abstractly. This development, Piaget says (1970, p.703) has biological presuppositions and epistemological consequences. Biological maturation provides the possibilities, but the individual must actualize them. This actualization, according to Piaget, "obeys the law of creodes [i.e. developmental pathway], that is, of constant and necessary progress such that the endogenous reactions find support in the environment and in experience" (p.712). Hence, all teleological entities develop toward the end state following the same trajectory (some might not reach it). The end state is a goal state in the sense that the development goes in that direction; it is not imposed because it is considered desirable.

The teleological entity

In principle, a teleological entity is anything that develops over time in the direction of the goal state, regardless of whether the goal state is natural (as in Piagetian cognitive development) or imposed (as in education, perhaps with some exceptions). In educational contexts the teleological entity most often refers to an individual – this is in keeping with education's historical interest in children, their upbringing and formation. However, teleological entities are not confined to individuals but can also refer to couples, groups, classes, organizations or whole nations, for that matter. But let us stay with individuals.

All goal-directed theories assume a starting point for the teleological entity, the individual that is to undergo some desired change. This is mundane but should be said nonetheless – the point of departure and goal state are not identical. Alexander Romiszowski (1984) suggested that the discrepancy between the current and the desired state of those who are meant to attain the goal should be defined as the basic educational problem. That evidently requires knowledge of the current state. But even if we knew the current state it may not be obvious what exactly is supposed to change and how it could or should change. How is the "current state" or point of departure more generally reflected in goal-directed theories? Theories seemingly differ wildly in which parameters if any they attribute to the individual in question. Let us look at Watson's classical behaviorism, briefly mentioned in Chapter 3. This theory takes the learning of behavior as its object, and describes it as a function of two parameters: stimulus and response. This is a highly idealized theory – in Suppe's terminology, it describes how the individual *would* respond *if* the stimulus was the only thing influencing his or her behavior. But what does this theory tell us about the individual? What attributes does this individual have, in perceiving and processing the stimulus and producing a (desired) response? We do not know. S-R theory treats the teleological entity as a "black box" about which nothing is known. This does indeed seem to be the case sometimes – educational theories treat the individual as a black box, providing no parameters to describe the teleological entity. Take educational technology (ET), a normative goal-directed theory which was popular in the 1960s and 70s, but which is largely discredited now. It comes in slightly different versions, which all basically say the same: learning a desired behavior, usually precisely described, is accomplished through small steps and successive reinforcement (e.g. Percival & Ellington, 1988, Romiszowski, 1984, Rowntree, 1974). In its simplest ideal-type form ET says that in order for students to acquire certain knowledge *(the goal)*, the teacher should present this knowledge in small pieces; give immediate feedback on students' responses or solutions; and not let the students pass on to the next level until the current one is mastered *(interaction with environment)*. ET is a goal-directed, prescriptive theory containing an *ought* (*should)*. It is a general theory about how the possibilities for achieving a certain outcome can be maximized. In Suppe's terminology, it describes what students *would* learn *if* their learning was a function of input, feedback and "control". Simple and crude as this theory may be, it is very useful for analytical purposes. It exemplifies both normativity, goal and manipulation of environment to facilitate optimal development toward the goal, which we shall come back to. But for the moment we are concerned with the teleological entity. And this theory, like S-R theory, does not tell us anything about the individuals under its scope (although it clearly makes many assumptions about them). So why are some educational theories silent about the very entity that takes or should take center stage? A possible explanation may be that the development in question is assumed to run from a "zero" state, where the individual has no (relevant) knowledge and no (relevant) skills, and toward a goal state representing such knowledge and skills. Nevertheless, if the individual has become a black box, I would say that simplification, which is both unavoidable and legitimate, has turned into oversimplification, which is illegitimate. In a professional field that concerns itself with people, it will not do to idealize away those people.

By contrast, Rosalind Driver's science education theory provides a rich description of the teleological entity (Driver, 1989, 1995, Driver & Oldman, 1986). It is an abstract individual student, created by a selection of parameters from a large class of students, including all science students in grade school. The individual student in the theory is abstract in the sense that it is not any concrete student.

This teleological entity is understood to be representative of that entire class of students, and all students in that class fall under the scope of the theory. Stephen Norris and I (1997) reconstructed Driver's theory using the conceptual resources of SC and in the following I shall draw heavily on our analysis. I should say, though, that this is not how Driver herself presents her theory, and that our reconstruction of it only addresses the structure of the theory, not its empirical adequacy. In our analysis we identified seven categories of parameters describing the teleological entity across Driver's texts: demographics, metacognition, nature of science understanding, affect, nature of students' conceptions, dispositions to think and engage, and content-specific beliefs. All these categories come with a number of sub-categories, a list of which is supplied in our article (pp.987–989). For my purposes here that level of detail is not necessary – our summary will suffice (p.986):

> There are only two demographic parameters: age, and a general background parameter. The metacognition parameters abstract aspects of students' evaluation of their ideas; the nature of science understanding parameters abstract students' broad understandings and appreciations of science in general; the affect parameters abstract aspects of students' individualism, responsibility and openness in learning new ideas; the nature of students' conceptions parameters abstract aspects of the value of students' ideas judged from an outsider's perspective; the disposition to think and engage parameters abstract aspects of students' active engagement in learning new ideas; and the content-specific beliefs parameters abstract students' beliefs about whatever natural phenomena are the focus of their science instruction.

The state of the teleological entity at any time *t* is defined by the ordered set of values of all parameters at time *t*. The teleological entity in Driver's theory is far from being a black box! As we can see from this example, describing the state of the teleological entity might be a very complex affair indeed. Now, whatever degree of complexity involved, the idea is that changes in these values should bring the teleological entity in the direction of the goal state G. That means that there is an intimate relation between the goal state and the parameters describing the teleological entity. And at this point two interrelated issues arise: the issue of how we should judge the proposed student parameters, and the issue of what use we shall make of them. It will be recalled from the previous sub-section that goal state G of Driver's theory comprises the modification of students' nonscientific understandings of various natural phenomena so that they become more scientific, modification of their views about what science is so that they become more accurate, and modification of their attitudes toward science so that they become more positive and science can play a bigger role in their lives. If we juxtapose goal state G with the student parameters, we see that the goal state is defined in terms of some of the student parameters but not in terms of all of them. The central aim of Driver's theory is alteration of content-specific beliefs and of the understanding of the nature of science such that they match the conventional beliefs of science and about science. Thus, two of the student parameter categories are clearly connected to the goal state: the category concerning understanding the nature of science, and the category of content-specific beliefs. Changes in the values of these parameters will bring the student closer to the goal state – on the assumption, of course, that the changes are the correct or desired ones. Alterations in parameter values in the other categories do not in and of themselves take the student in the direction of the goal state, although the categories do have some connections. For example, the goal concerning nature of science is connected to the student parameters concerning the nature of students' conceptions, but overall, Norris and I concluded in our analysis (p.989), the other student parameters have no clear definitional match with the goal state.

Where does that leave us? A couple of observations are in order. First, there is the question of abstraction of parameters. In Chapter 3 I argued that parameters make up the heart of any theory and therefore are a good place to start if you want to understand what a theory says about the phenomenon under its scope, but also if you wish to evaluate the adequacy of the theory. Which parameters? How many? Concerning Driver's theory, the question arises if she has selected too many student parameters, since only two of them explicitly match the goal state. Should, for example, demographics be included as a parameter, since changes in age by themselves do not bring students closer to the goal state? Second, it is vital for any goal-directed theory to have a selection of parameters concerning the teleological entity, precisely because these parameters are so closely connected with the description of the goal state. Third, if a theory includes entity parameters that are not directly related to the goal state, what role in the theory could they then play? Fourth, what sort of match should there be between goal state and the parameters of the teleological entity? That is by no means obvious. But there has to be some match, or else the theory cannot do its job, namely to tell us how the student parameter values change in the desired direction as a result of the student's interaction with an environment. Fifth, it is well worth mentioning that the value of what I judge to be the most central parameter in Driver's theory, content-specific beliefs, is a result of much empirical research. This parameter is an idealization in the form of an "average": the prevalent content-specific beliefs about natural phenomena, such as thunder and lightning, that students of a given age are found to hold. This average makes up the point of departure and the aim is to alter the value in the desired direction. Clearly a lot of careful work has gone into the construction of Driver's theory.

The environment

It is my distinct impression that the environment receives much more attention than the teleological entity. Yes, we are interested in students and their learning; we test and measure outcomes and achievements. But education in its professional parts is more concerned with the organization of material, social and temporal affordances, that is to say, the manipulation of the environment in order to facilitate the processes of learning, development and self-formation. In a sense, education is indirect – you do not influence the values on entity parameters directly, but through the entity's interaction with a (more or less) carefully organized environment. The pedagogue is a vital element in such environments, and we should not wonder that so much educational research and thought go into understanding and developing the role of the teacher. In fact, I think Hirst's *ought* is aimed at teachers – the question of "what should be done" is by and large a question of what teachers should do, not of what students should do.

Educational environments may consist of all sorts of affordances, and the environmental parameters can be any selected aspect of the environment that the theory constructor deems important. The values of environmental parameters may change as the state of the teleological entity changes; however, if the environmental parameters are idealized their value is constant for all states of the entity. Environmental parameters cannot be discussed completely independently of goal state and entity parameters, since it is interaction with environmental parameters that will move the entity in the direction of the goal state. Let us begin by looking at the simple ideal-type version of ET again. What does it say about the environment? That it consists of knowledge organized in small pieces, immediate feedback on answers and/or solutions, and stages of mastery. This is a much-stripped-down environment and provides a sharp but instructive contrast with the environment described in Driver's theory. It also illustrates the inter-dependence of goal state and environmental parameters (and potentially of entity parameters, had ET had any). Note the central role of the pedagogue in ET, even if he or she is not explicitly mentioned. The pedagogue organizes the knowledge, gives feedback, and controls the mastery stages.

Driver's science education theory is constructivist and, at least partly for that reason, portrays a rich learning environment. I shall again draw on Norris' and my analysis of Driver's theory (Norris & Kvernbekk, 1997). We categorize the proposed environmental parameters in six large categories. These are encouragement and opportunity from teacher; positive teacher feedback; instructional strategies; existence and presentation of standard science; student-student interaction, and resources. Again, all the categories come with a number of sub-categories (pp.990–992). We summarize as follows (p.989):

> Of the six categories, the first three include environmental parameters that are in the direct control of the teacher: the teacher's encouragement and provision of opportunity, the teacher's positive feedback to students, and the instructional strategies that the teacher employs. Category D contains a mixture of parameters, some whose values are under the control of the teacher (e.g., guidance to adopt scientific ways of seeing, shaping students' reasoning to the accepted view), and others whose values are outside the teacher's influence (e.g., concepts of standard science, culture and institutions of science). Category E contains parameters that fall partly under the teacher's influence and partly under the influence of the science students. Finally, Category F contains parameters that are controlled partly by the teacher and partly by other authorities.

The heart of any goal-directed theory is the interaction between the teleological entity and its environment. Specific interactions are supposed to bring about certain changes in the parameters describing the teleological entity. Which entity parameters are affected by which kinds of teacher encouragement, how and to what degree? How do different experiences with the physical environment influence entity parameters? Driver's theory is rich and complex, and the interactional possibilities practically endless. It would be unreasonable to demand that the theory should provide descriptions of all possible interactions and their supposed effects, but it does provide ideas about some such influences. For example, the instructional strategy of using contradictory experiences is designed to make students query their existing scientific understandings when these are not the conventional scientific ones. Interestingly, the theory places this strategy in a temporal sequence indicating how environmental parameters can, will or may change in tandem with values of entity parameters. Contradictory experiences are to be used early in instruction to make students reflect on their current understandings and become dissatisfied with them if they are not scientific, and to nudge students to generate new hypothetical understandings. Such a change in entity parameters exemplifies movement toward goal state G. How interactions happen is an empirical matter. It is also an empirical matter whether the entity, through interaction, actually does move in the desired direction. There is thus an intricate interplay of normative and empirical features in normative goal-directed theories. Note also the different kinds of *oughts* involved: students should move toward goal state G because G is desired, and they should move toward G because that it what we expect such interactions to deliver, if things go right.

Goal-directedness

Next we come to goal-directedness. How should we understand it? How do teleological entities display their tendency toward some goal state?

It will be recalled that goal-directed theories are governed by laws of succession (see Chapter 3). These laws determine which sequences of states of the model are possible; the model is this case being a teleological entity in interaction with an environment, perhaps with a special view to the changing values of the entity parameters but, as we have seen in Driver's theory, in tandem with changes in the values of environment parameters. Laws of succession can be deterministic or they can be probabilistic. Deterministic laws specify *one* trajectory through the state space; probabilistic laws tell us there can be different paths of change and assigns probabilities to them (if possible).

Let us begin our exploration by looking into the structure of classical theories of upbringing. Jürgen Oelkers (1994) calls such theories "paradigms" – in response, I take it, to their broad scope – and divides them into two large groups: *influence* and *development*. As Oelkers points out, these large categories are firmly rooted in the history of educational thought (he uses John Locke and Jean-Jacques Rousseau as examples) but they serve to organize our thought even today. Note the different prepositions, *on* and *of*. They are quite telling:

> In most theories *education* still is conceived either as "influence" (on body and mind) or as "development" (of body and mind), and most controversies in education still have to do with the struggle of these two paradigms.
> (1994, p.92)

In a sense, we can say that these two families of theories are inverse versions of one another. The teleological entity of both theories is the child. The *influence* theories famously treat the entity as a black box or a *tabula rasa*; nothing of what we learn is innate. The *development* theories, on the other hand, endow the newborn child with various attributes (needs, abilities, interests) and justify them in different ways, e.g. by religion, nature or evolution. Rousseau, Oelkers says (p.98), conceives of nature as a self-acting force in the child, a force which develops itself, and the task of education is to follow its track. Both theory families have the explicit temporal aspect that makes them goal-directed; from birth to the age – I presume – when children can take responsibility for their own development. But their inverse character is most clearly divulged in the idea of goal-directness. Let me use Ellen Key, Swedish reform educationist, as an example of a *development* thinker (Key, 1911). Her theory may be of historical interest only, but it illustrates well a certain way of conceiving goal-directedness, namely as change occurring under the teleological entity's own drive. Key bases her theory on a recapitulation conception of evolution. She conceives of evolution (of a species) as a continuous and unalterable movement toward a goal state termed "harmony" or "perfection". By means of the recapitulation thesis she establishes that the changes an individual undergoes in the course of a life-time are also continuous and unalterable, leading toward the individual's own goal state. By analogy she claims that this holds true even for mental development. When individuals are granted freedom to interact with the environment in accordance with their own needs, abilities and interests, they will tend toward the goal state by their own internal drive. It is perhaps a matter of some contention whether Key's goal-directed theory is normative or not. I would argue that it is non-normative – the goal state is built into the nature of the individual and the development simply goes in that direction. Her theory seems to fall under what Oelkers (p.100) calls a "strictly teleological" variety of development, which among other things means an irreversible movement. But while Key speaks of unalterable changes, we should not attribute to her the view that all individuals necessarily arrive at their own goal state. While development tends in that direction if left to its own devices, it can all too easily be thwarted by unfavorable circumstances.

By contrast, *influence* theories operate with external drives. If there are no entity parameters at the outset, then the inner mental states must be constructed from the outside, through influence exerted by more or less significant others. As Oelkers so aptly puts it, the Lockean terminology of objectives, influence and formation of habits casts the roles of child and pedagogue in the following way:

> [T]he child becomes the object of an external construction, the educator becomes the designer, who is no longer required to show consideration for

> "psychic" *preconditions*. He is master of the *tabula rasa* as far as it is under his control.
>
> (1994, p.96)

Both theories, Oelkers says, run on the assumption of distinct inner space. *Development* presupposes closed inner spaces; *influence* presupposes an opening up of the inner space to the outside. His description of *development* fits Key quite well:

> Nature develops "itself"; this implies both an agent and a space of development, namely the "soul"'s inner world of imagination, which is mysteriously directed to an (or *its*) objective.
>
> (p.101)

This is a good place to bring Piaget's theory into the picture. The theory is about the development of cognitive functions in the individual. At the outset let us briefly note that Piaget, like Key, adhered to some form of the recapitulation thesis and understood the growth of logic in the individual as paralleling the evolution of human intelligence. This assumption, Denis Phillips and Mavis Kelly (1975) point out, makes it unnecessary for Piaget to seek a large data base – any child can be used to provide data for his theory, since the development of logic in all individuals is assumed to follow the same pattern (p.354). The teleological entity of Piaget's theory is an individual child. Does the theory equip the entity with any initial parameters and parameter values? It would seem not. As Constance Kamii (1979) puts it, "While many rationalists stated that certain ideas, such as those of space, time, causation, and number, are innate, Piaget proved that the logico-arithmetical and spatio-temporal frameworks are constructed by each child" (p.23). At the point of departure, the values of all entity parameters thus seem to be zero, but the entity is endowed with biological presuppositions. The cognitive structures and functions are progressively constructed by interaction between subject and the external world. This is an active process, Piaget says (1970, p. 704), composed of actions, operations and transformations.

Piaget's theory, it will be recalled, is a stage theory. All individuals run through the same stages from birth to about 11 or 12 years of age: sensorimotor; pre-operational, concrete operational and formal operational – a development from simple to complex. The sequence of stages is invariant, according to Piaget:

> If we restrict ourselves to major structures, it is strikingly obvious that cognitive stages have a sequential property, that is, they appear in a fixed order of succession because each of them is necessary for the formation of the following one.
>
> (1970, p.711)

All cognitive development culminates in stage 4; the formal operational stage. Combine this with an invariant sequence, and I think it is fair to say that Piaget's theory assumes that there is only one path through the state space; the theory employs a deterministic law of succession. This is not a matter of different paths toward the goal state or different paths with different probabilities attached to them. Yet he also says that the evolution of cognitive structures is not entirely predetermined. The interplay of internal and external drives is intriguing. On the one hand, experience is not sufficient to explain the development of cognitive structures, much less its sequential character. On the other hand, children, without any teaching whatsoever, come to understand the principle of class inclusion and thus that there are more flowers than roses. Pedagogical interventions cannot change the order of construction, Piaget says; in fact, he warns against teaching children things prematurely. That prevents them from discovering or constructing it for themselves and therefore from completely understanding it. I shall come back to the issue of transition between stages below. Let me just say here that the goal-directedness in Piaget's theory is a matter of a deterministic law of succession. What changes is the inner space of the individual. What drives the change is a combination of maturation, experience and action of the social environment. Maturation is not sufficient to explain development because it contains no hereditary programming factor; the other two cannot account for the invariant sequence of the development (p.719). Like Key, Piaget's individual falls under what Oelkers calls "strictly teleological".

Before we leave this topic, let us look at the (possible) goal-directedness of Bildung theories. Ingerid Straume (2013) suggests that Bildung theories contain minimally a subject (a teleological entity), a social dimension (environment) and something she terms "movement". All of these can be conceptualized in different ways, to form different, contrasting and perhaps conflicting Bildung theories. The subject can be the self, the child, the disciple, the searching young person. Straume does not say, but I assume that these theories generally (but not necessarily) presuppose an inner space in the way Oelkers describes for the big theories of upbringing. In current Bildung theory the teleological entity is a critical and reflective one; a feature which makes me think that the temporal stretch of Bildung theories do not begin in childhood, but with somewhat mature individuals. Bildung in this respect is not for children. The "movement" is development, not just any development, but rather a new process that signifies a change in the ordinary ongoing development. Thus, there must be something that triggers the Bildung process, provides the jolt that gets it started. A trigger can be a disturbance in an individual's acquisition of societal norms, it can be a chance meeting or encounter with something new, something unknown which lacks a frame of reference. Triggers are provided by the social dimension, which offers the material for the Bildung of the individual; that with which the individual interacts. There is a significant difference between goal-directedness as implied by Bildung theory and goal-directedness as implied by for instance Key's theory. Key assumes an internal drive, a development that simply takes its course. In some ways Piaget's theory runs on the same assumption: the same cognitive functions develop in the same order in all individuals, without conscious effort. But Bildung processes require the awareness, will, intention and effort of the individuals undergoing them. Bildung is self-formation and you cannot do it against one's own will.

Classical Bildung theories tend to emphasize the social/material dimension, for example in the form of cultural heritage or tradition, and attribute to it the capacity to form or shape people in itself – more like an external drive and a focus on Bildung as a more or less tangible product. Nowadays, Straume says, the concept of Bildung is mostly used to refer to open processes with no particular goal state (p.21). This trait makes it possible to avoid conflicts over questions of values, ethics or cultural content more generally, and rather encourages critique of all forms of goal states for Bildung. Defined goal states, for example Bildung ideals, would be the very antithesis to free, critical and innovative thought. This leaves open the question of goal-directedness, since open processes can go in many different individual directions. Thus there are seemingly endlessly many possible paths through a vaguely described state space, to use SC language. However, the state space is not endless or unlimited, since not any development counts as a process of Bildung. Even if goal states in the form of set ideals or acquisition of specific cultural values and/or habits are ruled out, the open process generally implies goal states couched in terms of critical attitudes – even critical of traditional Bildung ideals. Hence, there is some direction implied, even in open processes.

Theoretical postulates

Naturally, people may differ in what aspects of goal-directed theories they deem most important or interesting: the goal state, the teleological entity in question, the environment, the idea of goal-directedness. Myself I have come to view the theoretical postulates involved in goal-directness as the crux of goal-directed theories. The selected parameters are the building blocks of the theory, but they do not in and of themselves tell us how the movement toward the goal state happens. For that, we need theoretical postulates to tell us how the parameters (supposedly) hang together. Together they should give us an understanding of how, exactly, the parameters of teleological entity and environment interact to move the teleological entity in the desired direction. This is a realm that lends itself both to empirical and conceptual investigation as well as to speculation.

In Chapter 3 I brought together the notions of parameters and theoretical postulates within the framework of modeling of phenomena. My understanding is that theoretical postulates concern the relationships between parameters, and it seems reasonable to suggest that postulates and models develop simultaneously. In goal-directed theories theoretical postulates basically concern the *how* of goal-directedness, the mechanisms by which the teleological entity tends toward the goal state. These lie at the heart of the theory and therefore at the heart of our understanding of the phenomenon. Let us begin by reviewing behaviorist learning theory.

John Broadus Watson (1878–1958), classical behaviorist, characterizes learning as a function of two parameters: stimulus S and response R (Watson, 1930). He understood behaviorism to be an objective experimental branch of natural science, without any references to an inner mental life (consciousness could simply not be studied). We should note here that this theory describes the behavior of an idealized population, not an actual one – in actual populations learning is evidently influenced by other parameters as well. This is the *as if* of theory construction; we treat the phenomenon as if all other influences can be safely ignored. The question now, however, concerns the relation between S and R. When I was a student, the standard interpretation of the S-R connection was causal: S causes R. How this happens is something of a mystery and the theory offers no explanations, since it omits any references to the understandings, interpretations and decisions of the individual. The teleological entity of this theory is a black box with no descriptive parameters. We may know *that* R obtains but we do not know *how* or *why*.

Let us leave that problem for the moment and instead look at the temporal aspect of the theory. At the outset, the duration of an S-R unit seems to be short indeed. It must be so, if some outside agent is to be able to connect an observed R to a given S. However short the duration, this unit still exemplifies goal-directness and is governed by a law of succession. Deterministically, if you think that S is causally sufficient for R; probabilistically, if you think S brings about R at least frequently enough to be of interest. The aim of Watson's theory was to predict and control behavior. Whose behavior is to be predicted and controlled by whom? S-R theory minimally presupposes a dyad: a responder and an administrator of stimulus. In passing, note here that the responder is the teleological entity, the idealized individual whose behavior we seek to shape. Now, unless we want to conceive of learning as a collection of independent S-R units, we need to figure out how to place them in longer sequences. What happens if we put together an S-R-S-R-S-R sequence (or as long sequences as we want)? In particular, how should we understand the relationship between R and S in this sequence? Causal? Sufficient? Probabilistic? Other? Perhaps longer sequences can be made sense of provided we do two things: shift focus from individual to dyad, and allow each parameter to play both roles. The learner's response becomes stimulus for the teacher; the teacher's response becomes stimulus for the learner; and the process more clearly moves through a state space simply on account of its taking longer. This sequential interpretation will, however, play out better with Skinner's neo-behaviorist theory of learning (e.g. Skinner, 1938).

Burrhus Frederic Skinner (1904–1990), neo-behaviorist, characterizes behavioral learning as a function of three parameters: S^D (discriminative stimulus), R^O (response, behavior) and S^1 (reinforcement, consequence). Reinforcement comes in two versions, positive and negative. Behaviorist language is nuanced and detailed. I will side-step all the details and look instead at the proposed relationships between parameters. The first thing to note is that they are probabilistic. Stimuli play two roles: they can cause or produce a response, or their presence in a context can signal that responding will have some consequence (in which case the stimuli are said to evoke the response, not cause it). As Skinner puts it,

> Three terms must therefore be considered: a prior discriminative stimulus (S^D), the response (R^O), and the reinforcing stimulus (S^1). Their relation may be stated as follows: only in the presence of S^D is R^O followed by S^1.
>
> (1938, p.178)

The term *reinforcement* denotes an operation or an action, namely the delivery of a consequence to a response. Reinforcement thus comes after the behavior. Roughly, if the reinforcement is positive, the response increases in probability – and this increase in probability must occur *because* the response has this consequence. If the reinforcement is negative, the response in question decreases in probability – and again it is demanded that the change in probability (frequency of behavior) happens *because* the response has that particular consequence. Reinforcement denotes the relation between behavior and environment – it influences and shapes future behavior. Neo-behaviorist learning theory thus has a probabilistic law of succession. There are several paths through the state space toward the goal, which is some desired behavior. Note that the theoretical postulates are empirical, and that we can recognize reinforcement as the basic principle of educational technology (ET). Many things have been said and still can be said about neo-behaviorist learning theory. But I'll say this for Skinner: he was admirably clear both as to the parameters and the theoretical postulates of his theory.

Before leaving behaviorist theory, let us again expand the unit into a sequence and see what happens. Skinner himself hints at temporal development, since a stimulus that evokes a response (rather than causing it) suggests that the individual has already learned the connection between S^D, R^O and S^1 and therefore must have some prior experience with it. But that is not exactly what I have in mind. What I have in mind is a sequence involving a dyad: say a learner and a teacher. If a teacher provides a stimulus, response by the learner will reinforce the stimulus. The teacher will perhaps think that this strategy worked well and could be repeated with different students. Reinforcement, e.g. praise, from the teacher, reinforces the response. The teacher's reinforcement becomes a new stimulus for the student, and the student's response becomes a stimulus for the teacher, and so on. All actions can play all roles and the two actors mutually reinforce each other.

Before leaving this sub-section altogether, let us take a look at how Piaget handles the questions of stage order and stage transitions. There are theoretical postulates concerning both. Children, according to Piaget's theory, go through an invariant sequence of stages characterized by an ability to master progressively difficult cognitive tasks and more abstract subject matter. The order of the stages, Piaget says, is *necessary*:

> To characterize the stages of cognitive development we therefore need to integrate two necessary conditions without introducing any contradictions. These conditions for stages are (a) that they must be defined to guarantee a constant order of succession, and (b) that the definition allow for progressive construction without entailing total preformation.
>
> (1970, p.710)

Phillips and Kelly (1975) find it highly problematic that a guarantee of a fixed order of succession is written into the theory, and I agree with their judgment. In SC vocabulary, the two conditions amount to a theoretical postulate. And it does not seem to an empirically grounded postulate, but rather a logical one – Piaget, we might say, is fond of necessity claims. Phillips and Kelly comment that "it is not clear to what extent invariance is empirically or conceptually grounded" (p.364). The biggest problem with it is that any other order of the stages is ruled out by definition. It will be recalled that Piaget himself rules out any form of innate, genetic predetermination which (perhaps) could explain the necessary, fixed order of successive stages.

What about stage transitions? Any account of transition from one stage to the next surely requires various theoretical postulates, unless one can point to a clearly identifiable mechanism. Kamii (1979) draws an analogy between the evolution of children's thought from one stage to the next and the evolution of scientific theories. The similarity centers on differentiation and integration: the cognitive functions of each stage become incorporated into the functions of the next stage, just as old theories become encompassed in broader more adequate theories:

> For example, when the child becomes a conserver, he does not reject his previous way of thinking. He still thinks that the liquid in the taller, thinner glass is "more" in a certain sense, but he has a very different way of apprehending this "fact" when he can coordinate a host of relationships and assimilate the old fact into a new system of relationships.
>
> (Kamii, 1979, p.18)

Cognitive structures within a stage become differentiated and refined, and at some point they become restructured, coordinated and integrated into subsequent structures. Thus, stage transitions are marked by an integration that results in a significant shift in a child's cognitive functioning. In the change from preoperational to concrete operational thought this shift is so dramatic that it results in qualitatively different processes of reasoning, Phillips and Kelly comment (p.365). It is unclear how such dramatic shifts sit with the proposed implicative relationship between the stages.

One last thing needs to be mentioned here: possible paths or trajectories through the state space. The goal state is the cognitive functioning characterized by the formal operational stage. How many paths are there to this goal state? Given the theoretical postulates concerning the fixed order of succession and the implicative relationship between stages, there seems to be only *one* path. Your current cognitive structures determine unique subsequent cognitive structures; the current stage *necessarily* determines the next stage. Piaget's theory therefore appears to run on a deterministic law of succession.

Means and ends

There are obvious similarities between goal-directed theories and means-end reasoning in that both contain a goal and an account of how to reach it, but there are also differences. In this section I propose to compare the two. We will begin with a characterization of means-end pedagogy.

Despite its centrality in practical pedagogy, means-end reasoning has been subjected to much criticism. Yngve Nordkvelle, in his discussion of the shifting relationships between technology and didactics, shows that means-end reasoning has been criticized for being technical, causal and instrumental, treating students as objects and by implication opening up for manipulation of students (Nordkvelle, 2004). The problem is the conception of the relationship between means and ends, which by critics is thought to be a purely instrumental relationship, one of causal sufficiency – the means always produces the end; hence, the possibilities of manipulation. We see the similarities to S-R theory, which indeed often is considered to lie at the bottom of means-end reasoning. If you want the R (the end), you implement S (the means). Nordkvelle concludes that this criticism was not particularly sophisticated, but that it still had a profound effect on Nordic educational thought – and still reverberates today, I would like to add. But as Robert Audi (1991) points out, the means-end relationship is diverse: it may be one of reciprocal determination, constitution or instrumentality. The latter can be understood as causal necessity, sufficiency, probability or possibility, and means may be treated as mandatory, permissible, simple or multiple.

The main difference between goal-directed theories and means-end reasoning seems to lie in the conception of means. If we assume the critics' version of means-end pedagogy, the means produces the end. The agent who controls the means therefore also controls the end; this agent being the educator. The student is a black box. This is different in goal-directed theories as understood by SC. Here a teleological entity changes toward a goal state at least partly as a function of his or her own interaction with the environment; the tendency toward goal state presupposing interaction with a *stable* environment. If the environment is unstable the goal may never be achieved. Consequently, we may seek to influence, stabilize and structure the environment so as to facilitate the desired kind of interaction. And, as we have seen, this is what goal-directed educational theories purport to do: tell us how we should organize the environment to ensure an interaction that will maximize the probability of attaining the goal. If the means is the teacher's action, then it is obviously within his or her power to bring it about. If the means is the interaction between student and teacher, then equally obviously it is not within the teacher's power alone. If the means is the environment, it is partly within the teacher's power, but equally within the student's power, since students are part of the environment. And the students decide how to interact with it.

Let us next look at means as constitutive or instrumental. Means-end pedagogy is generally understood as instrumental: means as instrumental to achievement of goal. Critics of means-end pedagogy take instrumentality to mean an external, causal or technical relation between means and ends, whereas a constitutive relation between the two is described as internal (e.g. Biesta, 2007). In SC vernacular, constitution and causation are two different theoretical postulates concerning the relation between means and ends. The constitution postulate signals a "for its own sake" approach: means do not contribute to some external goal; it is rather the case that implementing the means *constitutes* attaining the goal. When the activity (the means) is done for its own sake, it is its own goal. Or we might say that the means is an *instance* of the goal. Under either description the relation is internal. To be sure, there are educational activities of this kind and it is important that education has room for them. I have already suggested, however, that I think that *causation* is one of the most frequent and most important theoretical postulates of goal-directed educational theories. Causation denotes a manifold dynamic relation between causal relata and is therefore deeply connected to change, which is at the heart of goal-directed theories. It does not sound right to say that the interaction of teleological entity and environment is constitutive of the goal. If the interaction happens to instantiate the goal, the entity can hardly be described as tending toward it. On the one hand, the terminology of goal-directed theories may not accommodate the traditional means-end vocabulary, and especially not the *constitution* version. On the other hand, means-end is a simplistic way of viewing goals and their attainment. It is a form of input-output logic. Most importantly, the teleological entity is a black box and the *how* of goal-directed theories disappears. Input-output relations do not account for interaction; a feature that is central to goal-directed theories and that surely makes very good intuitive sense in educational contexts.

The biggest difference is the role accorded to the environment. Means-end pedagogy runs on an input-output logic and not only overlooks interaction, but the stable environment with which the teleological entity is supposed to interact. Means-end pedagogy focuses precisely on means and end, cause and effect, S and R, and it is all too easy to slide into the notion that the relationship between the two parameters holds *simpliciter*, in and of itself, and therefore can be transferred to all contexts – for example, if you think the relationship is one of causal sufficiency.

Summary

Normative, practice-oriented theories are by and large considered to be *the* form of theory that the field of education has. Thus, it should not come as a surprise that education is full of such theories. They come in different sizes and shapes, but they attempt to do the same thing: provide an account of how to attain a desired goal. Or, if the goal is innate, as it sometimes is, provide an account of how the development happens.

SC provides a certain view of which elements have to be present for theories to qualify as goal-directed educational theories. Using it as a lens therefore guides the search for elements and it guides the analysis of the theories one finds. Basically, goal-directed theories contain some desired goal state, a teleological entity, an environment with which the entity interacts, and a theoretical law describing allowable state transitions and providing us with an understanding of the goal-directedness involved in the theory. Goal-directed theories are dynamic; they deal with change over time. RV does not provide a framework that is capable of accommodating goal-directed theories. The standard view is that this is because educational theories are normative and tell us what *ought* to be the case rather than what *is* the case. The view taken here is that RV, with logical calculus, axioms and correspondence rules, does not have the resources to model the dynamic and changing behavior of teleological entities. SC, on the other hand, does – and this is crucial in education, where notions of process and continuous change are so prominent.

Different goal-directed theories "perform" differently on the proposed parameters. For example, SC guides us to look at what any given theory says about the teleological entity. In the case of Driver's theory, some of the parameters are definitional of the goal state and some are not. Does this suggest that Driver's theory employs superfluous entity parameters? If not, what role can teleological entity parameters play if their values are not directly related to a goal state? Stephen Norris and I suggested that they can be conceived as causally mediating between goal state and the other entity parameters, but we did not explore the issue in any depth. If, however, a theory is found to treat the teleological entity as a black box, that is a point of critique. It is hard to understand what a theory says about the development of the entity if the entity has no characteristics.

Under the lens of SC, theories like Driver's are shown to be very complex and detailed. On the one hand, this raises the issue of how many parameters are optimal for a theory to have. The jury is still out on that issue. On the other hand, SC also helps to organize the complexity and detail for better comprehension – it sorts the complexity into categories pertaining to teleological entity, environment, goal-directedness and theoretical postulates, and thus helps to get an overview and an idea of how the different parameters supposedly hang together. By the same token, SC helps us see where any theory is unclear or unfinished. I think that theoretical postulates may be a weak point in many theories – they may run on a number of assumptions about how parameters are related, but lack in specificity. A case in point is Bildung theories, which seem to lack any specificity concerning state transitions and the *how* of the change in question. But without a law of succession, the theory cannot do the job it is designed to do, namely provide a description of how the teleological entity moves toward the goal state, and in keeping with that, guidance on how to reach the desired goal.

5 Equivalence theories

It was argued in Chapter 2 that the field of education, despite its size, plurality and rather fragmented nature, exhibits a striking similarity when it comes to views about its theories. Educational theories are viewed as normative and their main function is to guide practice. That is to say, *one* type of theory is envisioned for the entire field. This type of theory is goal-directed in nature, and was the topic of the previous chapter. My analysis suggests that while goal-directed theories have a certain structure in common, whose backbone is a law of succession, concrete examples of such theory differ substantially among themselves concerning scope, entities, environment, interaction and the parameters selected for each.

Equivalence theories constitute a "black swan" in the sense that they are theories found in the field of education that do not conform to the traditionally conceived nature of educational theories. I shall argue that the field of education abounds with equivalence structures; we just do not call them *theories*. This could be because of an ingrained picture of goal-directed theories as educational theories, but I suspect it is rather because one might find it slightly odd to speak of the things I have in mind as theories. This is therefore a case where the meta-theoretical lens allows us to see something in the field that we normally do not see there. The most obvious exception to this is evaluation theory, which is called *theory* and which falls squarely under the umbrella of equivalence theories, but which in education is better understood as a sub-domain rather than as a concrete theory or collection of discernable concrete theories.

The natural sciences, on the other hand, have several examples of equivalence theories, and I shall take my point of departure there. The theoretical structure that is to be transplanted in the educational realm is well established, but the characteristics of the educational realm naturally require that the structure be adjusted to accommodate the material. Hence I shall proceed with great caution, especially because I shall attempt to make the case that the best use of equivalence structures in education is found in its explicitly normative entities – such as goals, ideals or evaluative judgments. I shall begin by presenting the type of theoretical law which is the main analytical tool of this chapter. Next I shall apply it to goals, ideals and evaluative judgments and I hope that my discussion will show how an equivalence-based structure allows us to see other things than the ones we usually see. Evaluation is an educational activity that puts the importance of construct validity in stark relief and this chapter therefore includes a discussion of realist and antirealist interpretations of the entities we are dealing with here.

Laws of coexistence

Theoretical laws are intimately connected to theory structure, and on the Semantic Conception of theories (SC) they are used with reference to entities *within* theories. In the previous chapter we met laws of succession, which specify the possible trajectories of teleological entities through some state space. In this chapter we meet laws of coexistence, which specify possible positions in a state space by describing equations that fix the states of the model in question and thus determine which states are equivalent. The adjustments mentioned above are necessary because the field of education does not lend itself well to equations, but there are phenomena in the field which lend themselves well to thinking in terms of equivalent states – hence we have equivalence theories.

Like all laws, laws of coexistence can be deterministic or statistical. Suppe (1989) thinks that statistical laws of coexistence strictly speaking are a version of laws of succession, since they say that "a system is such that it subsequently may assume only equiprobable states" (p.158). But equiprobability is not what we are after in educational equivalence theories, nor does determinism seem to be of any relevance, as I hope will become clear in the course of the chapter. We shall deal here with theories that simply pick out states that are equivalent. Laws of coexistence are well known in the natural sciences, and the ideal gas law provides an example (even though it is called a law and not a theory). This law is an equation of the form PV=nRT (I owe this example to Stephen Norris, personal communication). It provides the relationship among the thermodynamic parameters (pressure, volume and temperature); R being the universal gas constant and n the number of molecules. The ideal gas law is a law of coexistence: it defines all possible equivalent states that the model (P, V, T) can occupy. The technicalities here are not important, but the principle is. And the principle is that the parameters can assume different values, while the law defines which combinations of values will comprise equivalent states.

A couple of important caveats are needed before we can transfer this basic structure to the field of education. First, laws of coexistence in the natural sciences serve to limit what possibilities that can be realized at the same time. The ideal gas law, for example, constrains the values of P, V, and T of a gas at a given time. This is not necessarily how equivalence structures work in education. Second, despite their seeming symmetry, phenomena governed by laws of coexistence might have an underlying causal structure that rather suggests some form of asymmetry. Again, in the case of the ideal gas law, if V is kept fixed, an increase in T will cause an increase in P. But an increase in P will not cause an increase in T – the two parameters are asymmetrical in that sense. We shall see in this chapter that while parameters in educational equivalence theories might be considered to be asymmetric and accorded different weight, they are not causally related. Finally, we should note that this is quite different from laws of succession. The key feature of a deterministic law of succession is that the current state of some system determines unique subsequent states, such that there is one trajectory through the state space only. If the law is statistical, a number of different subsequent states may be assumed, and there are several possible trajectories through the state space. Laws of coexistence, by contrast, do not deal in change or development over time. So unlike goal-directed theories, equivalence theories do not have built into them temporality, development or sequencing. They are, in a sense, timeless.

This is now the theoretical structure I propose to apply to a selection of normative entities. That does not imply that I think that normative educational entities have anything in common with gases, ideal or not; nor do I think that educational theories of equivalence can be expressed as equations. But I do think that something interesting comes into view by using this particular lens. In passing, we note that already Auguste Comte (1968/1854) employs laws of coexistence in his discussion of "social statics" – how the different domains of a society are related to one another.

Goals and ideals

To set the stage for a foray into equivalence-based reasoning, let us momentarily return to goal-directed theories. It will be recalled that goal-directed theories supply a goal and an account of how to reach it. Nothing much was said about goals and goal states in Chapter 4 besides their being explicit normative entities that come in all sizes and shapes, from overarching vaguely described aims to highly specific ones. Generally, goals enjoy widespread – albeit perhaps implicit – agreement that the states described are desirable, good or worthy of achievement. Goals and ideals tend to receive much attention in educational thought, and not only because they are intimately connected to the traditional self-understanding of education as an intentional discipline, but because goals are central to all educational activity, right from kindergarten and up to the university (and of course other forms of activity as well). Goals naturally belong in political and various societal deliberations and debate – the aims of schooling, for example, are of interest to everybody.

Goals and ideals are formulated at different levels of abstraction: some superordinate and vague, some specific and precise. There are many different approaches to the investigation of goals. We can distinguish between types of goals and organize them in taxonomies (e.g. Bloom, 1956). We can discuss their legitimacy – something we perhaps should do more often, since goals need justification (ethical, political, social, educational) to avoid becoming something that educational actors simply take for granted. This is especially important because goals may conflict. We can also inquire into what function goals and ideals actually have, as opposed to the function we think they should have, and we can map desirable and undesirable side effects of pursuing the goals the way we do. We can inquire into the timing of activities and discuss at which time it is reasonable to evaluate achievement (or degree of achievement), and we can deliberate on what it makes sense to "do" with goals that already are achieved: should they simply be conceived of as the endpoint of a given process and filed away, or should we accord them some other kind of status and role (see e.g. Dewey, 1976)? I shall in the following do none of these things. Rather, I shall employ an equivalence-based structure to discuss the problem of what it means to have reached a goal state, or what it means to satisfy an ideal. This is where laws of coexistence become useful.

Goal states in Rosalind Driver's science education theory

Driver's theory is constructivist in spirit and it aims to provide an account of how students' nonscientific conceptions of natural phenomena can be modified so that they are more scientific. The theory also aims to account for how to make students' views about science more accurate and how to modify their attitudes toward science and allow science to take a more central role in their lives. In our analysis of Driver's theory, Stephen Norris and I (1997) particularly looked at three publications, Driver (1989, 1995) and Driver and Oldman (1986). All three works contain descriptions of goal states, and we grouped them in three broad categories: scientific concepts, nature of science, and scientific acculturation. Spelled out in detail, the goal states include the following:

Under the category *scientific concepts*, we find scientific view of phenomena (Driver, 1995, p.385); knowledge of scientific concepts (Driver & Oldman, 1986, p.109); scientific ideas and concepts (Driver & Oldman, 1986, p.109); scientific theory (Driver & Oldman, 1986, p.116); understanding accepted science (Driver, 1995, p.399); conventional science ideas (Driver 1989, p.92); and conventional scientific interpretations (Driver, 1989, p.96).

Under the category *nature of science*, we find scientific view of explanation (Driver & Oldman, 1986, p.106); seeing scientific knowledge as constructed (Driver, 1995, p.398); and seeing theories as provisional (Driver, 1995, p.398).

Under the category *scientific acculturation*, we find application of scientific ideas to everyday phenomena (Driver & Oldman, 1986, p.106); initiation into the culture of science (Driver, 1995, p. 395 and p.398); and acculturation into ideas and models of conventional science (Driver, 1989, p.103). We sum up the goal states as follows:

> Under the category of scientific concepts, the overall sense of the desired goal is that students acquire conventional scientific views of natural phenomena. Under the category of nature of science is the goal that students develop particular views about the nature of scientific knowledge and its origin. Finally, the category scientific acculturation refers, on the one hand, to the goal found under Category A [i.e. scientific concepts], and on the other hand, to the acquisition and inclusion as part of everyday living of a set of general attitudes and dispositions that might comprise a culture of science. We judge that the overall desired goal state consists of the combined goals of the three categories.
>
> (Norris & Kvernbekk, 1997, pp.985–986)

Now, what does it mean to have reached this quite complex goal? How can we understand it? I propose we treat it as an equivalence theory.

I realize it may seem odd to call this a theory. However, SC licenses such a terminology and some distinctly theoretical aspects will surface as we go along. Let us begin by noting that the goal state, as described above, has 13 parameters. Several of them are relatively superordinate and can be broken down into smaller, more precise goal states, in which case there will be even more parameters to handle. If we stick to the major categories, we reduce the number of parameters to three. This creates order and is presumably more manageable, but it also makes it more difficult to figure out if the students actually have attained the goal. Here we cross paths with a construct validity problem, which I shall come back to in a subsequent section. For the sake of the argument, let us accept Driver's description of goal states such as it is, and ask the question again: what does it mean to have reached this goal?

In grappling with this question we have (at least) two different approaches at our disposal. First, we can declare that one, and only one, state of knowledge and attitudes define goal attainment. That would mean that goal attainment is a state that satisfies all 13 parameters. The strictest version of this would be to insist that only one combination of values on the 13 parameters counts as having reached the goal. To make it virtually impossible for any student to ever reach the goal, we could demand maximum value or top score on all parameters. If we, however, judge that this approach is unreasonable, we have a second approach available to us. We can choose to say that different combinations of values all count as having reached the goal. If this is our strategy, we can understand and analyze goal states in terms of theories of equivalence. Whether one recognizes this as a type of theory in its own right or not, equivalence-based structures make important analytical tools. In this particular case, an equivalence theory should tell us which states – i.e. combinations of values on parameters – are considered equivalent: equivalent in the sense of counting as having reached the goal. We should note here that equivalence reasoning is based on difference, not on likeness. States are *different*, but we judge them to be in some sense *equivalent*. Equivalence can be cashed out as, for example, equally acceptable, of equal worth, etc. In the case of Driver's goal states, students can obtain different results, but still be judged to have reached the goal. It complicates matters further that several, if not all, of Driver's goal state parameters admit of gradation. Students can move from low to high values, and different combinations of low and high values may count as equivalent states. An equivalence theory contributes principles which make evident, ground and (possibly) justify the equivalence judgments that we make. See Figure 5.1 and 5.2 for an illustration of both approaches: the

Figure 5.1 Equivalence theory: One state only counts as having achieved goal

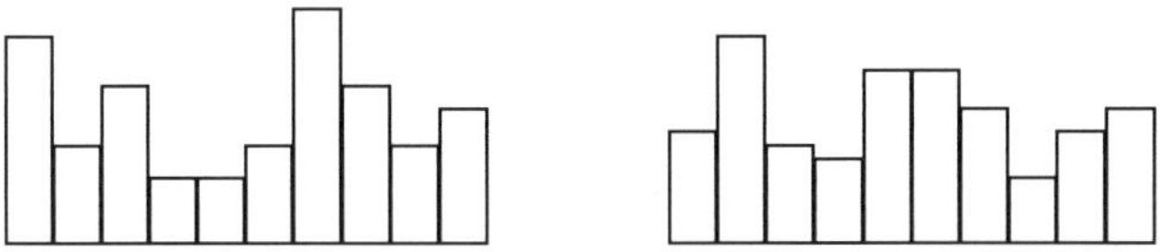

Figure 5.2 Equivalence theory: Two states, different but equivalent. Both count as having achieved goal

strict approach, with uniform scores on all parameters, and the equivalence-based approach, with different combinations of high and low scores – different, but equivalent.

Evidently it is not a straightforward matter to make judgments about equivalent states in many cases, and especially not when the overall goal state is as complex as it is in Driver's theory. I shall delve into the details of the equivalence approach in the next section. But first let me go back to the first approach – the one that says that only one state of knowledge (skills, attitudes) counts as having reached the goal. This is clearly a theoretical possibility, although it is not clear whether anyone actually holds such a view. Despite its restrictive character, even this approach admits of different interpretations. We can, for example, imagine only two values of a parameter (1 and 0). We can interpret it as demanding one specific combination of values on the parameters, which is very strict. Or we can interpret it as demanding that all values lie above a certain defined limit, which is slightly less strict. However we interpret this approach, it requires precise goals. Unless a goal is sufficiently precise, it is difficult to judge whether it is achieved. Many educational thinkers argue for the importance and usefulness of precise goals, and Ralph Tyler's view is classic:

> The most useful form for stating objectives is to express them in terms which identify both the kind of behavior to be developed in the student and the content area of life in which this behavior is to operate.
>
> (Tyler, 1949, pp.46–47)

This is expressing goals in behavioral terms. It is generally criticized for being way too restrictive and controlling. But if we look at formulations of goals that Tyler himself considers to be exemplary, they fall short of the strictest interpretation. Such examples as "To write clear and well-organized reports of social study projects" (p.47) and "Familiarity with dependable sources of information on questions relating to nutrition" (p.47) do satisfy Tyler's requirement of kind of behavior and content area. But surely there are different ways for reports to be well-organized, and familiarity is a fairly vague parameter which may assume many different values. It seems to me that it is more reasonable to interpret Tyler in terms of equivalence theory, since familiarity clearly can manifest itself in different, but equivalent ways. Different, but of equal worth.

Critical thinkers and critical thinking

Critical thinking has been discussed in educational circles for decades. Today it is listed as an ideal or a desired outcome in practically every university program around the globe. I am going to analyze it here as an ideal, but I should note that critical thinking can also be conceived of as a theory. Critical thinking theory is a normative theory about how we should go about thinking, providing standards and criteria for gathering and using various types of data and information, for making inferences and value judgments. As a result of this conception, Norris says, "testing for critical thinking is often seen as an attempt to determine whether examinees are following in their thinking the standards and criteria that have been laid down" (1989, p.23). That is to say, critical thinking theory is a normative goal-directed theory; the goal in this case being better understood as an ideal.

One of the most influential authors in this field is Robert Ennis. He has published extensively on critical thinking, and I have selected for analysis his version of the ideal (Ennis, 1987, 1996). I am not going to enter the debate about critical thinking, nor shall I make any judgments about the adequacy or consistency of Ennis' viewpoints. What I am after is to demonstrate the potential of equivalence theory, and Ennis' version is eminently suited for this purpose. Ideals and goals are closely related and belong to the family of deeply value-laden normative entities. Ideals, perhaps, tend to be somewhat vaguer and "further away" from current or actual achievement. Some ideals may not be achievable, but most of them are probably meant to have a regulative function. They give direction to the work; they comprise the basis for evaluating the desirability and legitimacy of various aspects of educational activity, and they comprise – at least contribute to – the basis for assessment of behavior and achievements. The ideals we keep also speak to the kind of people we wish to develop, what attributes we think they should have – as for example seen in different *Bildung* ideals (just to make it clear: these ideals also apply to ourselves). In this section we are dealing with critical thinkers. So how can we recognize a critical thinker, were we to come across one?

Ennis begins by providing a definition of critical thinking: "Critical thinking is reasonable reflective thinking that is focused on deciding what to believe or do" (1987, p.10).

This definition includes both dispositions and abilities and is therefore cashed out in terms of both. Below I reproduce Ennis' description of critical thinking in its entirety. Its sheer complexity in terms of number of parameters is really the crux of the matter and besides no abbreviated version can do justice to an ideal that consists of the following (Ennis, 1987, pp.12–15):

A. Dispositions

1 Seek a clear statement of the thesis or question
2 Seek reasons

3 Try to be well informed
4 Use and mention credible sources
5 Take into account the total situation
6 Try to remain relevant to the main point
7 Keep in mind the original and/or basic concern
8 Look for alternatives
9 Be open-minded

   a Consider seriously other points of view than one's own (dialogical thinking)
   b Reason from premises with which one disagrees – without letting the disagreement interfere with one's reasoning (suppositional reasoning)
   c Withhold judgment when the evidence and reasons are insufficient

10 Take a position (and change a position) when the evidence and reasons are sufficient to do so
11 Seek as much precision as the subject permits
12 Deal in an orderly manner with the parts of a complex whole
13 Use one's critical thinking abilities
14 Be sensitive to the feelings, level of knowledge, and degree of sophistication of others

B. Abilities

1 Focusing on a question

   a Identifying or formulating a question
   b Identifying or formulating criteria for judging possible answers
   c Keeping the situation in mind

2 Analyzing arguments

   a Identifying conclusions
   b Identifying stated reasons
   c Identifying unstated reasons
   d Seeing similarities and differences
   e Identifying and handling irrelevance
   f Seeing the structure of an argument
   g Summarizing

3 Asking and answering questions of clarification and/or challenge, for example:

   a Why?
   b What is your main point?
   c What do you mean by "…."?
   d What would be an example?
   e What would not be an example (though close to being one)?
   f How does that apply to this case (describe a counterexample)?
   g What difference does it make?

- h What are the facts?
- i Is this what you are saying: "...."?
- j Would you say some more about that?

4 Judging the credibility of a source

- a Expertise
- b Lack of conflict of interest
- c Agreement among sources
- d Reputation
- e Use of established procedures
- f Known risk to reputation
- g Ability to give reasons
- h Careful habits

5 Observing and judging observation reports; criteria:

- a Minimal inferring involved
- b Short time interval between observation and report
- c Report by observer, rather than someone else (i.e., not hearsay)
- d Records are generally desirable; if report is based on a record, it is generally best that
    - 1 The record was close in time to the observation
    - 2 The record was made by the observer
    - 3 The record was made by the reporter
    - 4 The statement was believed by the reporter, either because of a prior belief in its correctness or because of a belief that the observer was habitually correct
- e Corroboration
- f Possibility of corroboration
- g Conditions of good access
- h Competent employment of technology, if technology is useful
- i Satisfaction by observer (and reporter, if a different person) of credibility criteria (item B4)

6 Deducing and judging deductions

- a Class logic
- b Conditional logic
- c Interpretation of statements
    - 1 Double negations
    - 2 Necessary and sufficient conditions
    - 3 Other logical words and phrases: *only, if and only if, or, some, unless, not, not both*, etc.

7 Inducing and judging inductions

- a Generalizing
  - 1 Typicality of data
  - 2 Limitation of coverage
  - 3 Sampling
- b Inferring explanatory conclusions and hypotheses
  - 1 Types of explanatory conclusions and hypotheses
    - a Causal claims
    - b Claims about the beliefs and attitudes of people
    - c Interpretations of author's intended meanings
    - d Historical claims that certain things happened
    - e Reported definitions
    - f Claims that something is an unstated reason or unstated conclusion
  - 2 Investigating
    - a Designing experiments, including planning to control variables
    - b Seeking evidence and counterevidence
    - c Seeking other possible explanations
  - 3 Criteria: Given reasonable assumptions
    - a The proposed conclusion would explain the evidence (essential)
    - b The proposed conclusion is consistent with the known facts (essential)
    - c Competitive alternative conclusions are inconsistent with known facts (essential)
    - d The proposed conclusion seems plausible (desirable)

8 Making value judgments

- a Background facts
- b Consequences
- c Prima facie application of acceptable principles
- d Considering alternatives
- e Balancing, weighing, and deciding

9 Defining terms, and judging definitions in three dimensions

- a Form
  - 1 Synonym
  - 2 Classification
  - 3 Range
  - 4 Equivalent expression
  - 5 Operational
  - 6 Example-nonexample

- b Definitional strategy
  - 1 Acts
    - a Report a meaning (reported definition)
    - b Stipulate a meaning (stipulative definition)
    - c Express a position on an issue (positional, including programmatic and persuasive definition)
  - 2 Identifying and handling equivocation
    - a Attention to the context
    - b Possible types of response
      - i The simplest response: "The definition is just wrong"
      - ii Reduction to absurdity: "According to that definition, there is an outlandish result"
      - iii Considering alternative interpretations: "On this interpretation, there is this problem; on that interpretation, there is that problem"
      - iv Establishing that there are two meanings of key term and a shift in meaning from one to the other
      - v Swallowing the idiosyncratic definition
    - c Content

10 Identifying assumptions

- a Unstated reasons
- b Needed assumptions; argument reconstruction

11 Deciding on an action

- a Define the problem
- b Select criteria to judge possible solutions
- c Formulate alternative solutions
- d Tentatively decide what to do
- e Review, taking into account the total situation, and decide
- f Monitor the implementation

12 Interacting with others

- a Employing and reacting to fallacy labels, including
  - 1 Circularity
  - 2 Appeal to authority
  - 3 Bandwagon
  - 4 Glittering term
  - 5 Name calling
  - 6 Slippery slope
  - 7 Post hoc

8 Non sequitur
9 Ad hominem
10 Affirming the consequent
11 Denying the antecedent
12 Conversion
13 Begging the question
14 Either–or
15 Vagueness
16 Equivocation
17 Straw person
18 Appeal to tradition
19 Argument from analogy
20 Hypothetical question
21 Oversimplification
22 Irrelevance

b Logical strategies
c Rhetorical strategies
d Argumentation; Presenting a position, oral or written

1 Aiming at a particular audience and keeping it in mind
2 Organizing (common type: main point; clarification; reasons; alternatives; attempt to rebut prospective challenges; summary, including repeat of main point)

Ennis comments that "This is only an overall content outline. It does not incorporate suggestions for level, sequence, repetition in greater depth, emphasis, or infusion in subject matter area (which might be either exclusive or overlapping)" (p.15). To view this description as an outline may seem like something of an under-statement. There are two main categories, A and B. If we count all the major sub-categories, the number is 26. If we count *all* items, including sub-sub-categories and on occasion also sub-sub-sub-sub-categories (B92bi–v), we get up to around 150 items (give or take a few, depending on how you count). How should we deal with this ideal? Is it usable? More specifically, can we use it to recognize a critical thinker, should we meet one? Does it make sense to think that anybody can satisfy an ideal like this?

It is important to say here, before I embark on my analysis, that ideals serve different functions, and the questions we ask of them depend on which function(s) we endow them with. If they are meant to be superordinate and regulative and understood to be out of reach, we need not ask what it means to have reached it. Ennis holds that the ideal of critical thinking, as he describes it, should be part of school curriculum organization. This can be done in various ways, but, he argues, teachers accomplished in critical thinking are necessary if teaching critical thinking is to be successful, appropriate materials must be available, and there must be careful continual evaluation of what occurs. Thus, I infer, Ennis himself assumes that there *are* people who qualify as critical thinkers. And while the ideal is truly extensive, it is also fairly concrete. It is perhaps not unreasonable to view it as attainable.

For the sake of the argument, let us presuppose that it is legitimate to ask what it means to be a critical thinker on Ennis' conception of critical thinking. Furthermore, I shall view the (approximately) 150 items as parameters. What should we do? Again, we have different strategies to choose between. We can say that one, and only one, state of dispositions and abilities represents satisfying the ideal; a state which satisfies *all* parameters. We can choose to demand specific values, say top score, on all parameters, or we can choose to settle for minimum requirements. To demand one state of dispositions and abilities would be an unreasonably strict and restrictive approach, given the enormous complexity of the ideal. Can we imagine anybody who would satisfy all the parameters, and how should we go about investigating it? Alternatively, we can view different people as qualifying as critical thinkers, even if they exhibit different properties and different combinations of abilities and dispositions. In that case, our reasoning is equivalence-theoretical: different combinations (and scores) count as equivalent in the sense of all of them qualifying as critical thinking.

It is my contention that a theory of what it means to be a critical thinker lends itself well to analysis in terms of an equivalence-based structure, with a law of coexistence that indicates which states (combinations) are equivalent, such that those who satisfy the different states all count as critical thinkers. This requires that the theory characterizes the ideal itself, that it defines some sort of cut-off point between acceptable and not acceptable combinations (unless we want all possible combinations and scores to count as critical thinking), and that it provides principles for which states should be considered equivalent. That is to say, such a theory should be able to explain why acceptable states that are different are judged to be equivalent.

I am not saying that such a theory actually does exist or that it is easily formulated. The critical thinking ideal is large and detailed, and quite possibly we need a radical approach. First we have the combinations problem: the combinations of dispositions and abilities that are identifiable as different but equivalent states. With 150 parameters the number of possible states is enormous, and it would be unreasonable to demand of a theory that it should identify them all. One way of coming to grips with this issue would be to argue that some of the parameters are necessary, and identify acceptable equivalent states on the basis of those parameters only. And Ennis provides some guidance on this issue. For example, he holds the first 13 listed dispositions to be essential for the critical thinker, while the fourteenth (to be sensitive to others) is judged to be important but not constitutive (p.16). I understand Ennis to use "essential" and "constitutive" interchangeably. If the 13 dispositions are constitutive of critical thinking, they are necessary and thus must be present in anybody who wants to qualify as a critical thinker. Necessity means that the dispositions *must* be present for the label of critical thinking to apply; if any of them is missing we are not dealing with critical thinking, and the person in question is not a critical thinker. Concerning abilities, he says that the basic areas are those of clarity (B1–3), basis or basic support (B4–5), inference (B6–8) and interaction with others (B11–12) (p.16). For the record, B9–10 comprises advanced clarification. These four basic areas are described as constitutive (p.23) and must therefore be thought to be necessary for critical thinking. And while abilities are necessary, they are not in themselves sufficient – we must have the dispositions as well. I suppose we could turn the statement around and say of dispositions that they are necessary but not sufficient in themselves – we must have the abilities too. As Ennis puts it,

> The actual practice of critical thinking ... requires us to combine these abilities and to employ them in conjunction with the critical thinking dispositions and knowledge of the topic.
>
> (p.24)

Let us for a moment concentrate on the dispositions. If all of them are constitutive of critical thinking, then presumably only people who possess all 13 count as critical thinkers. But suppose we think this is too complex to use and that we never shall be able to ascertain for ourselves whether a person actually qualifies as a critical thinker? Maybe we even think it is rather unfair, since we know people who should count as critical thinkers but who miss out on one or two of the dispositions? Is it possible to think that it is sufficient for you to possess some of the dispositions and still count as a critical thinker? Is it possible to shift the status of some of them and make them correlative rather than constitutive? Perhaps theory construction in this area must begin by developing an argument to the effect that only a manageable number of these dispositions and abilities should be considered constitutive or necessary and thus have to be present in all combinations that represent equivalent states of being a critical thinker.

Ennis touches upon this very problem in his discussion of Perkins, Jay and Tishman's triadic theory of critical thinking dispositions (Ennis, 1996). In passing, "theory" here seems to mean an account of what dispositions consist of *and* an account of which dispositions critical thinking consists of. Perkins, Jay and Tishman (1993) propose we see dispositions as having three components: inclination, sensitivity and ability. The components are understood to be individually necessary and jointly sufficient. Ennis argues that neither sensitivity nor ability should be viewed as essential components of every disposition, because people might have a disposition without being sensitive to situations calling for its use, and furthermore that it is possible to have disposition, e.g. to seek clarification, without having the ability to ask pointed questions. Thus, he concludes, while sensitivities and abilities are not necessary conditions for dispositions, they are vitally important – without them, dispositions are not of much use (p.167). So how should we understand the relationship of components to dispositions, and of dispositions to critical thinking? Perkins, Jay and Tishman begin with a list of seven dispositions (1993, p.6). But, as Ennis comments: "The authors have elaborated the list so that it incorporates approximately thirty-seven inclinations, and thirty-three sensitivities (all of which also seem to be dispositions), making up to seventy dispositions in all" (1996, p.169). He is well aware of the problem of many parameters, but does not invoke the conception of equivalence structures to handle it. Rather, he suggests two other ways of handling it: one is to construct taxonomies, such that you create order in the system by employing superordinate and subordinate categories (p.174). The second is the distinction between constitutive and correlative categories. In response to Perkins, Jay and Tishman, Ennis thus developed a simpler system for critical thinking dispositions, consisting of three basic broad dispositions: "(1) to 'get it right' to the extent possible, (2) to represent a position honestly and clearly, and (3) to care about the dignity and worth of every person" (pp. 170–171). The first two are constitutive, the third is correlative, and together they have 12 sub-categories. By "correlative" he means that it is not part of the definition of critical thinking, but it is desirable for all critical thinkers to have. At this point, therefore, enters the matter of the definition of the phenomenon in question. For all parameters to fall under the definition, a fairly abstract and minimal definition is required, which is flexible in that it can accommodate a broad phenomenal range. So we have a definition, we have necessary parameters, and we have parameters which are unnecessary but desirable. We have thus narrowed down somewhat the number of possible combinations – the necessary parameters must be there for anybody to count as a critical thinker, but the three sub-parameters of the correlative parameter make for different combinations of dispositions. So should we think of these as different but equivalent?

While the first problem concerns combinations of parameters, the second concerns values of parameters. Different values on the parameters will yield different states. For example, what Ennis (1987) calls "Try to be well informed" evidently admits of gradation, from "not trying very hard" to "working tirelessly to be well informed". How hard must you try, and how well informed must you be? It is easy to imagine people having high and low scores on different parameters, and yet qualify as critical thinkers because we judge the states to be adequate and equivalent. Different, but equivalent.

I think that an equivalence-theoretical approach to the question of what it means to have reached or to satisfy goals and ideals is quite apt. In fact, one could imagine replacing the necessity approach delineated above with an equivalence-theoretical approach. To think in terms of necessary parameters is very strict and it has the consequence of excluding people from the class of critical thinkers if there is one of these parameters that they do not satisfy. Instead, we could recognize that people may possess different sets of characteristics and still qualify as critical thinkers. This is a flexible way of thinking, but it requires that we have some idea of which states we should think of as equivalent. That is precisely the job of an equivalence theory: characterize equivalent states and provide principles (postulates) for why we should see certain states as equivalent. One such postulate could for example concern how absent (or zero score) parameters are made up for by other parameters. However, nobody says the construction of such a theory is an easy task.

Evaluation

The term evaluation comes from the Latin *valere*, which roughly means to attach value to something. In some form or another evaluation permeates work life in general and educational activities, from kindergarten to university, in particular. As D. C. Phillips (2018) puts it, "There can be little doubt that evaluations have been carried out ever since the dawn of civilization – for evaluation is a part of effective governing" (p.3). Evaluation is a large and diverse sub-domain in the educational landscape. Practically everything can be evaluated: performances, achievements, essays, books, skills, strategies, processes, policies, staff, leaders, students, personalities, results, aims, designs, data, hypotheses, arguments, theories, and so on. The landscape of evaluation contains normative and empirical elements, many models, many purposes, many criteria, many objects of evaluation, many approaches, many perspectives, and quite possibly many unintended effects. What we tend to refer to as "evaluation theory" often denotes this sub-domain – thus exemplifying Bromberger's first main use of the term "theory", namely as denoting a field (see Chapter 3). I shall restrict myself to a discussion of criterion-referenced evaluation in the form of grading, which seems to lend itself eminently well to an equivalence-based analysis.

Grading

Grades and their use in education systems have been debated since the Jesuits invented them, as they are of concern to students, parents, teachers, politicians and employers alike. I shall skip all discussion of informational value, ethical and professional dilemmas, pain and pleasure, encouragement and discouragement, and focus on grading as a form of equivalence-based reasoning. That is to say, I shall include ranking in the mix since ranking implies a comparison that grading does not. Michael Scriven (2007) provides the following definition of grading:

> This is the operation of placing evaluands in one of a set of categories (the grades) which are defined in three ways: (a) each evaluand in a particular grade is superior in terms of X (the evaluative property within the large group of properties indicating m/s/w (sic) that is being used as the basis for grading) to all in a lower grade, and inferior to all in higher grades; (b) each grade is named with a term that has some degree of independent meaning in the vocabulary of m/s/w (sic), a meaning that must of course be consistent with condition (a); (c) the set of grades is exhaustive; i.e. all evaluands are included in one or another.
>
> (p.12)

Suppose now we grade papers. We place them in one of a set of categories, usually A through F. The placement is done in terms of certain evaluative properties or criteria. There are many intriguing issues surrounding criteria, such as what kinds of entities can serve as criteria, where our criteria come from, and how we justify them. The term originates in the Greek word *krinein*, which means to assess or state the value of something. We see here the close connection between criteria and evaluation – they both concern determination of value. Thus, we find ourselves in a normative landscape, very different from physical equivalence theories. And yet, I shall argue, criterion-referenced grading can be viewed as an equivalence theory.

Universities make no secret of the criteria they use to evaluate student achievement. These criteria are public, and presumably quite universal in academia, although they may vary from discipline to discipline. The criteria are not arbitrary (or should not be) because they are intimately connected to the aims of the university and are often formulated based on these aims. Let us look at the grading of master's theses as an example. At my own department we have agreed on the following criteria for evaluating MA theses, here rendered in simplified form: delineation of topic and clarity of research question; understanding of the field as shown in literature review; consistency of research question, research method and theory; research ethics concerning referencing, data collection and data storage; whether the conclusion follows from data and theory; tidiness of structure of the thesis; clarity in language; critical reflection on implications of the study, and so on. The role that equivalence-based reasoning can play does not come into view until we add ranking to the mix. Ranking and grading, Scriven points out, perform different jobs and neither can do the job of the other. The grade contributes the absolute reference to a set of external standards, whereas the rank contributes an inter-evaluand comparison. Furthermore, he says, "Each provides answers to questions the other cannot answer: ranking answers the quest for the best and the better; grading answers the quest for true quality, good enough quality, etc." (p.13). What I need from ranking is not the "best" and the "better", but the comparison.

The equivalence-based reasoning in criterion-referenced evaluation is fairly straightforward. No two master's theses are alike. History of education and educational psychology make for rather different master's theses. Nevertheless, they can be placed in the same grade; let us say B. That means that they are different, but found to be equivalent in the sense of being of equal worth. Some observations are in order. First, while grade may be decided mainly on general agreed-upon criteria such as those listed above, more specific criteria also come into play. These criteria are field-dependent and pertain to the thesis in question, such as treatment and understanding of central concepts and theories, misunderstandings, whether important sources are missing, and so on. Such specific criteria are hardly written down; they vary from thesis to thesis. I contend that a large measure of flexibility is necessary here, the result of which is that the actual set of criteria used to evaluate candidate H's thesis is not the same as the set of criteria used to evaluate candidate J's thesis. Second, and most importantly, examiners use the same criteria in different ways. They judge the degree of satisfaction differently, and they weigh the criteria differently. One examiner may hold that consistency of research question, methodology and theory is the single most important criterion, whereas another may hold that research ethics is the most important. A low score on one of the criteria might be made up for by a high score on another criterion. Again, we see that the number of possible states any thesis can assume, given the set of criteria, is large. And yet we judge that some are equivalent, equally adequate, and deserve the same grade. The job of an equivalence theory would be to contribute postulates to explain and justify the equivalence judgments that are made, especially when examiners use the criteria differently and still set the same grade. I am not sure that such a theory exists at the moment, and I am certainly not suggesting that it would be a simple task to formulate one. But I am fairly certain it would be a good thing – it would help to keep our criteria explicit and increase their legitimacy. Clear and agreed-upon criteria are necessary but not sufficient, since we also need postulates to determine difference and equivalence on the basis of those criteria. Third, the criteria used in the university to evaluate student achievement are not arbitrary. They are intimately connected to the basic aims of higher education and safely anchored in the same epistemic normativity as the aims and the normative structure of science. If the aims of the university are drastically changed, we can envisage a change in the criteria for evaluating student achievements. In a worst-case scenario, critical reflection would cease to be a criterion because critical, independent thinking is no longer relevant. Criteria are, after all, not hewn in stone, but must relate to the overall purpose in which they are anchored.

Realist versus antirealist interpretations

In the educational areas of interest in this chapter, we not only meet complex goal states and ideals, missing or unarticulated postulates; we also meet basic philosophical problems. In the previous sections I have discussed criterion-referenced evaluation and what it means to have reached a goal or satisfied an ideal. The focus on equivalence-based reasoning allowed me to evade the obvious problem one faces in such judgments, namely construct validity. I side-stepped this problem in a previous section and now it is time to return to it.

Suppose you employ Driver's theory and make the judgment that a student has attained the goal state. How trustworthy is your judgment? Or suppose you grade a student paper and make the judgment that the student's understanding of the basic tenets of Piaget's theory is rather confused, but that the ability to talk with and handle children seems excellent. How much confidence should we have in your judgment? How justified is the grade you give the paper? Or suppose you explain a student's low score on tests by low motivation. Is your explanation correct? Judgments such as these are central not only to evaluation, but to much everyday reasoning in general: we effortlessly attribute knowledge, understanding, abilities, properties and traits or lack thereof to people. Trustworthiness arises as an issue because the judgments make inferences to unobservable entities, traits or processes. Many if not all such attributions can be described as inductive or abductive inferences, where we infer the presence of some unobservable trait or entity, such as understanding, motivation or the ability to inspire trust, from the presence of certain observable signs or indications. The problem of construct validity among other things concern the justification of such inferences – the relation between our judgments about unobservables and the grounds on which we base these judgments (Norris, 1983). The problem is a deep and long-standing philosophical problem: how can we distinguish between traits that truly belong to an individual and traits that he or she does not possess but are attributed to them by an observer or an evaluator (Ladyman, 2002)?

Samuel Messick makes the point that construct validity concerns "all assessments, whether based on tests, questionnaires, behavioral observations, work samples, or whatever" (1995, p.5). Fundamentally, he claims, judgments of construct validity are evaluative judgments of the degree to which our empirical evidence supports the appropriateness of interpretations of test scores. In other words, we validate our judgments to justify the inferences we make about unobservable entities, processes or abilities (Nordahl-Hansen & Kvernbekk, 2020). Construct validity easily hooks up with the O/T distinction (see Chapter 3), with O-terms as indications of T-terms. But how should we understand the nature and ontological status of T-entities, which are unobservable but all the same loom so large in our evaluative practices? In the philosophy of science we find two main approaches to the nature and ontology of T-terms: realism and antirealism. Both approaches come in different versions, and I present here what I take to be the standard version of both.

Realists think that T-entities, such as motivation, learning or personality, exist and that it is possible to say something about them (Hacking, 1982, Ladyman, 2002). We can attribute causal powers to motivation and accord it a dynamic role in learning; we can refer to unobservable entities to explain unobservable ones, and claims containing T-entities can be true or false (on the correspondence theory of truth). Antirealists, on the other hand, are generally empiricists and standardly regard observation (experience) as the prime source of knowledge. They are suspicious of T-entities and causation, and they are reluctant to move beyond observation and experience. Bas van Fraassen (1980, 1989), who is one of the main developers of SC, is also a prominent antirealist – by his own description a constructive empiricist. He rejects realism among other things because he thinks it leads to an inflationary ontology – realists commit themselves to the existence of T-entities described by scientific theories. Van Fraassen advocates agnosticism concerning the existence of T-entities, and we might be well advised to be cautious – the history of science is full of theories once thought to be successful and true, but that later turned out to be false and the T-entity was found not to exist after all (for example, phlogiston). Antirealists hold that either T-entities do not exist, or that we have no good reason to think that they do.

What do T-terms do for antirealists, if they have no referents? Richard Braithwaite (1968) in a classical formulation puts it like this:

> ...electrons... are logical constructions out of the observed events and objects by which their presence can be detected; this is equivalent to saying that the word "electron" can be explicitly defined in terms of such observation. Every sentence containing the word "electron" can be... translated without loss of

meaning into a sentence in which there occur only words which denote entities ... which are directly observable.

(pp.52–53)

The same holds for traits, attributes and processes: they are constructs that are abstracted from observed behavior. The T-term is just a label for observables. We should note two things about this. First, this is the empiricist criterion of meaning at work: T-terms must be connected to observation in order to have cognitive meaning. Second, Braithwaite is very clear that T-terms can be exhaustively translated into O-terms and his view exemplifies how antirealists in general define T-terms – by equating them with the procedures for measuring them. Presumably, this is over-optimistic since it assumes perfect operationalization, T=O. Third, and this is the crux of the matter, for antirealists, T-terms are abbreviations of a class or a form of derived talk. As Stephen Norris (1983) puts it, "According to logical positivism [antirealism], theoretical talk in effect is merely a shorthand way of speaking and has no other significant import" (p.56). T-terms have no referents (or we remain agnostic about it) but are simply summaries of observations. Antirealists need not worry about construct validity, since they assume identity between T-term and O-terms.

Construct validity problems are for scientific realists. Realists are allowed to think that T-entities exist. They can, for example, hold that abilities are attributes of people rather than classes of their behavior, and that inner processes such as learning or cognitive development actually take place. They do however face the problem of justifying that unobservable entities are real, since obviously no observational test can determine that question, whereas of course the view is open to them that T-terms refer to unobservable entities that have (or can have) observable manifestations. Still, the construct validity problem remains for the realists: how to justify the inferences we make about unobservables. Am I right to attribute a process of deep learning to a student, based on my observation of his or her behavior?

Let us look again at critical thinking (Ennis, 1987, 1996). On Ennis' view, critical thinking consists of two basic constituents: abilities and dispositions. Both of these are T-entities. You cannot observe them directly, but you can identify them by observing (what you take to be) their concrete manifestations and attribute them to people. Our understanding of, and quite probably application of, Ennis' detailed ideal depends on whether we interpret it realistically or antirealistically. A realist may say that abilities and dispositions are something that we *have*. They do not in themselves necessarily tell us anything about behavioral manifestations, but they will tell us something about behavioral possibilities. In so far as Ennis thinks that dispositions and abilities can be used to explain observable behavior, he betrays realist tendencies. T-entities can only be used to explain or influence other entities if they exist and can be endowed with the requisite (often causal) powers. It is my hypothesis that this is what Ennis actually means. But things may not be so simple. Ennis says that abilities and dispositions together *constitute* critical thinking. Norris (1983) argues that *constitute* usually indicates an antirealist understanding of

T-terms – it suggests identity between a class of events or operations and the T-term in question. This is even more complex than it appears. For a full-blown antirealist thinker, abilities and dispositions, which are T-terms, will be constituted by various operations (described by O-terms). Ennis does not discuss this explicitly, but many of the sub-categories he employs are activity-oriented – e.g. report, stipulate, define, consider, decide, select, monitor, employ – and can be interpreted as being constitutive of abilities and dispositions. But Ennis adds a second layer, since he says that abilities and dispositions (whether themselves constituted by classes of behavior or not) *constitute* critical thinking. An antirealist interpretation of Ennis' views thus would say that critical thinking is a summary of abilities and dispositions, which themselves are summaries of a wide range of specific behaviors.

I have already suggested that I think Ennis' views should be taken in a realist spirit. At least, I would argue, this is not an unreasonable interpretation. Ennis is an educationalist, and educationalists in general think of abilities as something you can *develop* and afterwards *possess.* If this is how he thinks, the choice of the term *constitute* may give rise to misunderstandings when the topic is the relation between a T-term and its referent. In realist terms, critical thinking is an ability that you *have*, not just a class of behaviors. It is a dynamic power that can manifest itself in all the different ways that Ennis describes; it can influence other entities, for instance understanding, or other abilities, for instance learning to learn; and it can in turn be influenced by them – something it cannot if it merely is a summary of a class of observations. With a realist interpretation comes the problem of construct validity, since it is by no means obvious which behaviors should be observed for it to be justified for us to infer that a person actually possesses the ability and the disposition to think critically. And thus we are back to equivalence-based reasoning: which different combinations should we regard as equivalent and use them as a basis for judgments of construct validity of the term critical thinking? Unless we declare ourselves to be antirealists, of course.

Summary

I have in this chapter discussed the understanding and application of normative entities and activities that are central to both theory and practice in education, namely goals, ideals and criterion-referenced evaluation in the form of grading. Goals and ideals are found as parameters in goal-directed theories, and it might seem strange that they should somehow make up theories in their own right. But there is nothing in SC to preclude the same parameters from appearing in different types of theories.

The phenomena discussed in this chapter are explicitly normative and value-laden, but the theories are theories *about* and not theories *for*. They concern how we should understand such entities, not how to attain them. The same holds for grading, which is clearly normative because it is about deciding the quality and value of something – this is not a goal-directed theory but an equivalence-based one, centered on the relationship between difference and equivalence in the form of equal worth or adequacy. If these are accepted as theories in their own right, they will serve as counterexamples to the thesis that all educational theories are goal-directed theories *for*. Yet the most important thing is not to furnish such theoretical structures with the label *theory*, but to demonstrate the analytical power and potential of laws of coexistence. Such laws, I claim, are effective tools in approaching, understanding and handling complex normative entities such as goals and ideals.

Laws of coexistence are a type of theoretical law that can also be accommodated by Received View (RV), but applied to empirical entities. It will be recalled from Chapter 3 that RV operates with correspondence rules; rules that tie together T-terms and a given set of O-terms, such that lawful connections can manifest themselves directly in the phenomena. This is not the case in SC, which does not embody the O/T distinction. RV can accommodate equivalence, but not in normative entities – these simply do not figure in RV. Normative entities of the kinds we have looked at here fall outside the scope of RV among other things because they do not fit into axiomatic, deductive systems.

I have included a brief discussion of realist and antirealist interpretations of T-terms and T-entities in this chapter. Realism and antirealism are two basic approaches to the ontology of T-terms, and to other fundamental issues that follow in train: notably truth, explanation and causation, which I have evaded here, but will return to in Chapter 7 and 10. In this chapter I wanted to focus on T-terms and T-entities because they loom large in education: do attributes, abilities and processes really belong to people? If we think so and attribute them to people, we face a construct validity problem. This is a serious matter in education, because it may matter much to the people we evaluate and assess what kinds of abilities we attribute to them. SC has no built-in preferences concerning realism or antirealism. Its basic tenets are compatible with both approaches, and its main advocates differ on this issue. Van Fraassen calls himself a constructive empiricist and denies several realist tenets, Suppe calls himself a quasi-realist, and Giere as I understand him is mainly a realist. I will make one last observation here, since I have realist inclinations myself. If realism implies that realists are committed to the existence of any theoretical entity, then realism is not compatible with SC. SC employs idealizations, which by definition do not exist and therefore are not allowed in a strict form of realism. This is why I opt for caution and careful considerations concerning commitment to the existence of T-entities. A scientific realism for SC must be a modified sort, so that idealized entities do not stop theories from being true.

6 Interlevel theories

In this chapter I shall introduce a third type of theory found in the field of education. Interlevel theories exhibit a more complex structure than the other types of theories, for two interconnected reasons: they treat phenomena that involve different levels of aggregation, and in order to represent such phenomena the interaction of different theories is required. I shall argue that the Received View of theories (RV) is incapable of accommodating this form of theory, whereas the Semantic Conception (SC) contributes important analytical tools, although perhaps not all the tools that are needed in this case. Behind the analysis to be presented here lie two other sources of inspiration. One derives from sociology, namely the concepts of grand theories and middle range theories. The other derives from the philosophy of biology, most notably the employment in biology of grand theories and middle range theories to deal with an enormous phenomenal complexity. It may seem odd to import perspectives from biology to help analyze educational theory – sociology, after all, customarily belongs to the same family of disciplines as education and therefore could be deemed more relevant at the outset. In the philosophy of biology we find carefully worked out meta-theoretical analyses of a similar kind to what I am attempting here, and detailed examples are always useful. I am inspired by their thorough discussions and analyses of evolutionary theory, employment of SC and of the concepts of grand and middle range theories. Complex phenomena require complex theory structures for their representation, and philosophers of biology have shown how it can be done. But we proceed with caution – transfers, even only inspirational ones, from one field to another are never straightforward. To forestall any misunderstandings, I would like to note that I am not going to import any biological content or assumptions; I am going to build a parallel formal structure for analyzing interlevel theories.

I select socialization theory as my main example of an interlevel theory. This theory is not practical, it is not normative and it is not goal-directed, and as such it represents a counterexample to universalistic claims concerning the nature of educational theories. One can raise the objection to my example of choice that socialization is not an educational process and therefore does not belong to the field of education. This objection presupposes a fairly narrow delineation of the discipline or field of education. I argued in Chapter 2 that the field is large, unruly and fragmented, with porous boundaries and hybrid topics, and this in itself makes it difficult to determine whether some phenomenon falls inside or outside the field. More importantly, socialization is often invoked by Bildung theorists as a contrast to Bildung and therefore figures in educational thought. And of course, socialization is a process that happens to all people, children and adults alike, and is for that reason of interest to educationalists. There are, however, other examples of interlevel theories in education: for instance, theories of group dynamics, theories of school development, frame factor theory and others. I aim to show in this chapter that the notion of a grand theory, as I shall employ it, is a potentially very fruitful analytical tool in education. But first we have to inquire into the interlevel condition.

Levels and their relations

Throughout my analysis, I will indicate what I take to be central features of interlevel theories in education that an adequate conception of scientific theories should capture. As a point of departure, let us tentatively adopt Kenneth Schaffner's characterization of the interlevel condition (1980, p.84): "...the main point of the use of the term "interlevel" is to draw attention to the use of different levels of aggregation functioning in the same theory (or model)".

Schaffner is a philosopher of biology. As I said above: we proceed with caution. In the social sciences it is common to use the individual level as one of the levels. Some form of collection of individuals then makes up some form of aggregate level; for instance, family, group, institution, organization, society. The idea of different aggregate levels in one and the same theory is perfectly conceivable, and we should of course be as clear as possible as to which levels we are dealing with. The main issue concerns the relationship between the levels. How should we understand it?

Schaffner describes the relation between levels roughly as a part-whole relation. An entity e_2 can be said to be at a higher level than entity e_1 if e_2 has e_1 as one of its parts. Schaffner further requires that the defining properties of e_2 not be simple sums of e_1s, but that some additional "organizing relations" be present. Individuals e_1 are part of population e_2. Thinking in terms of parts and wholes is nothing new. We may see it as a way of handling complexity, whether in the natural or the social sciences.

However, the terms are rather vague and merit a brief exploration. It is not easy to define what a whole is or what a part is; nor is it easy to define the organizing relations that supposedly ensure that the whole is more than the sum of its parts. D. C. Phillips' exposition of various attempts to come to grips with part-whole relations suggests that a distinction commonly is made between external and internal relations (Phillips, 1990). Primarily, he says, the distinction concerns whether or not the parts interacting are affected by the interaction. Externally related parts are not so affected, whereas internally related parts are so affected because they themselves are partially constituted by the interaction. Hence, internally related parts change if any of their relations change; if a part is removed both it and the whole will change. We can picture that a whole consisting of internally related parts is in constant flux, and Phillips is skeptical of this form of holism because it makes it difficult to obtain knowledge of both parts and whole:

> ...the theory of internal relations makes the attainment of knowledge impossible, in principle. For to have knowledge of A, in the sense of knowing the defining features of A, all of A's relationships would have to be known; but since A is dynamically or reciprocally related to everything else in the whole of which it is a part, the whole must be known before A can be known.
>
> (1990, p.78)

Phillips is right to be skeptical of this way of reasoning, which seems to lead to an impasse. There are other problems as well. What should we take it to mean that the whole is "more" than the sum of the parts? Schaffner's organizing relations cannot be conceived of as parts, because if we add more parts, we would still need organizing relations to ensure that the whole is more than their sum. And how should we understand "sum"? How can we *add* parts? Would it not seriously restrict what can count as parts if they somehow have to be additive? We would do better to avoid these conceptual blind alleys and instead adopt a different way of looking at the part-whole issue. What exactly do we need here? I propose we minimally need a perspective that endows the whole with different properties than the parts. There are other things to be said about a whole than about the parts. But we also need a flexible concept of a whole – this is important in order to avoid demands for drawing up the boundaries of the whole. I shall briefly discuss Gregory Bateson's concept of context to indicate what kind of understanding of wholes and interlevel conditions that I think might be fruitful (Bateson, 1972). He summarizes his concept of context in the following way:

> ...I speak of an action or an utterance as occurring "in" a context, and the conventional way of talking suggests that the particular action is a "dependent" variable, while the context is the "independent" or determining variable. But this view of how an action is related to its context is likely to distract the reader – as it has distracted me – from perceiving the ecology of the ideas which together constitute the small subsystem which I call "context". ... It is important to see the particular utterance or action as *part* of the ecological subsystem called context and not as a product or effect of what remains of the context after the piece we want to explain has been cut from it.
>
> (p.338)

This gives us the following picture: events and actions contribute to the building up of the context that they themselves are a part of. A context thus becomes a whole, concretely defined, that is constituted by different parts – the whole is nothing independent of or completely distinct from the parts. The parts are not "inside" the whole; they rather constitute the whole. Take the alphabet, for example. It is a whole that is constituted by letters. The letters, in turn, are organized in a specific order, and together they make up the whole that they are all part of. The English alphabet has 26 letters and the Norwegian alphabet has 29, but both make up wholes that fall under the category of alphabets. The Greek alphabet has 24 letters and the organizing relations are different from English and

Norwegian, but the letters still constitute their own whole. Every part contributes to the whole, but is not identical to it – the letter A has different properties than the alphabet.

With this understanding of the part-whole relation, the interlevel condition will primarily concern *constitution*: the parts together constitute the whole. I say primarily – I do not want to preclude other possible relations. A couple of comments are in order. First, importantly, the interlevel condition goes both ways, as it were: while actions and events contribute to the constitution of their own context, they also at least partly get their meaning from the same context. Second, Bateson thinks in terms of hierarchies here and insists on a logic of class inclusion (which he takes from Russell and Whitehead). This means that you can build context upon context upon context, all the time such that the whole (the meta-context) is constituted by its parts (the contexts in question).

I tentatively conclude that at least parts of Bateson's concept of context are suitable for coming to grips with and deepening Schaffner's interlevel condition, because it directs our attention to relations between levels (parts and wholes, individuals and systems). It demystifies both parts and wholes and makes them manageable and applicable. As an extra bonus we avoid both extreme individualism (where the whole has no informational value for the parts) and extreme holism (where the parts have no informational value for the whole).

Grand theories

The guiding idea of a grand theory is that it takes a complex theory structure to account for phenomena with parameters at different levels of aggregation. Grand theories can handle such phenomenal complexity, since they are composites constituted by middle range theories. Again we meet a part-whole relationship, this time between middle range theories as parts and the grand theory as the whole. This guiding idea, however, requires some tweaking of the terms, so let me make clear what is tweaked into what.

The term "middle range theory" was developed by sociologist Robert Merton (1996 [1949]). Sociological theory, Merton says, "refers to logically interconnected sets of propositions from which empirical uniformities can be derived" (p.41). In passing, we note that this definition clearly is reminiscent of RV. But here it is his idea of middle range theories that interests us:

> ...*theories of the middle range:* theories that lie between the minor but necessary working hypotheses that evolve in abundance during day-to-day research and the all-inclusive systematic efforts to develop a unified theory that will explain all the observed uniformities of social behavior, social organization, and social change.
>
> (p.41)

What Merton presents here is a hierarchy of bodies of knowledge at different levels of generality or abstraction. Middle range theories are intermediate, located between descriptions of particulars on the one hand and general theories that are too far removed from the phenomena to account for them on the other. Middle range theories deal with delimited aspects of phenomena; they are developed in interaction with empirical data and provide accounts and explanations of the phenomena within their scope. As examples Merton mentions the theory of role conflict, the theory of formation of social norms, the theory of normalization, the theory of social mobility, the germ theory of disease, and the kinetic theory of gases (the latter two to suggest that the same theory-building techniques and epistemic interests are shared across science boundaries). In passing, these are exactly the kind of theories that SC aims to accommodate. What then about grand theories?

The notion of "grand theory" was coined by sociologist C. Wright Mills (1959). He used it to refer to highly abstract theorizing far removed from the reality of social phenomena and not amenable to empirical testing: a kind of theorizing he was skeptical of. This skepticism he shared with Merton, as we have seen, who suggested middle range theories as more fruitful for sociological investigation and understanding than the quest for total systems of theory. Merton used a variety of terms to characterize grand theories or total systems of theory, such as "all-inclusive unified theory", "single all-embracing theories" and "theoretical frameworks". I shall henceforth call them grand theories, as that seems to have become the established term.

A given middle range theory may be consistent with and subsumed under a variety of grand theories, Merton suggests; an observation he thinks might be scary to those who believed that systems of sociological thought should be logically close-knit and mutually exclusive sets of doctrine (it must be remembered here that this was originally published in the late 1940s. Today's sociologists may have other beliefs about their discipline). Merton offers a number of examples to illustrate this relation between middle range theories and grand theories, and concludes that the grand theories of sociology are sufficiently loose-knit, internally diversified and mutually overlapping to allow this relation of subsumption, problematic as it may be.

However, the kind of hierarchy of abstraction or generality that Merton describes does not provide us with what we need to account for phenomena that encompass different levels of aggregation. As announced above, we need to tweak the terms somewhat. More specifically, we have to endow middle range theories with a new function and the concept of grand theories with a slightly different content. I propose that we view the grand theory as a composite of middle range theories. That is, a grand theory is a whole and the middle range theories constitute the parts, and their relationship is to be understood in terms of Bateson's concept of context. In some respect the conceptual tweaks are also inspired by Merton, at least partly so. In his analysis of the relationship between middle range theories and total systems of theory he among other things says the following, worth quoting at length:

> Sociological theory, if it is to advance significantly, must proceed on these interconnected planes: (1) by developing special theories from which to derive hypotheses that can be empirically investigated and (2) by evolving, not

> suddenly revealing, a progressively more general conceptual scheme that is adequate to consolidate groups of special theories.
>
> To concentrate entirely on special theories is to risk emerging with specific hypotheses that account for limited aspects of social behavior, organization, and change but that remain mutually inconsistent.
>
> To concentrate entirely on master conceptual schemes for deriving all subsidiary theories is to risk producing twentieth century sociological equivalents of the large philosophical systems of the past, with all their varied suggestiveness, their architectonic splendor, and their scientific sterility.
>
> (1996, pp.48–49)

In other words, Merton thought that sociology stood to gain from keeping a double focus and by bringing concrete and abstract levels of theorizing into connection and communication with each other. This surely holds for education as well. The perspective offered above, with grand theories as composites of middle range theories, is one way of achieving it. This perspective puts us in a position to reinterpret the relation between middle range theories and grand theories, and some changes follow in train. The issue of consistency between middle range theories and between middle range theories and grand theory, as outlined by Merton, no longer occupies such a prominent position. The part-whole perspective shifts our focus from consistency to *interaction*: how different middle range theories interact *within* a given grand theory to provide an adequate representation of the phenomenon in question. Or more precisely, how middle range theories together constitute the grand theory which accounts for the phenomenon. The grand theory is the whole, the composite; it is constituted by the middle range theories and cannot be identified with any one of them. Grand theories are not necessarily interlevel theories; that depends on the nature of the object within their scope. But all interlevel theories are grand theories, since it takes the interaction of different middle range theories to account for interlevel phenomena. It stands to reason that grand theories have a highly complex structure to account adequately for interlevel phenomena, which themselves are complex in nature. Without a complex theory structure we risk oversimplifying and reducing such phenomena and thereby also misrepresenting them.

To summarize briefly, my proposed conceptual tweak requires that we detach ourselves somewhat from Merton's analyses and from his way of using the concepts. As we have seen, for Merton the difference between grand theories and middle range theories is mainly one of generality or abstraction and empirical content. I retain the concepts because they signal much of what I am after. Middle range theories still deal with delimited aspects of (educational) phenomena, but as parts in a grand theory they take on a different function. Grand theories are necessary to show that each middle range theory taken by itself is insufficient to characterize the phenomenon – the characterization is provided by the grand theory. Moreover, the grand theory aspires to satisfy the interlevel condition that applies to the phenomenon of interest. It should be noted, though, that "whole" in this context does not indicate "all". This is not a case of "adding" theories that each deal with one or two aspects of some phenomenon so that they together deal with all aspects (assuming that could be done). "Whole" here simply means the context that is constituted by the parts. In every concrete case we have to decide which parts it is wise to include and what kind of whole we want them to constitute.

Socialization theory as a grand theory

I had better make it clear at the outset that my aim in this section is not to launch a new socialization theory, nor to express an opinion on the merits of existing theories. Furthermore, I shall not analyze one specific socialization theory but extract parameters and postulates from different approaches, old and new, and discuss them using SC and the concepts developed above. My aim is to lay bare the structure of grand theories as accounts of interlevel phenomena.

Let me begin by painting a broad picture of socialization, as a background to identifying the different levels of aggregation in this theory. Socialization is a process that always takes place in societies, whether people are aware of it or not. As I understand it, the conscious cooperation of people themselves in this process is not necessary – it is something that happens to us all, something we undergo. A theory of socialization therefore has to encompass an individual level. Urie Bronfenbrenner (1979), in his classic ecological approach to socialization, argues at length that the society (or environment, as he prefers to call it), in which the learning of individuals take place, can be conceived of as a set of nested structures. That implies that a person's development can be profoundly affected, albeit indirectly, by events occurring in settings in which the individual himself or herself is not present. For example, conditions of parental employment will exert a powerful influence on child development, through such factors as flexibility of job schedules, availability of day-care arrangements, quality of health service, and so on.

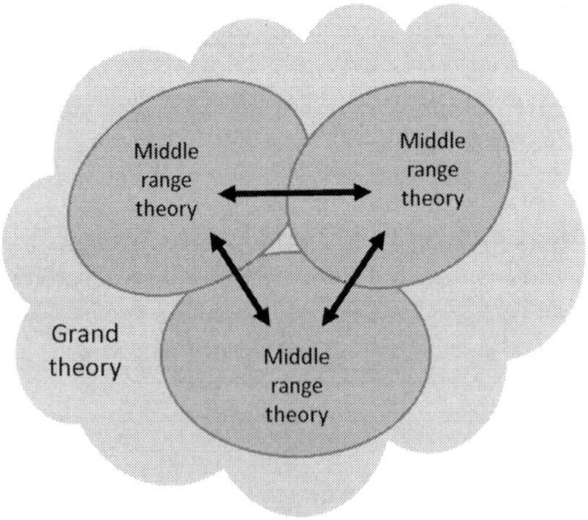

Figure 6.1 Grand theory: Interacting middle range theories

Anton Hoëm, a Norwegian sociologist of education, views societies as social systems representing the adaptation between social entities internally and between social entities and their surroundings (Hoëm, 1978). Modern societies are enormously complex, characterized by an increasing degree of differentiation and specialization, which in turn creates a need for coordination. Social structures comprise such entities as hierarchies, roles, positions, institutions, technologies, different settings and their mutual relations, all of which serve to restrict, promote, hamper or reinforce ways of transmitting culture. Social structures, therefore, are a candidate for the aggregate level of socialization theory – people are socialized in some context. Finally, let us note that social structures are not static; rather they evolve over time.

No matter how we define the concept of socialization, such theories have a tremendously wide scope. At their core we find a notion of change, since socialization implies change. The theories deal with how people become social beings: which agents contribute to the process and in what respects, how cultural patterns and societal forces influence or shape the process, and so on. Let us now look at which middle range theories might enter into socialization theory. My point of departure is the observation that most theories of socialization seem to center around three main concepts: individual, culture and society (e.g. Bronfenbrenner, 1979, Hoëm, 1978).

Possible middle range theories

Throughout the entire history of educational thought the development of the individual has been a major theme. Ideas about how people learn and develop invariably influence how educationalists, broadly speaking, structure the environment to facilitate learning that is considered desirable. It is obvious, though, that a lot of learning takes place outside formal educational settings. We all participate in several formal and informal settings or arenas, such as family, day-care center, school, organizations, work, voluntary activity, friends. Our participation in these arenas contributes to our development in various ways, significantly or not so significantly. We acquire knowledge, beliefs, prejudices, attitudes, values, habits, patterns of interpretation and behavior, and form our identity when moving in a larger or smaller variety of settings.

Socialization theories aim to incorporate the totality of the individual's development process. The learning that takes place in formal educational settings is just one part of this process. Independent of the number of arenas, however, one central concept seems to recur: learning. No doubt learning is an important mechanism in socialization processes, and no socialization theory could reasonably leave it out. Nevertheless, learning alone cannot constitute a complete socialization theory.

Learning implies learning *something*. There is no process of socialization without a content. Therese Sand's works on refugees and immigrants in Norway will serve as an example (for example Sand, 2008). Her studies highlight both the critical role played by the content as well as the fact that socialization applies to adults. In the case of adults we often use the term re-socialization, to identify the special kind of socialization process which occurs when there is a significant shift of cultural setting, as the case is with refugees and immigrants. The process of re-socialization runs parallel to a process of "unlearning", "forgetting" or "suppressing" the cultural baggage one brings to the new setting, termed "de-socialization" by researchers in this field. Culture is here not perceived as some objectified entity; the stance taken is rather interactional: there is a two-way relation between individuals and culture.

Refugees coming to Norway from, say, some Asian or African country, meet a different country, a different climate and a different culture. They are assigned different roles and given different social status. The conditions for practicing the "old way" of life are radically changed. Furthermore, on arrival they do not have the qualifications necessary for interpreting the new reality, nor for mastering familiar tasks and tasks new to the new surroundings. So a process of re-socialization begins. What do they have to learn to make a good life for themselves in the new country? Obviously the demands of change are immense, including adaptation to a new climate, learning the systems for banking and medical care, coming to terms with different sex role patterns, different norms for sanctioning behavior, and so on. They learn the values, norms, gestures, social codes, communication forms, behavioral patterns and knowledge of the people already living in the society – in short, the content of the re-socialization process is constituted (mainly) by the culture they meet in the new country. It is of course perfectly possible to learn *about* values and behavioral patterns without internalizing them and making them one's own. Sand's data show how refugees may have two sets of values, norms and behavioral patterns and switch between them according to which setting they are in.

"Culture" can be defined ideationally, as a more or less coherent system of concepts and rules and meaning that underlie and are expressed in the ways humans live, and thus refers to the socially transmitted patterns of behavior that are characteristic of a given group. It can also be defined more comprehensively as incorporating all kinds of material products. Sand's empirical findings underline the importance of material conditions and natural surroundings for re-socialization.

The point of this short and highly step-motherly foray into culture, social and material surroundings is to suggest that while learning may be a necessary condition for socialization, it is not sufficient. Some notion of cultural transmission is needed. Are the two of them, then, sufficient to account for socialization?

I have already suggested that it is reasonable to suppose that a theory of socialization also needs a notion of social structures as one of its parts. The content in itself, the ways of transmitting it, the roles of the agents in the socialization process – all vary in accordance with the society in which they occur. At this point it becomes particularly important to hold on to the interlevel condition as I discussed it in the previous section. Bateson warns against viewing context – here society – as something with fixed and identifiable boundaries, which invites thinking in terms of "inside" or "outside". Bateson thinks in terms of parts which serve to constitute the context they themselves are part of. He also admits that it is extremely difficult to escape using words such as "in" or "inside" when we speak about contexts (as witnessed in this section!), and I therefore wish to draw explicit attention one more time to the understanding of "context" and "society" that I employ, as wholes constituted by their parts, not as boundaries with parts inside them. This is vital because it means that the relationship between parts and wholes is dynamic. On the one hand, society or social structures do influence individuals, their beliefs and actions; on the other hand, society is constituted by individuals and influenced by them. The context is not unchangeable. There is no implication here that individuals are or should be aware of how they contribute to the constitution of the context. The context is huge and each individual is but a small part. Nevertheless, it is important to hold on to the principled understanding of the part-whole relation here.

The above meanderings yield three components: learning, cultural transmission, and social structures. Again, a couple of observations are in place. First, I am not going to insist that the proposed components together are both necessary and sufficient for an adequate account of socialization. I am, however, inclined to think that they are necessary, in the sense that if any one of them is absent, the resulting account of socialization will be inadequate because some central feature will have been omitted. Second, the proposed components are to be understood as middle range theories. These treat different kinds of phenomena. Socialization theory is a grand theory and cannot be identified exclusively with any one of its middle range theories. It is an interlevel theory because the components are on different levels of aggregation. Third, there is the question of whether the interlevel condition places restrictions on what kinds of topics the middle range theories must deal with. I shall come back to that issue subsequently.

Levels of aggregation

The middle range theories of socialization theory describe different phenomena at different levels of aggregation, and the grand theory thereby becomes an interlevel theory. The aggregate levels require comment.

It is not obvious how many or which levels of aggregation a socialization theory should encompass; socialization theories may have different emphases. Theories of learning (or development) focus on the individual. On SC they can be viewed as theories with laws of succession, which specify a pattern of psychological development and typical interactions with one's environment. As argued in Chapter 4, it is plausible to view the law in such cases as an indeterministic law of succession. That means that for a given current psychological state, the law allows the system (the individual) to assume a number of different subsequent states. We should note a couple of things here. First, that the kind of development we talk about here is not goal-directed in the normative sense. No socialization theory, as far as I know, holds that the process has or should have an aim, let alone an aim that can be specified in any way. We do not ask if an individual has attained the goal of socialization (however more circumscribed goal-directed processes can take place "within" or as part of the very broad socialization process). Socialization theories are empirical and aim to map or represent the process and its main agents, and the state space is in principle infinitely large. Second, following from the first, there is the question of whether it is possible to assign probabilities to various subsequent states. If not, an upshot will be that it is impossible to give any predictions as to the socialization pattern of an individual. Anton Hoëm's theory suggests that some prediction is possible when the number of settings is restricted (Hoëm, 1978). If the values and interests a child meets in school harmonize with those of his or her family, socialization may be what Hoëm terms "reinforcing". If the two sets of values and interests conflict, the socialization pattern is more likely to take the form of de-socialization (unlearning) and re-socialization, or of a rejection of the values represented by school, school being a new setting whereas family is the primary setting.

A theory of cultural transmission will have the *dyad* as its smallest possible unit; however, not to the exclusion of other possible units. The requirement is that these units be social; that is, consist of more than one individual – or else cultural transmission makes no sense. Individuals are members of groups and contribute to building the group as a context for themselves and for others. The *group* is therefore a possible aggregate level in a socialization theory. A middle range theory could conceivably have as its object the interaction between individual and group and the ways in which the content of the socialization process is transferred and modified.

Lastly, *society* can serve as an aggregate level, depending on the emphasis of the theory. Society can be defined and delimited in various ways, but is "bigger" than group level in that different groups also are parts of a society and contribute to the constitution of a societal context. The interlevel condition is thereby accommodated; between individuals and groups, between groups and society, or between individuals and society – different socialization theories may have different foci. A complex socialization theory may even contain a number of aggregate levels. The interplay of all involved middle range theories is required in studies of the relationship between the involved aggregate levels. The parameters that define the state space of socialization theory must therefore be interlevel parameters.

Brief interlude: Other grand theories in education

I have in this chapter singled out socialization theory for detailed analysis. I take socialization to be a topic that falls within the pluridisciplinary field of education, as this field is described in Chapter 2: diverse, hybrid, and with porous boundaries. To forestall objections based on narrower and (shall we say) more traditional views of the field of education, I would like to make it clear that I think there are other grand theories in education dealing with interlevel phenomena. For example, theories of school development are interlevel theories – "school" is an aggregate entity in which we find many individuals, and any theory of school development would have to look at both the organizational level and the individual level. I also think that upbringing can be analyzed as a grand theory. For example, Gert Biesta's discussion of H. H. Groothoff's definition of upbringing (*Erziehung*) suggests quite clearly that Groothoff conceives of theories of upbringing as grand theories (Biesta, 2011, Groothoff, 1973). In Biesta's rendering, Groothoff

> ...argues that such theories must encompass the following elements: (1) a theory of becoming a human being; (2) a theory of interpersonal interaction; (3) a theory of emancipatory learning; (4) a theory of contemporary social life and its perspectives on the future; (5) a theory of the ends and means of education and their interrelationships; and (6) an account of the specific ends and means in the context of the different domains and institutions of Erziehung
>
> (Biesta, 2011, pp. 184–185)

Groothoff, writing in the 1970s, thinks that such an encompassing theory is no longer possible, partly because the field of upbringing has become much more complex than what it once was. This judgment surely is based on the assumption that a theory of upbringing must not only be encompassing but *all*-encompassing to be adequate. This is an assumption that is not built into the concept of grand theories, where the point is the interaction of the middle range theories in question, coupled with the understanding that all theories are simplifications of the phenomenon. It is not Biesta's business in his article to discuss theory structure, but to me it is a fairly straightforward judgment to make that Groothoff's theory of upbringing is a grand theory. A highly complex grand theory too, consisting as it does of six middle range theories. All six are required to account for the phenomenon of upbringing. One can even argue that it is an interlevel theory, given parts (2), (4) and (6) above, which at least have a whiff of aggregate levels about them.

In fact, I think that a number of topics in educational research can be fruitfully conceptualized as grand theories as I have laid out the term: a whole constituted by interacting middle range theories.

Laws of interaction

It should by now be sufficiently established that the different middle range theories in socialization theory treat entities at different levels of aggregation. Middle range theories can be more or less thematically connected, or perhaps not at all, but whatever their connection they cannot reasonably be unified into a single theoretical framework. So how then should we understand the structure of a theory which is a composite of other theories?

Bringing back into play the conceptual apparatus introduced in Chapter 3, I suggest that socialization theory, as an interlevel theory, may plausibly be viewed as involving two distinct state spaces, one individual and one aggregate or systemic. Interlevel theories therefore involve laws of interaction that describe the transformations between the two spaces. Such accounts require the interaction or joint effort of the middle range theories, and the laws in interaction tell us how two or more theories interact and what the results might be. The two proposed levels of aggregation clearly satisfy Schaffner's interlevel condition: the requirement as to when an entity e_2 – in this case social structures – can be said to be at a higher level of aggregation than entity e_1 – in this case individuals. The total state space of an interlevel theory is thus defined by parameters on each level and parameters pertaining to the transformation between levels.

My analysis of socialization theory owes much to meta-theoretical discussions in biology; in particular to a view of evolutionary theory developed by among others Richard Lewontin (1974) and Paul Thompson (1989), and to theoretical developments in ecological theory (Castle, 2001). Evolutionary theory is by and large understood as a composite of theories of natural selection, heredity and variation. And to make the history of evolutionary thought very short: Thompson states that the "difficulty that this understanding of evolutionary theory poses in connection with a formal account of the theory is that it is not a unified theory" (1989, p.12). Not only that, the component theories describe mechanisms that operate on different kinds of entities and on different levels of organic organization. In response to this problem, Lewontin proposed that evolutionary theory be understood as involving two distinct state spaces, a phenotypic and a genotypic one, and furthermore that the theory involves laws describing the interaction – or transformation, as he prefers to call it – between the two state spaces:

> It would appear that both genotypes and phenotypes are state variables and that what population genetic theory does is to map a set of genotypes into a set of phenotypes, provide a transformation in the phenotype space, then map these new phenotypes back into genotypes, where a final transformation occurs to produce a genotype array in the next generation.
>
> (Lewontin, 1974, p.13)

Before proceeding, let me interject a brief linguistic comment. When the theoretical laws that we meet with in this chapter were introduced in Chapter 3, they were termed *laws of interaction*, following the semantic convention of my meta-theory of choice. Both Lewontin and Thompson mostly prefer the term *laws of transformation*. While the terms have the same referent, they may have different connotations. *Laws of interaction* may connote the interaction of the middle range theories in question and thus direct our focus to the constituent theories that act as parts in the grand theory. *Laws of transformation*, on the other hand, may connote changes taking place *in* and *between* the two state spaces, and thus direct our attention more to the effects of the middle range theories – their interaction is required to account for the transformations in and between state spaces. One set of connotations may be more apt than the other, depending on context. I shall use *laws of interaction* to describe the transformations that take place between the two state spaces. The changes that take place in each state space I take to be described by laws of succession, which we also met in Chapter 4.

Transformation between levels

According to Bas van Fraassen (1970), "the most satisfying approach to interaction is no doubt the procedure of regarding the interacting systems as constituting a complex system" (p.332). He then modifies his statement somewhat, admitting that this is not always a feasible approach since the systems in question can be rather dissimilar. Van Fraassen's preferred approach is not what I am after, however. To treat interacting systems as one single large system serves to obscure the features of interaction that we are after in interlevel theories, where the point is precisely how middle range theories interact to produce an adequate account of a complex interlevel phenomenon. To see the necessity and the contribution of each theory, surely we need to keep them apart and heed their respective boundaries (to the extent possible). If we wish to go for van Fraassen's approach, we should opt for the modified version – the middle range theories of socialization theory are quite different and treat entities at different levels of aggregation.

But there are other features of van Fraassen's approach that might serve us better. On his version of SC, interaction of theories can be described by means of a "next-state function". This means that there can be inputs to a system as a result of its interaction with another system, and with the effect that the state of the system is changed. The laws of interaction specify the possible outcomes – to the extent that this is possible, we might add. In van Fraassen's own words,

> A system with input has state space H and a nonempty set of inputs D. These inputs change the state of the system in a manner described by the "next-state function" $H \times D \rightarrow H$
>
> (1970, p.332)

This may seem formal and technical, and it may not be entirely clear from this formulation that this is an interaction between two systems and not a transition within one system (it is perfectly possible to imagine a system that creates its own inputs). However, the next-state function is more applicable than appears at first glance, so let us explore some possibilities. First, D could be construed as input that comes from the system's *interaction* with another system. The input is thus to some degree produced by the system itself. By means of the next-state function, the laws of interaction will tell you something about the possible outcomes of this input. Thus, the system's interaction with another system will affect its behavior and $H \times D$ is mapped into H. Van Fraassen's notation is perhaps a bit confusing here, since the point of the next-state function is that the state of the system changes – the formula $H \times D \rightarrow H$ does not by itself show the change. To make the change explicit, the next-state function could be rendered as $H_{state} \times D_1D_2 \rightarrow H_{state+1}$ to show the successive states of the system. This is what I take a law of interaction to do.

A slightly different way of conceiving of D is to construe it as the output of another system that serves as input for H. I am not sure that van Fraassen would accept this formulation of the next-state function, since it leaves out explicit interaction between systems, although it leaves systems open for input. However, the wording is apt, concerning the state spaces of interlevel theories specifically and theoretical integration more generally.

I would also like to suggest that as it stands, the next-state function in the context of interlevel theories describes only half the story. This is because interlevel theories have (at least) two state spaces, one state space for each aggregate level. The other half of the story therefore concerns H_1, which produces new output that serves as input for the other system, which then changes as a result. Thus, we get a "double" next-state function, where the sequence of transformations in principle may continue indefinitely. That is a useful figure of thought in education.

Before we apply this structure to socialization theory, a couple of clarifications are in order. First, we see that interlevel theories make use of two types of theoretical laws: laws of succession and laws of interaction (my wording here thus differs from Lewontin's). Laws of succession describe the changes occurring at each level of aggregation under input determined by the theory operating at the *other* level. While van Fraassen's next-state function treats laws of succession as deterministic, the appropriate law of succession in the case of socialization theory (or indeed all educational theories that account for changes over time) is indeterministic or statistical. There is not only one possible state transition trajectory in the state space concerning the individual's behavior. Rather, for any given state there is a number of possible next states. The same holds for trajectories of change at aggregate levels: for any given state of a social system there is a number of possible subsequent states. Second, the transformations occurring between the levels should also be conceived of as indeterministic. There is no way, I submit, to predict exactly what the results of such transformations might be. This is perhaps also one of the reasons why laws of interaction are harder to come to grips with. It is hard to pin down exactly what happens in such transformations, although processes of aggregation and aggregate effects are well known in the social sciences.

With these caveats in mind, let us explore the implications of the double next-state function for socialization theory. I have argued that socialization theory can be conceived of as a grand theory with middle range theories interacting to produce an account of the transformations occurring between two (or more) aggregate levels. The theoretical law involved in this transformation is one of interaction; hence, both

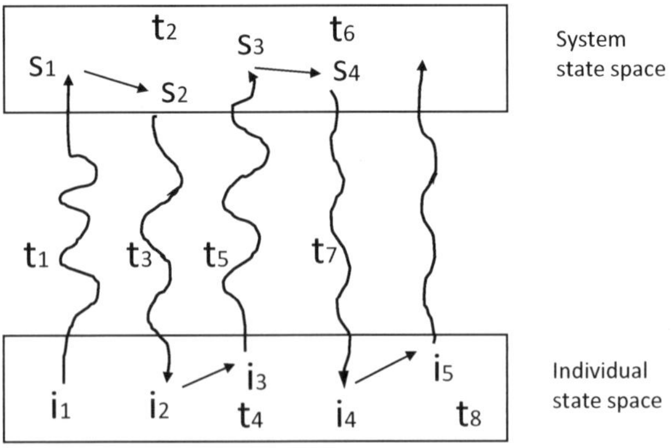

Figure 6.2 Grand theory: Two state spaces and transformations in and between aggregate levels
Adapted from Thompson (1989, p.13)

levels must be taken into account when the possible outcomes of the interaction are specified and examined. This is why it is required that interlevel parameters be utilized in defining the state space. Let me again use Therese Sand's research on the re-socialization processes of refugees as an example (Sand, 2008).

First, we require descriptions at the individual level. Such descriptions can trace the individual through a number of settings, such as family, school, bank, shops, workplace, social gatherings, and so on. The main process at this level was earlier identified as learning, broadly understood, and so the individual will develop in accordance with the laws of succession employed in learning theory. By means of the next-state function, the state transition law of learning theory will indicate how the individual (as an idealized entity) behaves under inputs determined by the theory operating at the level of aggregated effects; for example social norms from country of origin being gradually replaced or modified by norms or cultural content more generally encountered in the new context. The individuals, participating in different social settings, bring input to the group in the form of new cultural content, values, fashion, recreational activities, and so on, all of which serve to create changes at the group level. By means of the laws of interaction the input is transformed into aggregated group or systemic effects and the next-state function indicates the state transition ($\text{System}_{\text{state}} \times \text{Input}_{\text{from individuals}} \rightarrow \text{System}_{\text{state} + 1}$). Changes at the aggregate level in turn provide the individuals with new inputs and create new possibilities for learning and experience, as the model above depicts ($\text{Individual}_{\text{state} +1} \times \text{Input}_{\text{from system}+ 1} \rightarrow \text{Individual}_{\text{state} + 2}$). It is vital that the middle range theories somehow accommodate this mutual input into the levels, or else the grand theory will not be able to account for transformations between the levels.

To return briefly to the question about predictability that I dismissed above: can a grand theory of this kind, with a double set of indeterministic laws of succession and an indeterministic law of interaction, have predictive power? It seems unrealistic to predict with any accuracy what might be the aggregate effects of refugee children spending more time in domestic settings, or how exactly changed systemic conditions will affect individual behavior and learning. However, rough estimates could be possible, and Anton Hoëm's theory, briefly alluded to in a previous section, does allow such prediction. On the other hand, I would argue that it is a mistake to view the processes involved in socialization as having one unique terminus. Many different state transition paths and outcomes must be allowed.

Interlevel theories and conceptions of theory structure

I am advocating a view of interlevel theories in which each middle range theory is in some sense dependent on the other(s). Any formal account of the structure of grand theories must capture their interactive character. It is precisely the interaction between the middle range theories that enables the grand theory to give an adequate account of phenomena such as socialization.

SC accommodates complex theoretical frameworks like this, I have argued, by allowing the interaction of constituent theories. Thus, grand theories are not unified theories, but theoretical structures composed of relevant middle range theories. Admittedly, the resulting theoretical structure is dauntingly complex. RV, on the other hand, does not accommodate grand theories, let alone interlevel theories. A clue is found already in Merton's description of sociological theories as logically close-knit and mutually exclusive sets of doctrine, interconnected sets of propositions from which one derives empirical uniformities (Merton, 1996, p.41) – a view of the nature of theories evidently reminiscent of RV. Since a view advocating exclusiveness cannot accommodate his idea of consistency between middle range and grand theories, he declares that grand theories must be sufficiently loose-knit and internally diversified to subsume a given middle range theory.

The exclusiveness doctrine refers to the axiomatic structure of a scientific theory and to the procedures for specifying the meaning of theoretical terms proposed by RV. It will be recalled from Chapter 3 that on RV, a scientific theory is an axiomatic-deductive system, which when interpreted consists in a deductively related hierarchy of generalizations describing the behavior of the phenomenon. The empirical interpretation of the symbols in the theoretical vocabulary is provided by the correspondence rules, which in effect assign empirical meaning to the T-terms by partially defining them in terms of the observation vocabulary, the O-terms. Definitions are partial when T-terms are defined by reference to an open-ended number of observational situations or procedures. Translating T into O is, however, not the whole story of the meaning of T-terms. As Carl Hempel observes, if T-terms are completely defined in terms of O-terms (T=O), then they cannot play their intended role in explaining the observations. Nor can the meaning of all T-terms be given exclusively in terms of other T-terms, on pain of circularity or infinite regresses. The response to this situation for Hempel is to invoke the notion of meaning postulates:

> ...the meanings of theoretical terms are determined in part by the postulates of the calculus, which serve as "implicit definitions" for them; and in part by the correspondence rules, which provide them with empirical content.
>
> (1970, p.149)

The crucial point about the determination of the meaning of T-terms to be noted here is its "internal" character. Both meaning postulates and correspondence rules are integral parts of a scientific theory, and taken together with the axiomatic-deductive structure (the calculus) they ensure exclusiveness in "sets of doctrine". No interaction of theories is thus possible; each theory is thought of as a unified structure kept together by a deductive system and strong internal meaning relations. Thompson (1989) also points out that since the correspondence rules of a theory by their nature can provide no role for laws and terms of other theories in the relating of a particular theory to phenomena, it follows that two distinct theories cannot be used interactively (p.41). Concerning SC, this brings up the question of restrictions on middle range theories called into service in the same grand theory: how different or distinct can they be?

Merton's point about mutually exclusive sets of doctrine is paralleled by Thompson's point about unified theories. The criticisms Thompson levels against various attempts to axiomatize evolutionary theory in accordance with the canons of RV precisely concern the fact that in order to have a unified theory to axiomatize, evolutionary theory is invariably reduced to or identified with one of its component theories. The same is the case with socialization theory, I have argued, and I would like to extend this argument to grand theories in general. To reduce the grand theory to one of its constituent theories is to distort the theory and to misrepresent the phenomenon within its scope. Even if each constituent theory should allow axiomatization, RV cannot capture the distinctive features of their interaction. Thompson concludes:

> [Evolutionary theory] is a genuine scientific theory even though its structure is that of a complex framework of interacting theories. ... Specifically, a theory functions to explain and make intelligible phenomena, to predict phenomena, and to integrate our knowledge of phenomena. If an entity functions in these ways but fails to fit a particular conception of theory structure, this failure counts against the conception of theory structure and not against the status of the entity as a theory.
>
> (1989, p.52)

Socialization theory can provide further inductive support for Thompson's judgment. It is a genuine theory, which surely can be fleshed out and refined, but which by its structure counts against RV and in favor of SC.

Theoretical integration

In Chapter 2 I characterized the field of education as an internally diversified, fragmented and unstable academic landscape with shifting and porous borders. Interlevel theories, understood as grand theories in the sense discussed above, represent one possible way of combatting fragmentation – they serve to integrate different theories in larger frameworks and can thus bring order and unity at least to small areas or pockets in the landscape. A brief foray into issues of interdisciplinarity, unity and theoretical integration is therefore in order, to shed further light on the specific characteristics of interlevel theories.

Why should we want to join theories together, and what does it actually mean to integrate them? Traditionally, theoretical integration is discussed in terms of reductionism in service of the unity of science (see e.g. Nagel, 1961). If one theory can be reduced to another more general or more basic theory, the two can be said to be integrated. However, if we employ the root notion of reduction, then one of the supposedly "integrated" theories disappears or becomes obsolete – the idea being that the more basic, general theory can do all the work of the reduced theory. All terms and explanations of one theory can be translated into and replaced by the terms and explanations of the basic theory. This is evidently not the form of integration that we are after. In the case of interlevel theories, reduction is counter-productive – it is precisely the point that the middle range theories are not reducible to one another, nor is the grand theory reducible to either of the middle range theories. Reduction would destroy the ability of the grand theory to account for the phenomenon under its scope.

At the outset, "integration" can mean any combining of two or more things and a good many relations are possible. For example, Agnes Tellings (2001) discusses integration in terms of reduction, synthesis, horizontal and vertical addition of theories. Her discussion raises several interesting issues. For example, she points out that the superiority of the integrative framework should be defended by arguments independent from the original theories (p.286). I agree. In the case of socialization theory this would mean that we consider the grand theory to be superior to the constituent middle range theories. This we do, in terms of the grand theory's superior capacity to account adequately for socialization – each of the middle range theories, by themselves, would provide a partial and distorted account of socialization. This is an important point! It is why we construct a grand theory in the first place. But then Tellings goes on to argue that integrated theories neither disappear nor remain intact, and that we should explain what has been changed or omitted from the original theories as they got integrated (p.286). This, I think, does not capture the role of middle range theories as I have described it. I would rather argue that they should retain their separate identities in order to do their job, which is to interact and work together so that the grand theory can do *its* job, which is to represent some complex interlevel phenomenon. This point does not, however, speak against Tellings' analysis; it rather goes to show that interlevel theories do not conform to various widespread forms of theory integration.

We could say that interlevel theories run on the same principle as interdisciplinarity, given that different theories are selected and put to work in a grand theory. The middle range theories I have tentatively identified as parts of socialization theory could conceivably all come from the field of education, although any theory focusing on social structures and aggregate levels would more clearly belong to sociology. At any rate, the aim is the same: to bring together information, data, concepts and theories from different disciplines or fields to further our understanding of topics that are beyond the scope of any single domain or theory. The most common or traditional understanding of interdisciplinarity, Henrik Thorén and Johannes Persson note, is as a collection of disciplines coordinated by a higher-level concept (2013, p.339). The disciplines thus coordinated are brought into cooperation with one another; or perhaps conversely – their cooperation allows them to be coordinated by some higher-level concept. Traditionally this contrasts with multidisciplinarity, where we have disciplinary perspectives on a topic but no cooperation between them. Socialization theory clearly shares those features of interdisciplinarity which highlight cooperation, in this case understood as interaction, between disciplines or theories. As far as the grand theory can be viewed as a higher-level concept, there may be a sense in which it coordinates the middle range theories. But as I argued in a previous section, the relation between middle range theories and grand theory is best understood as a part-whole relation.

Where does this leave the problem of unity? I am not particularly worried by the fragmented state of the field of education; like Ewald Terhart (2016), I think we have to make do with the field that we have (see Chapter 2). But: we can create little pockets of order and unity even in fragmented fields. Philosopher of biology Harold Kincaid argues that the best form of unity we can have is when

> ...two theories are linked by, or perhaps incorporated into, an *integrated interlevel theory*. An interlevel theory thus unifies two disparate theories by employing explanations, confirmation procedures, etc., invoking both levels, and by providing evidence that the events and entities of one theory depend upon and are constituted from those of the other.
>
> (1990, p.590, emphasis in original)

Thus, Kincaid concludes, there can be unity without reduction. I concur.

Summary

The possibility of interacting theories is, I believe, of utmost importance in such disciplines as education. It requires that we select theories which can feed into each other. Such selection happens against a large background of knowledge and assumptions concerning the phenomenon in question, and the selected theories must be capable of interaction or integration – an integration, I have suggested, that can take many forms. The possibility of interacting theories is crucial for a discipline which traditionally takes as its intended scope such complex phenomena as upbringing, group processes, socialization and school development. Adequate accounts of such phenomena require descriptions on different aggregate levels, as well as portions of knowledge imported from other disciplines. It is of vital importance to keep the interlevel condition in mind – middle range theories are all necessary, but they are to be conceived of as parts in a whole, a grand theory. If this whole is reduced to and identified with one of the parts, you no longer have an adequate representation of the phenomenon.

I have argued in this chapter that SC is well suited to accommodate the interactive character of grand interlevel theories. I have attempted to show that it is a sufficiently flexible and rich conception to allow the interplay of theories, through laws of interaction. In the case of socialization theory, the interaction of different middle range theories is required to describe the transformation between individual and systemic (aggregate) levels. The levels involved can be described as two distinct state spaces and the laws of interaction describe the transformation processes between them. Furthermore, the next-state function indicates that laws of succession are also involved, since transitions occur at each level, providing the input to the other level and occasioning transitions there. This kind of theoretical framework does involve two types of theoretical law. It is important to note that types of laws are not exclusive to types of theory. To complicate things even further, take school development: this is a kind of theory that will involve state transitions at an individual level and state transitions at organizational level. It involves (indeterministic) laws of succession at both levels and laws of interaction between levels, and will thus have the same basic structure as socialization theory. In addition, school development theories are normative and goal-directed, since the efforts at development have a more or less defined goal state and are made on assumptions of improvement.

I have also argued that RV is incapable of accommodating the interactive character of socialization theory, or interlevel theories more generally. The procedures for specifying the meaning of T-terms preclude interaction of different middle range theories. Therefore, the interlevel condition cannot be accounted for since it is precisely the interaction of the middle range theories which makes possible the transformation between aggregate levels.

Like equivalence theories, interlevel theories provide a counter-instance to the view that all educational theories are practical and goal-directed. Interlevel theories are theories *about*, not theories *for* – although as I briefly suggested above, there are theories that are interlevel and goal-directed at the same time. Interlevel theories are complexly structured theories about complex phenomena. The normative twist adds a further dimension, of course.

Faced with such counter-instances, proponents of the unified nature of educational theories can employ one of two strategies. They can rely on a narrow definition of the field of education and deny that the proposed counter-instances count as counter-instances. I have already placed socialization squarely in the field of education, given the state of this field, but even if socialization is counted out, school development surely must be counted in. The other strategy is to abandon the notion of *the* nature of educational theories and instead adopt a pluralistic view, as I have done here.

7 What makes an educational theory good?

In this chapter, we find ourselves squarely in the landscape of epistemic normativity. The distinction between good and bad theories is not an empirical one; it is a normative one. How do we or how should we judge the quality of educational theories? Which criteria should we use? The problem of theory evaluation has many ramifications. It also has an extra layer: assuming we use a given set of criteria and judge that the theory in question is good, how do we then justify our criteria? How do we ground them, make the case that they are legitimate and possess the required normative force?

Let us begin by distinguishing briefly between internal and external criteria. Thomas Kuhn famously distinguished between paradigm-internal and paradigm-external criteria (Kuhn, 1970). My proposed distinction is slightly different: by "internal criteria" I simply have in mind criteria that come from "inside" scientific activity and (mainly) applies to the products of such activity: theories, models, hypotheses, equations, historical narratives, and so on. Internal criteria are time-honored and universally known (but perhaps not universally employed). Carl Hempel, for example, lists precision, consistency, conceptual clarity, evidential support, simplicity or parsimony, and the probability of the theory or hypothesis (Hempel, 1966). Advocates of narrative research propose a very different set of criteria: including plausibility, evocativeness, uniqueness, coherence, familiarity, engaging plots, and moral persuasiveness (e.g. Bruner, 1986). This set, too, is meant to be *internal* and apply to the products of such research. External criteria do not come from inside science and research. They originate elsewhere, for example in society, or in considerations that do not belong to the inner life of science and research. Here we find such criteria as practical relevance, usefulness, innovativeness, and profitability. We do not have to choose either internal or external criteria – different combinations may be deemed appropriate (which itself is a normative judgment). Conceptual clarity, evidential support and practical usefulness would, for example, be a powerful combination. Surely, there are other possible criteria as well. The point here is just to show that there are different criteria to choose among, and that they can be combined in different ways. There is good reason to think that people will evaluate the same theory differently, because they use different criteria, or weigh the criteria differently if they use the same set.

I am not aiming to provide a definite answer the question posed in the title of this chapter. I rather aim to shed light on certain pertinent topics surrounding the issue, as well as highlighting the contribution I think that the Semantic Conception of theories (SC) can make.

Inroads to theory evaluation based on the Semantic Conception

SC provides a different approach to theory evaluation than do the sets of criteria exemplified above. As far as I can tell, SC by itself does not contain or provide any specific criteria, but we can extract some clear ideas about what to look *at* and look *for*.

It will be recalled from Chapter 3 that theories do not describe the phenomenon within their scope in all their complexity. Rather, theories characterize the phenomena in terms of a few selected parameters abstracted from them. The parameters together make up an abstract and idealized replica or model of the phenomenon in question. The theory is about this model, and only indirectly about the phenomenon. This selection implies that theories in fact are simplifications of their objects – many causes, factors, relations and attributes that are characteristic of the phenomena fall outside the theory. I venture the claim that all theories bear this out: all theories, not just the ones examined in this book, will be found upon unpacking to be simplifications of the phenomena within their scope. Let me briefly invoke again Ronald Giere's highly useful analogy of maps to drive the point home: (1) Abstraction implies simplification in that many features and details of the landscape are left out when we represent a landscape on a map, and (2) simplification is necessary to make the map useful. If all details were represented, the map would be the same size as the landscape; it would not give you the information you need, and would be unwieldy and unmanageable and thus of no use. As an irresistible aside: this latter point is wonderfully treated by Lewis Carroll in the novel *Sylvie and Bruno Concluded*. In the novel we meet Mein Herr, who is discussing the intricacies of map-making with the narrator. How large should maps be to be useful? The narrator suggests six inches to a mile as a general measure, to which Mein Herr replies that in his country they made a map on the scale of a mile to the mile but that using it raised a problem:

> 'It has never been spread out, yet', said Mein Herr, 'the farmers objected: they said it would cover the whole country and shut out the sunlight! So now we use the country itself and I assure you it does nearly as well'.
>
> (Carroll, 1988, p.557)

I take the "nearly" to point to the information that maps can give at a glance and that the landscape itself cannot; for instance, information concerning the relative location of villages, distances, north and south, roads, footpaths and potential shortcuts. Let us note two features concerning maps here: there is a purpose behind their construction, and they can misrepresent the landscape and lead the traveler astray. And it is of course possible for the traveler to misread the map.

According to SC, the major "elements" found in theories are parameters, theoretical postulates and theoretical laws. Let us begin by looking at parameters, since these make up the building blocks of theories. The parameters in many ways make up the heart of a theory and are a good place to start if you want to understand how a particular theory represents the phenomenon within its scope. Ultimately, theory evaluators must make their own judgments about the goodness of a given theory, but a few general suggestions for what to consider are possible.

First, identification of parameters is intimately connected to the articulation of the theory. We should not only worry about conceptual clarity, as one of the time-honored criteria would have us consider, but also the clarity of articulation of the entire theory. Researchers often do not tell the readers or users what the parameters of the theory are; occasionally they call them "central concepts", sometimes it is difficult to understand whether a concept should count as a parameter or not, and of course on some occasions the theory is clearly articulated. The point is important. If a theory is so vaguely articulated that readers or users are unable to identify its basic building blocks, then the readers do not know what the theory *says* about its object and, hence, are in no position to judge its adequacy.

Second, a theory evaluator should consider the number of (possible) parameters. There are no rules as to how many parameters a theory ideally should have. That depends on the nature of the phenomenon, the purpose of the theory, and the researchers' judgments – it is after all they who select the parameters. Disagreement about whether the selected parameters are essential, central, peripheral, or unnecessary is to be expected. This is reminiscent of the criterion of simplicity, although it does not suggest that we should go for as low a number of parameters as possible. Let us look again at S-R theory (Watson, 1930). Obviously many things can be said and have been said about behaviorist theory, but that need not concern us here. Viewed as an example *of a theory*, classical behaviorism is simply beautiful and eminently well suited to illustrate a number of issues. Classical behaviorist theory is very precise in the sense that we know exactly how Watson characterized the learning of behavior, since he explicitly tells us which parameters he has selected. So how should we think about this theory? We may judge at the outset that the learning of behavior is a fairly complex phenomenon, and we may have strong background assumptions concerning how such a phenomenon should be characterized. That is to say, there is a parallelism between theory construction and theory evaluation. A researcher who constructs a theory uses several sources in the selection of parameters, such as his or her prior knowledge of the phenomenon, other existing views, data and various background assumptions. The same is the case when we evaluate parameters in a given theory: we use prior knowledge and various background assumptions. What sort of and how many parameters do we think a theory about behavioral learning should have? Watson, as we have seen, selects two parameters to characterize the phenomenon: stimulus S and response R. Both S and R are observable entities. Are these, then, sufficient to characterize behavioral learning? This theory is not only a simplification of the phenomenon, I would say – it is an oversimplification. Simplification is perfectly legitimate; oversimplification is not. Two parameters would in general seem like a very small number of parameters to represent behavioral learning. But we should also consider what these parameters represent and form a picture of what is *not* there that *should have been* there, given the nature of the phenomenon. Then it becomes clear that what we have is observable input and observable output, but that the individual whose responses we are interested in (the teleological entity, see Chapter 4) effectively is rendered a black box. There are no descriptive parameters at all. The theory is silent as to the processing of stimulus and the deliberation of response; it provides no clues as to *how* the response is connected to the stimulus and we may well wonder how adequate it is as a representation of the learning of behavior.

The flip side of this coin is theories with too many parameters. Generally, if the number of parameters is very large, the theory is unwieldy and not usable. Nobody can handle fifty parameters and their various relations. But what considerations should go into a possible reduction of parameters? Let us look at an example and return to Rosalind Driver's science education theory from Chapter 4. There I suggested that she selects too many student parameters, although they all make good sense when viewed on their own (Driver, 1989, 1995). In stark contrast to Watson, whose theory has no parameters characterizing the teleological entity in question, Driver's theory has seven: demographics, metacognition, nature of science understanding, affect, nature of students' conceptions, dispositions to think and engage, and content-specific beliefs (all of them come with a number of subcategories). It will be recalled that her theory also contains a number of environmental parameters, as well as a number of parameters related to the goal state of the theory. This makes for a complex theory and perhaps one that is difficult to employ (theory use will be returned to in Chapter 10). If we wish to reduce the number of student parameters, how could or should we reason about it? In many cases it would be natural to look at the *object* of the theory and make judgments about the centrality and/or representational importance of the suggested parameters and weed out parameters that are unconnected or peripheral or somehow deemed not necessary. However, Driver's theory is a normative goal-directed theory and I suggest it would make more sense to look at the *purpose* of the theory and then make a judgment as to whether the proposed parameters are all necessary. The purpose of Driver's theory is found in the goal state G, the state to which the students aspire. Thus, all student parameters should be clearly linked to the goal state to defend their place in the theory, and that I suggest is not the case. For example, change in demographics, say age, will not in and of itself bring the student any closer to the goal state. Removing this parameter from the theory would not affect what the theory *says* about the phenomenon within its scope, and no damage would be done to the theory's adequacy.

Third, the question of the number of parameters naturally leads to the question of how the parameters are thought to hang together. In Chapter 3 I suggested that this is a job for the theoretical postulates of a theory (though not to the exclusion of other functions). Evidently, parameters can be related in many different ways. It is quite common in education to interpret such relations as causal. Causation in education is a highly contested issue, but to me this interpretation is apt since practical domains of education are concerned with how to achieve desirable changes. That is, educational practice essentially involves dynamic causal relations. Suppose now we interpret the relation between S and R as causal: how then should we understand it? Causation comes in different forms: deterministic, necessary, sufficient, as INUS conditions, probabilistic, counterfactual, frequent, infrequent, strong and weak. Our understanding of the S-R relation will be very different according to which of these interpretations we employ, and our judgments of the adequacy of the theory will vary accordingly. A probabilistic relationship between S and R surely is more reasonable than a deterministic one. However, it may well be that Watson, since he was a behaviorist, leaned toward antirealism and therefore dismissed causation altogether. If so, the S-R relationship is one of correlation and understood as the co-variation of S and R. At this point, we can also consider various assumptions underpinning the theory: for example, whether S is the only thing that influences (or determines) R, whether all individuals are thought to be alike, etc. These assumptions are part of the *as if* of S-R theory. Idealizations may be difficult to handle, but it is important to discuss whether we think they fall within the limits of the acceptable.

However that may be, I hope this demonstrates that SC provides inroads to evaluation. SC can serve as a toolbox for theory evaluation, for critical discussion about theories more generally, without emphasizing any particular evaluative criteria.

Truth

Does an educational theory have to be true to be good? Interestingly, none of time-honored criteria mentioned in the introduction to this chapter mentions truth. By "truth" in this context, I shall mean what I take to be an intuitive understanding of it: that claims in general attempt to describe how things are in the world. In this sense, empirical support is intimately connected with truth – it is that which gives us good reason to think that our theories are true of their objects. There are several theories of truth and they have different answers to the question of what it means for a truth bearer to be true. We have the correspondence theory, the coherence theory, the pragmatic theory, the redundancy theory, the deflationist theory, Tarski's theory, and perhaps more (Kirkham, 1997). Of these, the intuitive understanding delineated above is best captured by the correspondence theory of truth – surely, this is our everyday understanding of truth, and it is the approach I am going to take in this section. But first I need to lay out a couple of preliminaries.

The first thing to note is that not all educational theories have to be true (in the correspondence sense) to be good. Many equivalence theories, for example, deal with normative and/or conceptual issues and make no empirical claims. Judgments to the effect that different states of goal attainment are equivalent are not *empirical* judgments. They are not supported by empirical data, but by logical or normative (or other) reasons. Equivalence theories are better judged in terms of adequacy, of being up to the task, or of bringing clarity, sense and direction to murky educational practices. All of this is perfectly legitimate, but not what I want to explore in this section. I am therefore leaving this kind of theory out of the discussion.

The second thing to note is that educational theories, like other scientific theories, are complexly structured entities. As such, they pose particular problems for any truth theory, including the correspondence theory. When we add the element of *as if*, things get even more difficult. Take S-R theory again. This theory treats behavioral learning *as if* it consisted only of the selected parameters, *as if* stimulus and response are the only parameters with a non-negligible influence. One effect of simplification is that theories are not literally true about the phenomenon under study. In fact, S-R theory is obviously false about actual, existing people, since their learning depends on a host of other factors besides stimulus and response. So in what sense, if any, can we accord a truth value other than falsity to this theory? I shall ask the same question of Driver's theory. Driver's theory poses an extra challenge, since normative claims hardly can be said to be empirically true or false. But, as I argued in Chapter 4, Driver's goal-directed theory, despite its normative character, has an empirical heart. It claims that students move toward a certain goal state as a function of certain interactions with the environment. Whether this happens or not is an empirical question.

The third thing to note is that proponents of SC have different views about truth. The issue of truth here becomes exceedingly complex because it involves views concerning realism and antirealism and their finer details, including for example existence of unobservables and treatment of T-terms – briefly touched upon in Chapter 5. Bas van Fraassen (1980, 1989) is after empirical adequacy, not truth – he is an antirealist (although not a logical positivist). I shall return to his views and devote a (short) sub-section to them below. Frederick Suppe (1989, 2000) subscribes to a form of scientific realism that holds that theories are counterfactually true; they describe what the phenomenon *would have* been *if* the selected parameters were the only ones exerting any influence on them. It could be argued that people in general would be more interested in factual truth, rather than counterfactual truth. Ronald Giere (1988, 2004) is also a scientific realist in that he holds that models are representational devices, but otherwise finds that truth is not the real crux of the matter. For example, discussing the harmonic oscillator, he first distinguishes a sense of "truth" which he dismisses as being of no epistemological significance: the relationship between a set of equations and their corresponding model is one of truth since the equations are true of their model. It is of no significance, however, because the model is defined as something that exactly satisfies the equations – they match because they are so defined. Models are the means by which scientists represent the world. But models are not linguistic entities, Giere argues (1988, p.80) and therefore do not admit of truth or falsity. A theoretical hypothesis, on the other hand, asserting some sort of relationship between a model and the phenomenon of which it is a model, is a linguistic entity and so can be true or false. What we are really after is the relationship between the model and the phenomenon, the real system. Whereas van Fraassen (1980) suggests isomorphism as the desired relationship between model and phenomenon, Giere rightly points out that in the natural sciences isomorphism is often explicitly ruled out. The relationship, Giere thinks, is better conceived as one of similarity, specified in terms of relevant respects and degrees. And he concludes,

> That theoretical hypotheses can be true or false turns out to be of little consequence. To claim a hypothesis is true is to claim no more or less than that an indicated type and degree of similarity exists between a model and a real system. We can therefore forget about truth and focus on the details of the similarity. A "theory of truth" is not a prerequisite for an adequate theory of science.
>
> (1988, p.81)

Isomorphism and similarity will be returned to below. But first I would like to briefly state my own position on this issue, again betraying realist inclinations. I take truth to be a *value*, and in general I take researchers to have a commitment to truth. And here I do mean truth in the correspondence sense – a claim is true if the state of affairs it claims to be the case actually is the case; i.e. there are so-called truth makers in the world that determine the truth value of the theory. I take this to be the commonsense view of truth, the intuitive way of thinking about truth that we all grew up with. But of course, as already suggested above, things are not simple, and I shall have several qualifications to make as we go along.

Rosalind Driver's science education theory will again serve as an example (Driver, 1989, 1995). It will be recalled that Driver's theory is a complex normative goal-directed theory which states that the teleological entity (an idealized individual student) moves toward the goal state at least partly as a function of its interaction with an (organized) environment. The goal state is broadly conceived and incorporates a number of different but related sub-goals. The teleological entity is described in terms of a number of parameters, and so is the environment. The theory contains at least two idealized parameters – both, incidentally, idealized in terms of mean values. There is the parameter of content-specific beliefs which represents the "mean" beliefs about natural phenomena held by a certain age-group, and there is an environmental parameter idealized to the kind of experiences that generally have positive effects on students' changes in the desired direction. Both idealizations, we should note, are results of much empirical research. Despite its complexity the theory clearly amounts to a simplification with a built-in *as if* to it. So in what sense, if any, can this theory be said to be true?

Before we can investigate that question, a brief foray into the correspondence theory of truth is in order. The theory is intuitive because it foregrounds the relation between theory (claim, belief) and reality and thus the idea that our representations purport to tell us what some aspect of reality is like: a theory (or any truth bearer) is true if it corresponds to some fact, situation or state of affairs in the world. The truth-making relation is called correspondence, and the elements of reality that make theories true are called facts (truth makers). The claim that there is a laptop on my desk is made true by the independent fact that there actually is a laptop on my desk. If there is no laptop on my desk, the claim is false. Thus, the correspondence theory also defines what it is for a claim to be false.

There is nothing particularly positivist about the correspondence theory of truth, even if it is sometimes so labeled. Otto Neurath, famous logical positivist, explicitly rejects the correspondence theory: "*Statements are compared with statements*, not with 'experiences,' 'the world', or anything else", he says (1959, p.291). Nor is there any reason to think that adopting the correspondence theory should commit us to the view that there is exactly one true (and complete) description of the phenomenon in question. Common sense is sometimes worth listening to, and it is a common enough fact that the same phenomenon can be described in different ways, and that these ways may be compatible, all true, all false, or in genuine conflict with each other.

Isomorphism

Isomorphism denotes a perfect one-to-one, bijective relationship between two structures or sets. Whatever details we find in the phenomenon is mapped onto some entity or relation in its representation. Margaret Morrison (2007, p.214) claims that SC is deeply intertwined with isomorphism, such that abandoning SC will liberate us from reliance on isomorphism as the way of representing phenomena. This view surely is wrong – SC fully accommodates the fact that theories are simplifications of the phenomena under their scope. However, it may well be that when Suppe states that theories are not literally true of their phenomenon, he envisions isomorphism as the ideal – a theory is *literally* true if it somehow maps all details of the phenomenon. What are we now to make of the correspondence theory of truth?

The correspondence theory of truth is more properly understood as a family of related theories rather than as one single theory (David, 2004). According to Richard Kirkham (1997) there are two major types of correspondence: congruence and correlation. Congruence is a strong form of correspondence and demands isomorphism between all elements, structures and relations in the theory and its corresponding phenomenon. On this understanding of the correspondence theory of truth, no scientific theory will ever be true; some factors, causes and relations characteristic of the phenomenon will always fall outside the scope of the theory. This is certainly the case for Driver's theory, despite occasional suspicion that it aims at completeness. There are many descriptors concerning individual characteristics, relationships, school culture and social surroundings that are omitted from the theory. But does it follow that the correspondence theory of truth cannot be applied if completeness is unattainable? Instead of congruence we could turn to correlation as the basic truth-making relationship. Giving up isomorphism would at least do two things for us. First, it would allow us to focus our attention on the whole of the theory rather than its particular elements, and second, it opens the path to truth in degrees or approximate truth – the idea that a theory can be more or less true, or roughly true. This move is not without its own problems, since truth becomes fuzzier when grey areas are allowed. Furthermore, while approximate truth may be indispensable to scientific realists, it seems to have eluded a precise characterization (Ladyman, 2002, p.232). All the same, it is a useful notion in that it allows us to think of a theory as roughly true even if some of its details are false. It is hard to avoid approximate truth if we think that our theories tell us something about what the world is like.

Reference

This is a topic we have met before, as the problem of the existence of T-entities (unobservables). It also belongs in an exploration of the correspondence theory of truth. The correspondence relation, Marian David says, stands and falls with the general theory of reference (David, 2004). Let us look again at Driver's theory. Should we demand that all parameters and postulates have referents, or else the theory will not be true? I think not. Realists need not commit themselves to the existence of every entity referred to by a T-term. As van Fraassen argues, we are better off being agnostics about existence, and the history of science bears this out – many postulated entities have been shown not to exist after all, the most famous historical examples perhaps being phlogiston and luminiferous ether. Moreover, I do not think that the intuitive idea of correspondence entails any such demand.

It might also be the case, van Fraassen points out, that theories contain structures for which there is no correlate in the real world. This too is the case with Driver's theory – it contains parameters that have no referents, the most obvious one being the goal state (although it is intended to refer in the future). Her theory also contains idealized parameters; both are averages, which must be said to be frequently used in the social sciences. Perhaps we should describe averages as semi-idealized – they can after all be realized in some instances.

Suppe (1989) finds it unreasonably strict to demand that all parameters refer for a theory to be true. Most, if not all, theories contain idealized parameters and an absolute reference requirement would render them all false (or a non-realist theory of truth would have to be applied). But if we allow parameters with no reference, other questions come to the fore, such as whether some central parameters should be required to have referents, or how many no-reference parameters a theory can contain and still be thought to be true. We also face the problem that theories are general. They characterize classes of phenomena, not individual instances. And what does a class refer to?

Reference is a problem that does not go away. It remains even if we give up the congruence version of correspondence and its requirement of isomorphism and instead adopt the correlation version. John Austin (1950), who defends the correspondence theory, says that correspondence between truth bearer (which in his case are statements, not theories) and phenomenon is conventional, such that "there is no need whatsoever for the words used in making a true statement to 'mirror' in any way, however indirect, any feature of the situation or event" (p.125). Here we recognize correlation, the weaker type of correspondence. Thus, a theory can be deemed (roughly) true even if a number of properties, relations and elements are left out, and even if the theory contains structures not found in the phenomenon.

Truth makers

I do not know whether Driver's theory is empirically true or not; that is a question for a separate investigation. What I would like to briefly look at in this sub-section is the question of what would serve to make it true. General formulations of the correspondence theory tell us that theories (or any truth bearers) are true if they correspond to facts, also called truth makers. So what could the truth makers be in this case?

Let us make a small detour and begin by looking at a couple of simple examples. The claim that there is a lamp on my desk is made true by the fact that there actually is a lamp on my desk. Bertrand Russell (1971) provides the following example: the proposition that Othello believes that Desdemona loves Cassio is true if it is the case that Othello actually harbors such a belief. These things seem quite natural and easily recognizable from everyday life, and underscores the intuitive nature of the correspondence theory. But while things might seem intuitive and understandable, they are philosophically complicated. Over the decades, virtually every aspect of the correspondence theory has been problematized: most notably the relation of *correspondence* and the notion of *fact.* I am not going to rehearse these criticisms (see e.g. David, 2004, Glanzberg, 2018, Kirkham, 1997); I am rather going to side-step them and instead investigate some select points concerning truth makers. Some minimal idea of *fact* is needed, however, and I shall lean on John Searle's take on it:

> The whole point of having a notion of "fact" is to have a notion for that which stands outside the statement but which makes it true, or in virtue of which it is true, if it is true. On this account facts are not complex objects, nor are they linguistic entities; rather they are conditions in the world that satisfy the truth conditions expressed by statements.
>
> (Searle, 1995, p.211)

This makes fact a general term for all the different "somethings" in virtue of which a truth bearer (theory, statement, proposition, belief) is true. So what can we now say about Driver's theory? What kind of facts or truth makers would it take to make her theory true? What state of affairs would have to obtain? What kind of conditions in the world should we look for? And what kinds of facts should we allow?

It is by no means obvious which strategy is the better for coming to grips with the question of whether a theory such as Driver's science education theory is true or not. It seems unproductive to look at the constituent elements of the theory, look for possible corresponding facts, and then try to match them. It is not obvious that a given parameter, even if it has a referent, thereby has a fact tied to it. Isomorphism is unfeasible, not only because it is unreasonably strict, but because it hardly makes sense to think that a theory can be meaningfully partitioned into sentences each with an identifiable corresponding fact. The normative character of the theory poses an extra challenge, since we usually do not say of normative claims that they are true or false; at least not in the correspondence sense. Furthermore, the parameters constituting the goal state of Driver's theory have no referents – there is nothing for them to be isomorphic to *now*, although they are intended to refer at some point in the future, when the students have attained the goal. And yet, I have argued, Driver's theory does have an empirical claim at its heart: the claim that students (characterized by a given set of parameters) move toward a defined goal state at least partly as a function of their interaction with an environment (characterized by a given set of parameters). Driver uses the term *construction* to denote this movement, and I argued in Chapter 3 that it is best understood in terms of a statistical law of succession. The theory is true if this desired change actually happens. What should we look at to find that out? Could we formulate statements of fact that accommodate the theory's parameters, postulates and theoretical laws? More to the point, would we obtain sufficient truth conditions by testing the students' scientific beliefs regularly during the academic year and find that they do indeed move in the desired direction? How many of the students should exhibit desired changes and how big should the changes be? Are there facts we should hold to be necessary for the truth of the theory, such that if they do not obtain, the theory should be judged to be false? I do not know the answer to any of these questions. We should also keep in mind that Driver's theory is general and characterizes a class of phenomena. Like most general statements, it can be true of some of its instantiations, but not all – correctly describe the development of some individual students, but not all. But the theory clearly aims to be true at the general level – the values of some of the parameters are averages derived from empirical results.

But while theory testing is a vastly complex enterprise, we should not therefore think it is impossible or a waste of time. Considerations such as these make it easy to understand the allure of the notion of approximate truth. That would allow us to say of a theory that it is roughly true, more or less true, contains a grain of truth – expressions well known from everyday vernacular and seemingly well enough understood, despite the philosophical problems attached to approximate truth (Ladyman, 2002). Approximation seems to go well with the correlation version of the correspondence theory, and can be understood in different ways. For example, a number of truth conditions may obtain, but not all. The problem then becomes one of making a reasoned judgment about how many unobtained truth conditions can be tolerated before we have to describe the theory as more false than true. This is not settled by counting facts – degrees of evidential support demand astute judgment. And how many concrete instantiations of the theory should we demand the theory be true of before we deem it to be overall or generally true? This is not settled by counting either – again, astute judgment is required.

Empirical adequacy

While Bas van Fraassen is an advocate of SC, he also adheres to scientific anti-realism; specifically, a version of it termed constructive empiricism. Constructive empiricism comes through as a complex, fine-grained and sophisticated doctrine about the nature and aims of science and various aspects of science as an enterprise. The part of it that interests us here concerns empirical adequacy. But this is by no means easy to understand. On the one hand, van Fraassen (1980) spends much time working out a distinction between empirical adequacy and truth; on the other hand, he initially describes empirical adequacy as follows: "...a theory is empirically adequate exactly if what it says about the observable things and events in the world is true – exactly if it 'saves the phenomena'" (p.12). We should remind ourselves here what he takes a theory to be:

> To present a theory is to specify a family of structures, its models; and secondly, to specify certain parts of those models (the empirical substructures) as candidates for the direct representation of observable phenomena.
> (1980, p.64)

Such a theory, he says, is empirically adequate if it has "some model such that all appearances [i.e. structures described in measurement or experimental reports] are isomorphic to empirical sub-structures of that model" (1980, p.64). A couple of observations are in order. First, we see here the claim about isomorphism that Giere dismisses on the grounds that it often is explicitly ruled out, for example in textbooks. Second, van Fraassen employs the notion of empirical substructures, which adds a layer of complexity to theories that I have avoided in my discussions, and which may or may not be useful in the analysis of educational theories. It is not clear to me whether educational theories can be said to possess empirical substructures, and if so, whether that would contribute to our understanding of the phenomena in question. Third, it should be noted that empirical adequacy concerns observable phenomena. Constructive empiricists can retain an idea of empirical adequacy without committing themselves to any view that unobservable parts of a theoretical structure are also to be found in the actual phenomena. This last point invokes deep intricacies of realism and antirealism, briefly met in Chapter 5. Suffice it here to note that van Fraassen thinks that claiming that a theory is empirically adequate is less epistemically demanding than claiming that it is true. Both types of claims go beyond what we can know at any given time, he says, but you can believe that a theory is empirically adequate without believing that it is true. Hence, I take it, empirical adequacy requires judgment, not a counting of observable phenomena that can be said to find a place in the structures described by the theory – after all, van Fraassen says that a theory consists of a family of models and only parts of those models may have substructures that are isomorphic to structures described by data. It seems to be an open question how many cases of such isomorphism a given theory should have to be deemed empirically adequate.

So what should we do at this point? I consider truth to be a value, I have realist inclinations and I hold to a version of the correspondence theory of truth which rejects isomorphism and allows flexibility in the understanding of what it means to "correspond". Yet my analysis brings no solutions, only more problems. That is philosophy for you, I suppose.

Usefulness

Commitment to truth underlies many concerns, in research and in everyday life alike. Injunctions against researchers fabricating their own data, for example, make no sense unless understood against a background of assumed truth. But then, what? In the case of goal-directed educational theories, truth alone is hardly sufficient to make them good – we should be able to cash truth into practical value and put the theory to work. Goal-directed theories are constructed to make a difference for the phenomenon, to modify it in some desired direction. And thus enters *usefulness* as a possible criterion for evaluation of educational theories.

So do educational theories have to be useful to be good? In some ways *usefulness* represents and requires a different set of considerations. One thing is that usefulness is considered to be an external criterion; it does not come from inside science but instead means that we judge the value of something after we have put it to its intended use and observed the results. In the same conceptual landscape, we find (practical) relevance, effectiveness and fitness for purpose. A goal-directed theory is a good theory if its employment gives us the results it promises – if it does, we consider it effective, useful, practically relevant. As the old saying goes: the proof of the pudding is in the eating. Performance is the only valid test of the pudding. But as usual, things may not be so straightforward.

Usefulness and truth

Does a theory have to be true (in the correspondence sense) to be useful? The short answer to this question is no. Fraud stories, for example, are known to be false but are often beautifully coherent and enticing. They are useful to the disseminator if the recipient takes the bait and pays up; the disseminator thereby having attained his or her goal. Not so useful to the victims, of course, who lose their money. The history of science also bears witness to a number of cases of theories that are useful without being true. Most notably, Newton's theory of gravitation is not thought to be strictly true, but it still explains the motion of both the planets and the tides. Another example is Semmelweis, who postulated that childbed fever had exactly one cause, namely some (unknown) cadaverous matter transmitted to the women by doctors and medical students who came straight from autopsy. The solution was to have doctors and medical students wash their hands in chlorinated lime (i.e. bleach) before examining the patients: that would kill off the cadaverous agent, Semmelweis thought. As we know, his hygiene policy led to a significant drop in the death rate among the women. But his hypothesis is also now known not to be quite true (in the sense that there are other causes of childbed fever). And yet his hypothesis worked, we might say. He put it to its intended use and observed the results. While his theory was not exactly true, it was certainly useful – for the women, at least, if not for himself. In passing, it is worth noting here that usefulness, both in the fraud case and in the Semmelweis case, introduces an element of relativity: what is useful for some may not be so for others; usefulness comes to depend on perspective. On the other hand, we can imagine a perfect overlap between usefulness and truth (in the correspondence sense): if students actually move toward the goal state in the manner described by Driver's theory, then her theory is true. By the same token the theory is also useful, because it tells us how the students attain the goal, which is what we want for them.

We can also define truth in terms of usefulness or expedience, as William James (1975 [1907]) did. Like the correspondence theory of truth, the pragmatic theory of truth is perhaps better described as a family of theories with somewhat different central tenets. True statements are variably seen as "those that are useful to believe, that are the result of inquiry, that have withstood ongoing examination, that meet a standard of warranted assertibility, or that represent norms of assertoric discourse" (Capps, 2019, p.1). Whichever version one prefers, pragmatic theories shift our attention away from the question of truth makers and toward truth as a function of the practice we engage in. And this is of obvious interest and importance to the practice-oriented parts of the field of education, and to the theories that are employed with the purpose of achieving some desired change in the world. Thus, while the correspondence theory of truth tells us whether a theory is true or approximately true, it does not tell us what to do with this truth. Pragmatic theories of truth have their focus on the practical value of truth. Ideas are tools, William James argues, tools that help us interact effectively with our social and material surroundings. James may not be the most sophisticated of the pragmatists, but he brings out the connection between truth and usefulness in an admirably clear way:

> Any idea upon which we can ride, so to speak; any idea that will carry us prosperously from any one part of our experience to any other part, linking things satisfactorily, working securely, simplifying, saving labor; is true for just so much, true in so far forth, true *instrumentally*. This is the 'instrumental' view of truth.
>
> (1975, p.34)

We have here the essence of the pragmatic cash-value of having true beliefs. To say of a belief that it is useful because it is true is tantamount to saying of it that it is true because it is useful, James asserts. There is no difference between epistemic and pragmatic virtues. And the usefulness in question is linked to some sort of satisfaction – for example, an educational theory bringing about the results we want. We should note, though, that for James this precludes the usefulness of false stories, as in the fraud story above. But here again different perspectives come into play: fraud stories may be useful and thus true for the fraudster if the scam works, but not for the victim.

Relevance and effectiveness

As is clear from the above, the notion of usefulness is inextricably connected to goals, aims and intentions. Theories and research in general are useful to the degree that they contribute to fulfilling the perceived intentions. Since intentions may change with time, what is considered useful knowledge may change accordingly. But that depends on how widely or narrowly one defines usefulness. It should also be clear from the above that truth and usefulness are independent of one another. A theory may be true but not useful; useful but not true; both true and useful, and neither true nor useful. But as usefulness ramifies toward the notions of relevance and effectiveness, the issue of truth fades into insignificance and other considerations take over.

To set us off, let us look briefly at the evaluation of Norwegian educational research (see Strand & Kvernbekk, 2009, for a detailed discussion). In 2002, the Research Council of Norway (RCN) decided to conduct a wholesale evaluation of the quality of educational research in Norway. In 2004, the Evaluation Committee's report was published. Unsurprisingly, the overall conclusion was that the quality of educational research varied. But quality judgments depend on the criteria used. The Committee selected originality and creativity as criteria of quality – an interesting choice, since even common sense would have it that research can be creative and original without satisfying any of the time-honored internal criteria delineated at the beginning of this chapter. More to the point for my concerns here, however, is the claim of the Evaluation Committee that

> a considerable pressure is exerted on educational researchers to produce research that is useful in public debates and in the school system; which again forces the researchers to employ relevance criteria *rather than* scientific quality criteria in their assessments of academic texts.
>
> (RCN, 2004, p.9; translation here cited from Strand & Kvernbekk, 2009, p.271, emphasis added)

"Relevance" means "practical usefulness"; throughout the report the terms are used interchangeably. The Evaluation Committee thus constructed a contrast between relevance and scientific quality, intimating that more of the one implies less of the other. It must be added here that the Follow-Up Committee, appointed by the RCN in 2005 to work out a national strategy for development of Norwegian educational research, problematized the opposition of relevance and quality. And to be sure, a given theory can be both relevant/useful *and* of good quality (RCN, 2006). Neither committee clarified what it took relevance to be, besides equating it with practical usefulness.

Discussions of the relevance of research and theory to practice are endemic to education (and quite possibly to all professions). But as David Labaree (2008) points out, it is hard to define what constitutes relevance for educational research. It should not be viewed as an inherent property, such that a given piece of research is either relevant or not. Relevance, I submit, is better understood as a pragmatic property, as coming in degrees, and as essentially tied to context and perspective. Relevant for whom, for what purpose, and to what degree? As Labaree puts it,

> What might make research useful for some of these [i.e. teachers, principals, students, textbook producers, etc.] might at the same time make it useless for others. Relevance is in the eye of the beholder. In addition, research may be useful for helping to accomplish some educational ends but not others. Studies that seem relevant to people who are trying to raise test scores may not

> be at all relevant to those who are trying to improve critical thinking, enhance civic commitment, reduce the racial achievement gap, increase graduation rates, or enhance human capital production. These studies may not even seem helpful to people trying to raise student scores on other tests. In fact, what is helpful in attaining one goal may be harmful in attaining another, which, for example, is the argument made by proponents of critical thinking about the effects of efforts to raise test scores.
>
> (2008, p.422)

Labaree's viewpoint makes eminent sense to me. I shall return to the issue of relevance and usefulness in Chapter 10. I now turn to considerations of effectiveness.

"Usefulness" should not be equated with "practical usefulness". As will be argued in Chapter 10, both "usefulness" and "relevance" enjoy a much wider field of application. Practical usefulness usually means effectiveness, and with that a new set of considerations emerges. Effectiveness, I submit, comes in degrees, like relevance. It concerns the degree to which goals are achieved, the extent to which problems are solved and solutions found. To say of an educational theory that it is effective is to say that our implementation of it brings us the results we want. A theory judged in this way is like a course taken at the university. We normally do not say of courses that they are true, but we can say of them that they are effective – meaning that we get the results we want. We might also describe such a course by saying that it works, that it is adequate, or that it is fit for its purpose. There is nothing to stop us treating theories in the same way, especially not goal-directed theories. It is a good theory if it is effective; that is, if the theory achieves its goal, such that employing it brings us the results we want, as the theory promises.

As the Semmelweis story shows, a theory does not have to be true to be effective. If effectiveness in terms of results achieved is what we are after, we speak of the theory as a tool rather than a representational device. We do not say of tools or means that they are true, but that they are more or less effective. If they do not deliver as promised, we deem them ineffective and say that they do not work. Again, a couple of observations are in order. First, and importantly, educationists who wish to judge educational theories by their effectiveness in practice should not be accused of being wholly preoccupied with results. Processes of change are important in education and there are always ethical considerations to be made – the goal does not justify the tools, at least not in principle. Second, we can of course adopt William James' version of the pragmatic theory of truth and deem theories true if they produce for us the result we want. By "true" he means "useful" and "dependable" and this serves to distinguish true from false theories – false theories are not useful or dependable, James says. Effectiveness is thus intimately connected to instrumentality and many educationists are wary of it because instrumentality historically has a bad reputation in education. There is nothing wrong with wanting to achieve aims and obtain results, and instrumental considerations do have a legitimate place in education. However, as Labaree argues, worthy aims can cancel each other out, and effectiveness considerations are sometimes inappropriate. Third, effectiveness judgments run on an input-output logic. You put something in, and you get a result out. Effectiveness is generally considered a property of the input but it cannot be judged independently of the output, since the output decides how effective the input is. Thus, effectiveness judgments are highly complex and crucially turn on which success criteria you have adopted. That is to say, when does an outcome count as having reached the goal (see Chapter 5 for a discussion of this particular problem)? To what degree must the goal have been attained for us to judge that the input has been effective? For how long should we be able to observe the result? If knowledge learned is forgotten after one month, does the input (the theory) still count as effective? So while usefulness as effectiveness might be an important criterion for the goodness of at least some educational theories, it is by no means an easy criterion to handle.

Realism and antirealism

Deliberations on truth and effectiveness lead straight into deep philosophical problems of the sort we have met before, both earlier in this chapter and also in Chapter 5, such as the reality of unobservable entities and the nature of (scientific) knowledge. First let me reiterate the basic questions: must an educational theory be true to be good? Must it be true to be useful? Must it be useful to be good? The answer to all three questions is *no*. But let me shift the question somewhat and ask what makes theories or research successful. The question of success is much discussed by philosophers of science, in the context of scientific realism and scientific antirealism. Success, it seems, is mainly cashed out in terms of prediction and explanation. I shall have more to say about explanation in Chapter 10, but will inquire briefly into prediction below. Scientific realism is by and large the view that theories should be interpreted literally, as telling us about phenomena and their properties, unobservable and observable alike, and thus as being capable of truth or falsity in the correspondence sense. Antirealists are described by Ladyman as follows:

> They are empiricist in that they regard observation (experience) as the only source of knowledge; they are anti-theoretical entities; they are anti-causation, they emphasize verification and they downplay explanation.
>
> (2002, p.148)

We may all agree that generally speaking, science is vastly successful. But what accounts for this success? In 1975 Hilary Putnam put forward a global defense of realism, which has become famous as the no-miracles argument: "the positive argument for realism is that it is the only philosophy that doesn't make the success of science a miracle" (1975, p.73). The realist argument is that the success of science in predicting new phenomena and in explaining occurrences, results and events would be miraculous if the theories did not – in general – correctly identify the entities and processes that underlie our observations. As Putnam argued, if theories are false, how can they be successful? Science, realists argue, works so well because its theories are true (or approximately true). In particular, realism can account for the predictive success of theories. And to be sure, if predictions of phenomena, following from the theory, are subsequently observed, that is usually taken as strong motivation for a realist understanding of the theory in question and science in general. That is to say, a theory should be true to be useful.

However, there are counterexamples to the no-miracles argument. We already know that theories do not have to be true in order to work, which means that theories can be effective even if central T-terms fail to refer (e.g. Laudan, 1981), and Newton's theory is known to be false but still explains the tides (van Fraassen, 1989). Van Fraassen's constructive empiricism is hard to grasp because, as we have seen, it combines features of realism with an instrumentalist epistemology. On the one hand, he claims that successful theories latch on to actual regularities in nature (1980, p.40); on the other hand, he suggests that we can be agnostic about whether scientific theories are true or false or useful fictions – the important thing is that they enable us to predict and control phenomena. If predictions are made and subsequently observed, we should accept the theory but without believing it, since believing it would imply taking a position on the truth of its claims concerning unobservables. On this view, then, theories become tools, science becomes an instrument. Predictive successes will tell us that the theory in question is a good tool. But if we are antirealists, we will not know whether it is more than a tool.

I expect John Watson (1930) would have agreed with this. His S-R theory is empiricist in nature. It foregrounds observable entities, Stimulus and Response, and aims to map their correlation. What happens with the S as it is processed through a mind need not be of any concern to him – the point is the correlation of S and R. Watson can avoid all reference to unobservables, and he can also avoid all postulates concerning the relationship between S and R. For all practical purposes it is the predictive power of the theory he wants. If the theory can predict that stimulus S will elicit response R, his theory will be effective indeed. If what you want from your students is R, then you present S to them. S-R theory is confirmed if its predictions are realized and disconfirmed if they are not, and no unobservables or any assumptions concerning processes need be involved. On the other hand, as they stand S and R are generalized and abstract categories and would need to be filled with concrete content if any testing of predictions is going to take place. This might be tricky enough. And hard decisions would have to be made on how many individual predictions would have to be realized for the theory to count as empirically adequate.

Realism and antirealism are complex perspectives and pose daunting challenges to philosophers of science. I have simplified matters substantially in order to get at what I think are matters that also empirical researchers, including educational researchers, must face head on. Can we in the long run be neutral as to treating theories as truths about the world versus treating them as tools? And can we in the long run avoid taking a position on the truth of a theory and deciding whether to believe it or not? That depends on what you take the nature of knowledge and the job of theories to be.

Summary

Obviously there is much to be said about the evaluation of theories. Time-honored criteria for theory evaluation exist, and theory evaluators must decide for themselves which criteria apply in any given case. This is not self-evident, since theories are of different types and are constructed for different purposes. Some considerations about the quality of theories arise directly out of SC, such as parameters, their number, centrality and possible connections. This is an important exercise, I submit, because it will serve to make explicit the structure of a given theory and in what ways it represents a simplification of the phenomenon. Then we can judge for ourselves whether we think the simplification is legitimate for whether it crosses the thin line to over-simplication.

Commitment to truth is generally conceived of as central to the research process, and truth is therefore interesting as a criterion for theory evaluation. Applying the correspondence theory of truth to a sophisticated and detailed goal-directed theory is a complex undertaking that gets us embroiled in a number of intriguing problems. Given the job of goal-directed educational theories, truth may be an excellent quality but it may not be all that we want. Thus enter usefulness and effectiveness and judgments of the quality of theories by their results in practice. But such results should not be the sole criterion either, since that would neglect processual qualities and ethical qualms one might have. We should note, however, that a theory can be true, coherent and effective at the same time – these are not exclusive categories. Nor is there any reason why exactly one theory should be true of a phenomenon – educational phenomena are complex and surely more than one theory or one description can be true of them at the same time.

I have no definitive answer to the question of what makes an educational theory good. It may be that different types of theories require different criteria or that different uses of theories make different criteria necessary. I would not leave it entirely to the eye of the beholder, however. The issue will be returned in Chapter 10, in the discussion of different uses of theory.

8 Conceptions of practice

In many ways, practice is a commonsensical concept. We use it effortlessly in a wide variety of contexts, we seem by and large to take it for granted, and no big misunderstandings seem to occur in our talk about practice. But once we start digging into it, it may well transpire that practice is an even more difficult concept than theory.

A couple of things need to be said before we dive into a discussion about practice. It might seem odd to include a discussion about practice in a book about theory, and I should make clear that this chapter in that regard breaks with the flow of the previous chapters: it does not follow up the meta-theoretical framework laid out in Chapter 3 and employed in subsequent chapters. No particular theory or theory structure is to be discussed here. On the other hand, a chapter on conceptions of practice does have a natural place in this book, since practice is the phenomenon that many (if not most) educational theories are supposed to be *applied* to, in one way or another (see the discussion of educational theory in Chapter 2). Various conceptions of the relationship between theory and practice will be discussed in Chapter 9. Furthermore, it is not my ambition in this chapter to propose a definition of educational practice. I shall, however, entertain a hypothesis about what *kind* of concept (educational) practice is. This will, hopefully, emerge in the course of the discussion. But first a sketch of the conceptual and linguistic landscape surrounding practice.

Practice: Some initial meanderings

Usually the term practice connotes actions, habits, habitual ways of doing something. We talk about good practice, best practice, private practice, malpractice, practice that can be changed and improved. But what is it, that which is private and good? What, exactly, do we improve when we improve practice? Somehow we regard practice as an unproblematic term, despite the fact that the term, as Wilfred Carr (1995) points out, has a plethora of meanings (p.64). Any search for a unified definition is futile, Carr suggests, since the term simply does not have the unity required for any kind of definitive meaning to be had. This may well be right, especially if we want a definition to capture all possible and actual uses of the term. But then, maybe that is not necessary. And as suggested above, my quest here is not for a definition of practice.

Practice is a T-term, a theoretical term. However, it often seems to be treated as a fairly unproblematic O-term, observational term, especially if we treat practice as consisting of actions. And since actions by and large are observable, practice becomes an O-term. Moreover, we have the related but not identical view that practice is primary – it precedes theory and is therefore independent of theory. For example, in the early 1800s the German philosopher, theologian and educationist Friedrich Schleiermacher (1768–1834), stated that educational practice is much older than educational theory, and that practice thus not only precedes all theory but also possesses a dignity and a value that is independent of theory (Schleiermacher, 1994 [1826]). Practice gets its meaning from concrete experience and an already existing ethical insight. The Norwegian philosopher of education Reidar Myhre (1980) supports this view. Historically, he points out, practice definitely comes before theory in the sense that children have been brought up and taught long before there existed any explicitly formulated educational theories. It is the job of educational theories, he suggests, to employ an educational vocabulary to analyze and organize practice such as it is (p.177). That is to say, practice exists before you can analyze it. Practice will retain its relative independence even after such analyses have been performed, Myhre thinks, since its factors are too many and too unpredictable to be completely captured by theory.

The idea that upbringing has existed in practice long before it became theorized seems intuitively right, although it depends on what we take theory to be. Nevertheless, I would argue that practice is a T-term, in two different ways. First, let me return briefly to the distinction between O-terms and T-terms, which is discussed in Chapter 3. According to Ronald Giere (1988), the O/T distinction is a conflation of two distinctions: between the observable and the nonobservable on the one hand, and the theoretical and the nontheoretical on the other. Giere thinks all empiricists are guilty of this conflation, the net result of which is the O/T distinction. T-terms thus are not reserved for entities belonging to a scientific theory, but apply to all unobservable entities. Thus, motivation, understanding, personality, causation, intention and Bildung are T-terms. Practice becomes a T-term because it is an unobservable entity; unless you want to identify practice completely with directly observable actions – and I cannot imagine anybody who would want that. I would also say that teaching is a T-term; it should not be identified with a set of observable actions but rather encompasses different activities and intentions which together make up the concept of teaching.

There is also a second sense in which practice is a T-term. The Finnish philosopher of education Michael Uljens is highly critical of the idea that practice precedes theory, as intuitively right as that idea might seem (Uljens, 1998). The reason for his skepticism is that it reduces the role of theory to one of yielding deeper understanding to an already existing practice. Theory, Uljens thinks, rather has a constitutive role; meaning that educational practice is theoretically defined because it is theory that enables us to identify practice as educational in the first place, rather than, say, psychological. This by no means precludes other roles for theory, such as helping us understand practice better (p.96). His argument relies on the same kind of temporality that can be used to define practice as an O-term – a kind of what-comes-first argument. My own preferred view, to be explored in a subsequent section, is that practice qualifies as a T-term because it is a systemic concept that encompasses many entities, some of which are observable and some are not. But practice as a *whole* is unobservable. Moreover, it is not clear what Uljens takes educational theory to be; he speaks of it as an undifferentiated abstract entity, in the singular. He paints with broad strokes that fit his bird's-eye perspective and he refers to broad, comprehensive ideas about the distinctive characteristics of education.

My final meandering concerns what we tentatively can glean about *practice* from what is said about *theory*. Let me begin by introducing German philosopher of education Erich Weniger's (1894–1961) description of what he took to be a widespread understanding of theory and practice in his day, but which he himself was highly critical of:

> ...hier die wissenschaftliche Theorie mit ihrer unabhängigen Systematik, dort the praktische Erfahrung ... Dieses ist in der Tat die allgemeine Auffassung von dem Verhältnis von Theorie und Praxis: beide Teile reinlich geschieden, grau ist alle Theorie, die Praxis aber is gleich dem grüngoldenen Baum des Lebens [On the one hand the scientific theory with its independent systematics, on the other hand the practical experience ... Such is the common understanding of the relationship between theory and practice: neatly divided, all theory is grey whereas practice is like the green-golden tree of life].
>
> (Weniger, 1990, p.30)

Weniger's thoughts about theory and practice were first published in 1929 and may very well still be widely shared. I mentioned Weniger's notion of theory in Chapter 2, and will explore it more fully in Chapters 9 and 10. For the moment it suffices to note that the neat divide described by Weniger renders practice everything that theory is not: a pulsating lively activity, filled with intentions, content, actions, emotions, interactions and live, concrete individuals. Independently of Weniger, and much later, Wilfred Carr (1995) problematizes the strategy of pitting theory and practice against each other. Suppose that theories are (as indeed they are!) abstract, general and context independent. With a dichotomous understanding of the theory–practice relation, this will make practice concrete, particular, and contextual, as Weniger points out. But this picture, Carr says, yields a very narrow conception of practice which neglects the fact that practical problems can be general, not just particular (which subjects the curriculum should consist of), and directed to knowledge more than action (which factors prevent teacher collaboration at our school). We risk overlooking aspects of practice that are not particular or contextual, Carr argues. Thus, Carr's arguments illustrate the large *practical* significance of conceptual meaning. If you are hostile toward theory and advocate a particularized, action-oriented conception of practice, many important practical questions may go under the radar and be insufficiently treated.

Wolfgang Brezinka, German educational thinker, makes a sharp distinction between educational science or research and practical pedagogy (Brezinka, 1978). Research should map laws (or lawlike relations) whereas practical pedagogy should "map" rules about what should be and what should be done. Practical pedagogy is supposed to equip the practitioner with the knowledge he or she needs to perform goal-directed educational (erzieherische) actions. What, if any, view of practice can we glean from this? I suggest that Brezinka's description presupposes that practice is something relatively unambiguous or unequivocal, an activity that is relatively constant, uninterrupted and predictable and thus can be planned a long time ahead. If this is not the case, we cannot use practical pedagogical knowledge as a guideline for practice. All attempts at prescribing practice surely must rest on the assumption that all (educational) practice in principle is alike (or nearly so), such that the same approach is generally valid and can be employed most if not all of the time. Brezinka must assume that teachers work in the same way in all practice situations, or else it makes no sense to define the content of practical pedagogy as he does. We see much of the same effect of Paul Hirst's concept of theory (Hirst, 1966), also discussed in Chapter 2. It will be recalled that on Hirst's view, an educational theory organizes types of knowledge in a structure that "culminates in rationally justified principles for educational practice" (p.40) and its function is to determine what should be done. This understanding of theory allows for no variation in practice. Different interpretations of Hirst's view are possible. We can, for example, take it to mean that the theory is so detailed that it can determine what should be done in any given situation. This would mean that the theory accounts for the phenomenon in all its complexity. But if we then assume that practical situations can vary, we would need a new theory for every situation – and that is simply not feasible. Or we can see all situations as identical, such that the same theory would determine precisely what should be done in all situations. Paradoxically, this would render all students highly generalized, average entities – quite the opposite of what is wanted.

Donald Schön (1983) and his idea of the reflective practitioner implies a very different view of practice, namely as problematic and unclear. The practitioner has to enter into a dialogue with the situation, in which the situation "talks back" to figure out what the problem consists in. Thus, as a thought experiment, we can construct a continuum of practice ranging from nonproblematic to problematic. Brezinka and Hirst both seem to assume that practice is unproblematic, such that we know what teachers need to know and can furnish them with that knowledge. Schön is at the other end of the continuum and thinks that no research-based theory will do. If we also place a continuous-discontinuous continuum on practice, we can distinguish between acute and more or less long-term situations. Acute situations demand swift decision and action, as there is hardly time to reason about what the problem might be and how best to solve it. In lasting situations, the practitioner may think, hypothesize, try solutions and observe effects. I think this is where we find Brezinka and Hirst – they implicitly take practice to be continuous and nonproblematic. The two continua may be combined to produce acute nonproblematic and long-lasting problematic situations – this latter possibility seems to be how Schön thinks about practice in general. But evidently practice may also be nonproblematic, if for example the classroom climate is stable and the activities are well known and predictable to all involved parties.

A personalized conception of practice

I argued above that the way we talk about *theory* implies an understanding of practice, albeit implicitly so. In this section I shall look more closely at how we talk about *practice*. From this talk I shall extract a view of practice which tacitly assumes that practice is an individual and action-oriented concept. It is my hypothesis that this view is widespread and taken for granted, both by researchers and practitioners – practice is something that "belongs" to one person or category of actors, such as teachers (see also Kvernbekk, 2014). This is the view assumed in such expressions as "in my practice I emphasize" and "have you in your practice found that...", and so forth. To get us started, let us look at some examples of educational practice provided by the Norwegian teacher educator Roar Pettersen (1993): the philosophy professor who gives a lecture on Greek moral philosophy, the counselor who comforts a troubled teenager, the learning disability specialist who implements a behavioral intervention to improve linguistic skills in an autist, the math teacher who demonstrates the Pythagorean theorem, the teacher who chairs a class discussion on ethnic majority-minority issues, the preschool teacher who helps a five-year-old tie his shoelaces. These examples, Pettersen says, illustrate the great diversity of educational practice, both in terms of type of activities and types of practitioner (with recent developments in online teaching the list can be expanded even further). Pettersen refrains from trying to extract an explicit general definition of practice, and Carr, as we have seen, does not think that the concept is sufficiently unified for that to be possible.

However, a closer look at Pettersen's examples reveals that while they indeed differ in content, they share the same form. Grammatically speaking, they all have a subject, a verb and an object. Viewed slightly differently, they have an actor and a description of an action. I glean from these examples a conception of practice which encompasses the practitioner, and thus suggests an individualized or personalized conception. All Pettersen's examples focus on the practitioner and what he or she does: the professor who..., the math teacher who..., the counselor who.... They all *do* something in relation to other people. Practice becomes something that belongs to and is performed by an individual. Pettersen's views are reminiscent but independent of Wolfgang Schulz's views on practice. Schulz (1979) is crystal clear on the point. Practice, he says, consists of the actions, thoughts and judgments of the teacher. In the writings of two Norwegian educational researchers, Gunnar Handal and Per Lauvås (1992), we find this personalization made explicit:

> When I prepare my classes, when I think about how to do it, when I search for ideas in my own knowledge and previous experience, when I seek advice before making a decision, when I try to extrapolate what I have learned...
> (pp.33–34, my translation)

Hiding behind the "I" is the teacher. They, like Schulz, put actions, knowledge, ideas, judgments and ethical reflections into the concept of practice. In itself this is fine, since we do not want to identify practice with observable actions. But it also reinforces a personalized conception of practice, since we cannot get around the fact that it is the practitioner who acts, thinks and judges.

Much talk about educational practice centers on actions performed by the practitioner. It makes no difference to the personalized conception of practice whether practice also includes the knowledge, experience, judgments and values of the practitioner – it is still personalized. But there are other actors involved in educational practice. In some of Pettersen's examples they are only implicitly present. The math teacher who demonstrates Pythagoras' theorem is an example of practice. But the teacher is not alone; the students are implicitly present even if they are not mentioned. The same holds for the university professor; the students are implicitly present, without students in the lecture hall the professor would not do what she does. Students, patients, clients more generally are, however, not included in a conception of practice which says that practice consists of the practitioner's actions, decisions, judgments and professional knowledge. In a personalized conception of practice there is room for one actor category only. I defer to a subsequent section the question of whether the implicitly present actor groups such as students should be explicitly included in the concept of practice.

An internal goods conception of practice

We turn now to a very different approach to the concept of practice, namely Alasdair MacIntyre's (MacIntyre, 1996, first published 1981). This conception, when it was published, immediately struck a chord with both academics and practitioners, not least in the field of education. Part of its power of attraction, one might speculate, lies in its being a single, overall, holistic concept. As such it might help to keep large, untidy and fragmented fields together, and at the same time prevent highlighting certain aspects at the expense of others. Here is MacIntyre's well known definition of practice:

> By a 'practice' I am going to mean any coherent and complex form of socially established cooperative human activity through which goods internal to that form of activity are realized in the course of trying to achieve those standards of excellence which are appropriate to, and partially definitive of, that form of activity, with the result that human powers to achieve excellence, and human conceptions of the ends and goals involved, are systematically extended.
>
> (p.187)

A number of interesting things happen here. First, this is a *definition*, of the stipulative kind. It distinguishes practice from other kinds of activities, and can be used to determine whether an activity should count as practice or not. The definition is large and complex and leaves no doubt that practice is a T-term – practice is not presented here as a unified empirical entity admitting of direct observation. Nor do we find here any attempt to define practice in relation to theory. This is not a personalized conception of practice; rather, collective constructions such as "departmental practice" become possible. In addition, it points toward internal goods, standards and tradition, the latter implying a temporal dimension. This conception makes it possible to individuate practice and, hence, speak of *a* practice. Not *my* practice, but *a* practice.

The internal goods conception of practice needs some contextualization. By his own admission, MacIntyre defines practice in a way not quite in agreement with ordinary usage, including his own previous use of the term. That is to say, he stipulates a certain meaning for it because he wants it to serve a particular purpose in his social teleological account of the nature of the virtues. In turn, the motivation for his account of the virtues lies in his overall diagnosis of the social world: it is fragmented, the language of morality has fallen into disorder, and emotivism rules the day. Emotivism is the doctrine that all judgments, including moral judgments "are *nothing but* expressions of preference, expressions of attitude or feeling, in so far as they are moral or evaluative in character" (p.12). MacIntyre has a moral agenda and the concept of practice, defined as shown above, is part of his proposed solution. At bottom we find the concept of virtue and the idea of a good life. The concept of virtue, MacIntyre argues, demands a rich social and moral fabric. The development of the concept of virtue takes place in three stages, each with their own conceptual backdrop. These stages are practice, narrative order of life, and (moral) tradition. These three stages paint the picture of a long tradition of which virtue forms the core. Practice is the first of these stages – hence, MacIntyre's stipulative definition of it. Practice provides "the arena in which the virtues are exhibited and in terms of which they are to receive their primary, if incomplete, definition" (p.187).

MacIntyre's definition suggests a range of conditions an activity must satisfy to fall under the concept of practice: coherence, complexity, internal goods, internal standards, personal and shared involvement, and a continuing development as a result of this involvement. When Wilfred Carr, after having criticized attempts at defining practice in relation to theory, suggests that we understand educational practice "as the *achievement of a tradition* rather than as a form of craft knowledge or technical expertise" (1995, p.73, my emphasis), he is essentially inspired by MacIntyre. MacIntyre, in his turn, is essentially inspired by Aristotle. Engagement in a practice necessarily involves virtues, according to MacIntyre, since practitioners interact both with each other and with former participants through literature, traditional discussion and norms. Three virtues are internal to any practice, namely honesty or truthfulness, justice and courage. In addition, he thinks that a practitioner must submit to the internal standards of excellence of the practice in order to partake of the internal goods of that practice, something which Kenneth Wain (2003) argues is reasonable to view as a fourth virtue. Finally, it is important to say that the goals, ends or goods involved are multidimensional and only partly articulable. This points toward complexity, the necessity of virtues, and the significance for practice of tradition and community.

Educational practice

Activity and practice are not the same. The criteria provided by MacIntyre's definition should at least be understood as necessary conditions (if not sufficient as well) for an activity to qualify as a practice. So what kind of activities count as practices? The range of practices is wide, MacIntyre says. Falling under the concept are, for instance, arts, sciences, games, home making, and politics in the Aristotelian sense. Playing chess is a practice, tic-tac-toe is not. Architecture is a practice, bricklaying is not. Farming is a practice, planting turnips is not. Painting is a fairly prototypical example of a practice (pp.187–188). But teaching, MacIntyre states, is *not* a practice. In an interview with Joseph Dunne (MacIntyre & Dunne, 2002), MacIntyre unequivocally declares that teaching is not a practice but rather "a set of skills and habits put to the service of variety of practices" (p.5). This statement is a direct consequence of perceiving the criteria as necessary conditions – something that *must* be satisfied or be present for an activity to qualify as a practice.

So why is painting a practice and not teaching? This is where the notion of goods enters the picture. There are two types of goods one can gain by painting. There are goods externally and arbitrarily attached to any practice, such as prestige or money. More importantly, there are goods that are internal to the practice of painting, meaning that they cannot be had in any other way than by painting. Internal goods are identifiable and accessible only by participation in the practice: "Those who lack the relevant experience are incompetent thereby as judges of internal goods" (MacIntyre, 1996, p.189). Internal goods in their turn come in (at least) two kinds. First there is excellence: excellence of the product and excellence in the performance of the painter. Excellence must be understood historically, since standards develop and change over time. Furthermore, the standards demand obedience. Initiation into a practice requires submitting your own performances to be judged by the current standards. The second kind of internal goods is found in the practitioner's efforts to make progress, solve problems, be creative – the good of a certain kind of life. This latter kind of internal goods is unspecifiable outside the practice, and judgment of it is the privilege of the participants in the practice.

Let us back up a little and look again at the distinction between internal and external goods. MacIntyre's main, but by no means only, source of inspiration is *The Nicomachean Ethics* (Aristotle, 1987). Here the good is defined as that at which all things aim. But ends are different, Aristotle says (Bk.1, Ch.1): some ends are activities and some ends are results beyond activities. The highest good is something that is sought after for its own sake and not as a means to something else. A good is the *telos* of the activity, that for the sake of which we act. The form of activity which has internal ends sought after for their own sake is termed *praxis*. The form of activity which is done for the sake of something else, and thus has independent or external ends, is termed *poiesis*. On MacIntyre's view, painting qualifies as a *praxis*, i.e. a practice, whereas teaching qualifies as a form of *poiesis*. Teaching is an ingredient in every practice, but it is not itself a practice. Here is why:

> For it is part of my claim that teaching is never more than a means, that it has no point and purpose except for the point and purpose of the activities to which it introduces students. All teaching is for the sake of something else and so teaching does not have its own goods.
>
> (MacIntyre & Dunne, 2002, p.9)

The internal goods conception of practice has found fertile ground in the field of education and spawned much discussion; not least his view that teaching does not have its own internal goods. In the wake of Dunne's interview with MacIntyre, a special issue of the *Journal of Philosophy of Education* (2003) was published, featuring a selection of responses, both critical and supportive of MacIntyre. Some embraced the concept of practice and argued that teaching is indeed a practice, complete with internal goods and an integrity of its own (e.g. Dunne, 2003, Hogan, 2003, Noddings, 2003). They criticized MacIntyre's conception of teaching for being simplistic and impoverished. Yes, teaching is a means, Dunne, Hogan and Noddings argue, but it is also more than that – teaching encompasses many things that are not directly related to the subjects, and working with children can very well be thought of as having value in its own right. Kenneth Wain, on the other hand, agrees with MacIntyre – it would be tragic, he says, if teaching was a self-serving profession. Teaching should be regarded as a means because the good it serves is not intrinsic to itself but is the good of learner and community (Wain, 2003). Suppose we grant that teaching qualifies as a practice in MacIntyrean terms; who should we say the internal goods are *for*? Who can be counted as having access to the internal goods of teaching? Christopher Higgins (2003) suggests that internal goods must belong to the practitioner, for instance as excellence of character and a meaningful life. The practice of teaching must thus be understood in terms of its role in the teacher's quest to flourish. I shall come back to this viewpoint in the next section.

While MacIntyre evidently draws on Aristotle's distinction between *praxis* and *poiesis*, he for some reasons omits mention of it. His conception of practice owes much to the Aristotelian notion of *praxis*. Nel Noddings (2003) points out that on occasion MacIntyre classifies as practices what Aristotle classified as examples of *poiesis*, such as architecture. But architecture is not done for its own sake. The end of architecture surely is the buildings produced and their subsequent use, not the building of them. Aristotle organizes *poiesis* activities into a hierarchy. Leather is made for the harness-maker, who makes bridles for the military, who devises some military strategy the aim of which is victory. And military concerns take precedence – activities high up in this hierarchy are more desirable than subordinate activities, according to Aristotle. Teaching could conceivably be organized into the same kind of hierarchy, since it serves a number of other practices, activities and domains. That would make teaching a *poiesis*, not a *praxis*. Wilfred Carr (1995) emphatically opposes such a view, and it is instructive to look at his arguments. Carr is adamant that teaching is a *praxis*, an activity whose end exists only in the activity itself. *Poiesis*, in Carr's rendering of it, is a form of rule-following action; its point is to bring some product or artifact into existence. *Poiesis* is guided by *techne*, which is a nonreflective form of know-how. *Praxis* is a form of reflective action, which can itself transform the theory that guides it. The guiding theory of *praxis* is called *phronesis*, which is commonly translated as practical wisdom. With such descriptions of *poiesis* and *praxis* we should not wonder that Carr classifies teaching (or education) as *praxis*. But it is by no means evident that Aristotle's writings justify the description of *poiesis* as rule-following action and *techne* as nonreflective know-how. There is nothing to suggest that harness-makers should be incapable of perceiving and processing various obstacles or problems in their work and take measures to circumvent them.

Purposive practice

Taking stock, where has this discussion left us? I think the main thing to come out of it is a holistic vision of teaching. This is important because it counteracts reductive and (over)simplified ideas about practice and the role of the teacher. The internal goods conception of practice is not compatible with teaching understood solely in terms of skills and competences (McLaughlin, 2003), or solely in terms of theoretical knowledge, for that matter. MacIntyre's concept of practice usefully reminds us of the complexity of practice and, by implication, of the dangers of identifying the whole with one of its parts only.

Many educational thinkers have embraced MacIntyre's concept of practice. Some of them wish to subsume teaching under *praxis*, some do not. Those who do invariably take issue with MacIntyre's description of teaching, since teaching according to MacIntyre has no internal goods. But maybe the distinction between *praxis* and *poiesis* is not as clear-cut as commonly assumed. What is to prevent an activity from having internal and external aims at the same time? What is to prevent an activity from having instrumental value and intrinsic value at the same time? David Miller (1994) proposes we make a distinction within the concept of practice: self-contained practice and purposive practice. Self-contained practices are practices that revolve around internal goods and their achievements. Purposive practices exist to serve some aims beyond themselves. There is nothing to prevent a purposive practice from having internal goods, from being a coherent and complex form of social activity, from having a tradition and a long history, from being an arena where virtues can flourish, from having standards of excellence – and yet have aims beyond itself. Miller's own favorite example is medicine. A physician may satisfy all current standards of excellence and have access to all the internal goods of the medical profession, but this will not amount to much if his patients do not get better. We do not praise a surgeon, Miller states, whatever skills he possesses of whatever effective procedures he introduces, if the death rate from his operations is much higher than average.

I am not enamored of the distinction between *praxis* and *poiesis* – it has too much of an either/or character to be useful. Miller's concept of purposive practice, on the other hand, overrides the *praxis/poiesis* distinction and makes good sense concerning teaching, as far as it takes us. It provides the same vitally important antidote to the reductionist attempt to identify practice with the skills and knowledge of the practitioner, as MacIntyre's concept of practice does. In addition is provides direction. MacIntyre, however, writes as if all practices are self-contained. This, as Richard Smith (2003) points out, has the effect that his concept of practice denotes activity that has no direction, no ideas of where we want to go. In its turn, Smith argues, this leads to an even bigger problem:

> Without the element of purposiveness it is difficult to see what prevents a practice from falling into self-indulgence and self-absorption, from coming to resemble in this respect an endlessly sophisticated tea-ritual.
>
> (p.315)

Whereas Wilfred Carr makes *phronesis* the only acceptable form of knowledge for teachers and educators, Smith thinks that self-absorption and descent into virtuosity – meaning excessive attention to one's own skills and knowledge – are constant risks for activities that are guided by *phronesis*. This is surely not what we would want for the practice of teaching. An adoption of Miller's concept of purposive practice changes the discussion profoundly, since the unfortunate contrast between teaching for its own sake and teaching for the sake of something else disappears. Teaching can be both, at the same time.

In self-contained practices, internal and external goods are easily kept apart since internal goods are only specifiable in terms of the practice itself. External goods are independent. Things are more complicated in the case of purposive practices, Miller maintains. While external goods still are independent, internal goods are no longer specifiable exclusively in terms of the practice. The wider purpose that the practice serves must also be taken into account. Critical review or evaluation of the practice in question can of course still be undertaken by the practitioners, but they can no longer be viewed as having privileged – let alone monopolistic – access to internal goods. Others can have a say, in the light of the practice's wider cultural or societal purpose.

In summary, according to MacIntyre practice is a socially and historically established activity with internal goods and standards to which the practitioners must submit. Teaching is a servant to other practices and does not exist for its own sake. The internal goods conception of practices is not personalized since it exists independently of the practitioners who happen to partake of it at any given time. Practice should be understood holistically, with practitioners among the parts. Nevertheless, and perhaps paradoxically, with MacIntyre's concept of practice practitioners run the risk of becoming self-absorbed, as Smith points out. And as Higgins suggests, the internal goods conception of practice may reduce to the teachers', *qua* practitioners', quest to flourish. But educational practice consists of a second group of actors: the students. While their development, learning and Bildung may be the target, they are not portrayed as participants in the same way as teachers despite their presupposed presence in the activity. We now turn to the question of whether the students (or any client group, for that matter) should be explicitly included in the concept of (educational) practice. But first some notes on the identity of actions.

Interlude: The identity of actions

Some notes on actions and their description are needed to prepare the ground for a discussion about the possibility of a systemic conception of practice. I am quite aware that in recent decades there has been a shift away from actions to knowledge and judgment. Nevertheless, I think that *however* we define practice, actions surely are a central part of the activity. Furthermore, I think that the description of actions is a vastly underrated topic: a topic, moreover, of great theoretical significance.

Recall Pettersen's examples of educational practice. The professor who *gives* a lecture, the preschool teacher who *helps*, the math teacher who *demonstrates*, the teacher who *chairs* a discussion. What kind of descriptions are these? What kind of action is it to demonstrate something, or to chair something? What if anything is specifically educational about such actions? It is important to be aware that actions can be described in many different ways, all of which can be correct. We can ask what the math teacher is doing and receive different answers, for example, "drawing a triangle on the blackboard", "explaining what a hypotenuse is", "asking the students who Pythagoras was", "teaching the students to hate math", "working toward the defined learning outcomes in math", "fulfilling the intentions of the curriculum" or "securing mathematical skills of the future labor force". All these descriptions concern the math teacher's actions. All of them may be correct, but not necessarily at the same time since some of them are incompatible – satisfying curricular intentions is not compatible with students learning to hate math. The descriptions exhibit different degrees of abstraction and it is by no means obvious which level of abstraction we should aim for when we describe actions. Drawing and asking might be viewed as unproblematic O-terms, directly observable, even if a good deal of concrete details might be missed – there are many ways of asking questions: wording, tone of voice, gestures and posture. There is an interesting weighing of considerations to be made here: what detailed descriptions gain in particularity and concreteness they might lose in identity. There might be cases where it is important to describe the math teacher's movements in detail, but I think that the examples overall qualify as T-terms at a reasonably high level of abstraction. Take for example "explain" and "prepare". Both are verbs, both denote some kind of action. Both of them are T-terms – you cannot observe explanation or preparation directly – and both fairly abstract in that they refer to the actor's intentions more than to actual actions. "Explain" and "prepare" are not concrete actions, but rather point to what the actor wants to achieve with what he or she is doing. As MacIntyre puts it,

> Some of the answers [to the question "What is he doing?"] will characterize the agent's intentions, others unintended consequences of his actions, and of these unintended consequences some may be such that the agent is aware of them and others not.
>
> (1996, p.206)

According to MacIntyre, when we wish to address the identity of an action – that is to say, find out what is going on, what type of action or behavior we are dealing with – we must look at how the different answers hang together. If, for example, the teacher's primary aim is to satisfy general educational aims of human flourishing, it is a coincidence that society is provided with a competent labor force. If the primary aim is to prepare students for the math exam, then asking questions to check what knowledge and skills they have acquired is logical, whereas human flourishing is (perhaps) not even considered.

So what can we say about the identity of teachers' actions? In the first case the action can be placed in a context of commitments to general educational aims and ideas of what is best for students. In the second case the context may be mathematics as a practice in MacIntyre's sense, a professional ambition to initiate students into this practice and thus give them access to its internal goods and values. If the teacher's primary aim – contrary to expectation – is to make the students detest mathematics, the context is perhaps a personal story of professional and educational failure.

What is happening in these examples is that we add new contexts and levels of abstraction to the descriptions of the teacher's actions. Often these extra layers will have teleological overtones, which is hardly surprising given the purposiveness found in most (but not necessarily all) cases of educational practice. We cannot, MacIntyre says, characterize actions independently of intentions, and we cannot characterize intentions independently of the context that gives them their meaning. In other words, to look at the actor's intention only is not sufficient to understand or explain an action. Even intentions have to be explained, and we do that by placing them in a larger social context. In that way we – at least tentatively – can specify the identity of an action.

To look at actions in terms of levels of abstraction means that they, at least partly, get their identity as parts of a larger context. Historically, on the other hand, it has probably been more common to decompose complex actions into smaller parts. This can be interesting enough; what does a single action consist in? When does it start and when does it end? The idea of one single action makes good sense in many contexts, MacIntyre points out. In recipes, for instance, where each act is individually described: "Take six eggs. Then break them into a bowl. Add flour, salt, sugar, etc." (1996, p.209). Such separate, individual actions must be placed in some sequence or context or other to make sense. That is to say, we can understand the utterance "take six eggs", but the *point* of taking them comes from the context: the baking of a cake.

It is not uncommon to associate practice with actions, with something concrete that somebody does. Nor is it unreasonable. If we focus on actions, "improving practice" becomes a matter of performing other actions, or performing them differently, all based on more or less explicit criteria of what "better" means. But which level of abstraction should we look at? Which unit? Individual actions? Whole sequences? Or even higher levels of abstraction?

A systemic conception of practice

The personalized way of talking about practice is widespread, perhaps naturally so. But practice, I shall argue in this section, cannot be seen as "belonging" to the practitioner, the teacher, alone. There is another group of actors implicitly present in all cases of professional practice: students, patients, clients. An adequate conception of educational practice should explicitly include students – "students" here being a generic term for anybody in a relationship to any educator – small children, school children, adults taking evening classes. What might a concept of practice look like, that would accommodate more than one group of actors? What consequences might it have, to employ such an understanding?

The internal goods conception of practice is not necessarily personalized. MacIntyre does not mention any specific actor groups, and as far as I can see there is nothing in this conception to preclude the inclusion of students. It is easy, however, to interpret it that way – even such a complex notion seems to zero in on the teacher. Both Richard Smith and Kenneth Wain warn us of possible consequences of this focus: teaching risks becoming a self-absorbed activity as viewed only from the teacher's perspective. With no direction to the activity, focus shifts toward one's own internal goods and the perfection of one's own actions. The strongest example of a personalized understanding of MacIntyre's concept of practice comes from David Carr (2003). Interestingly, he criticizes MacIntyre for thinking instrumentally and viewing (moral) virtues mainly as a *means* to the pursuit of private and public goods. But, Carr claims, no personal or social reasons are required for aspiring to virtue, because virtues are ends in themselves and therefore their own reward:

> As a teacher, I may recognize a need to be self-controlled and fair, and also that my pupils are more likely to become self-controlled and fair by my good example – but as a *good* teacher, I will aspire to become self-controlled and fair *for its own sake* irrespective of any benefit to others.
>
> (2003, p.261)

While this may be right, the view is too narrow, too focused on oneself, to provide a good road into educational practice. It is this "irrespective of any benefit to others" that I think can be avoided by explicitly including the *other* in the concept of practice. This requires a different *kind* of concept.

Let us begin with Nel Noddings' discussion of MacIntyre's concept of practice (Noddings, 2003). Teaching, she says, is a fundamentally relational practice. This relationality is not worked out in principle, but she provides several examples:

> Teaching is thoroughly relational: the feeling of safety in a thoughtful teacher's classroom, a growing intellectual enthusiasm in both teacher and student, the challenge and satisfaction shared by both in engaging new material, the awakening sense (for both) that teaching and life are never-ending moral quests.
>
> (p.249)

In her argument *contra* MacIntyre that teaching has its own internal goods and standards, she says that the "goal [as a teacher] is to help students use my subject effectively for their own legitimate purposes. The hope is that, in working toward this goal, both of our lives will be enriched" (p.250). I agree with Noddings that teaching is relational, but it is unclear whether it means anything more than doing things together, sharing goals, both learning along the way. What I have in mind is something more radical: a systemic conception of practice.

A systemic conception of practice implies looking at practice as a *whole*. In parts, the following discussion will bring in perspectives already touched upon in Chapter 6, notably Gregory Bateson's concept of context (Bateson, 1972). In Chapter 6 this concept was put in the service of an analysis of interlevel theories and their interlevel condition; here I shall focus on the systemic level and tease out some implications for the concept of (educational) practice. The concept of context, however, cannot do all that work alone, so I will invoke a handful of other concepts from systems theory in my analysis (see also Kvernbekk, 2014). The point of departure, though, is Bateson's concept of context. It merits repetition:

> ...I speak of an action or an utterance as occurring "in" a context, and the conventional way of talking suggests that the particular action is a "dependent" variable, while the context is the "independent" or determining variable. But this view of how an action is related to its context is likely to distract the reader – as it has distracted me – from perceiving the ecology of the ideas which together constitute the small subsystem which I call "context". ... It is important to see the particular utterance or action as *part* of the ecological subsystem called context and not as a product or effect of what remains of the context after the piece we want to explain has been cut from it.
>
> (1972, p.338)

Importantly, here, as in Chapter 6, context denotes *whole*. Bateson uses such terms as whole, context, form, pattern and relationship more or less interchangeably – whichever terms he uses, the parts together constitute their own whole. This is how I propose we include students in the concept of practice: we employ the same logic of constitution as in Chapter 6. Practice is the whole, and the students make up one of the parts that constitute it.

Systems theory offers very different analytical tools from those we have met so far in this chapter. Bateson speaks about patterns, flexibility, context, difference, self-correction, communication, punctuation, change, and so forth. Ludwig von Bertalanffy, in a systems theory classic, speaks about organizational complexity, feedback, wholeness, directedness, and so forth (Bertalanffy, 1968). William Ross Ashby, a pioneer in the neighboring field of cybernetics, speaks of input, output, transformation, control, restraint, stability, and so forth (Ashby, 1984). These are certainly not concepts we normally use to describe, analyze or discuss educational practice or teaching. Together they make up a way of thinking which deals with form rather than substance and which carves up the world in unexpected yet hopefully productive ways. Like any perspective, the systemic one shines a light on certain aspects of phenomena while leaving other aspects in the dark. Surely, it rubs against customary, traditional perspectives and deeply ingrained ways of thinking about the world in general, and educational practice in particular.

Von Bertalanffy famously defines systems as organized complexity, made up of parts in interaction (1968, p.19). Complexity points to the number of parts and their internal patterns, whereas organization concerns the level of order/disorder in the system. Systems are wholes and therefore find themselves at a different level of abstraction and/or aggregation than the parts. I wish to analyze practice as a systemic concept, as a whole, and I shall focus on teachers and students as parts. For a formal analysis it does not matter how many parts are involved; so more than two actor groups can be included. What this basically means is that practice cannot be identified as "belonging" to any of the constituent groups – rather, they create it together. As von Bertalanffy argues, systems are not understandable by investigation of their parts in isolation. Constitutive systemic characteristics are not explainable from characteristics of isolated parts; their relationships and exchanges are far more important. All parts contribute to the composition of the whole and get part of their meaning from this whole. Obviously, a number of issues in this intricate and somewhat fluid landscape are deserving of elaboration. I shall focus on two that I judge to be of particular interest, namely punctuation and dormitive mistakes. But first, let me introduce an example.

Educational practice revisited

Imagine a preschool teacher student: let us call her Cecilie. After a period of pre-service training in a kindergarten, she reflects upon one experience in particular: one day she had been very meticulous in teaching the children the difference between acceptable and unacceptable behavior, and one of the children had asked her why she always yelled so much at them. I love this example and use it often. In all its simplicity it serves to illustrate a number of interesting issues. First, Cecilie makes the essential discovery that what she takes herself to be doing is not what others (the children) take her to be doing. If we accord Cecilie the role of actor and the kids the role of observer, it becomes clear that actor and observer have different views about what is going on. Cecilie describes it as the teaching of acceptable behavior; the kids describe it as yelling. For the sake of the argument, we shall ignore the fact that much teaching of acceptable behavior surely happens by yelling. Second, "teaching acceptable behavior" is not a description of a concrete action; it is rather a description of the intention that motivates the action. When Cecilie is asked to describe her actions, she responds by describing the intention. We note here that this description gives the action an identity – with knowledge of Cecilie's intention, an observer can understand what she is doing (it might not be self-evident). Her description is fairly advanced, it is at a high level of abstraction and to make sense it requires knowledge of the theoretical and value-laden notion of "acceptable behavior".

Cecilie describes her own action or sequence of actions as it appears from her own actor perspective – and perhaps her description reveals that she holds a personalized conception of practice. Teaching acceptable behavior is something a teacher does; and the example easily fits the general form of Pettersen's examples of practice. If Cecilie is judged to be successful in her endeavors, we may describe her practice as good or effective. We may also say of Cecilie that she has much educational knowledge and skills as well as good personal traits as a preschool teacher. This, however, is a personalized perspective. What would it look like from a systemic perspective?

Punctuation

It stands to reason that there are many different kinds of parts in the whole we call practice. I shall focus on teachers and students and the interactional patterns or relationships between them. Punctuation is the process of structuring a relationship. According to Bateson, punctuation is the basic epistemological act by which we draw distinctions and create differences and order. As Bateson himself puts it,

> ...we might ask: "What circumstances determine that a given scientist will punctuate the stream of events so as to conclude that all is predetermined, while another will see the stream of events as so regular as to be susceptible of control?" ... "What circumstances promote that specific habitual phrasing of the universe which we call 'free will' and those others which we call 'responsibility,' 'constructiveness,' 'energy,' 'passivity,' 'dominance,' and all the rest?" For all these abstract qualities, the essential stock-in-trade of the educators, can be seen as various habits of punctuating the stream of experience so that it takes on one or another sort of coherence and sense.
>
> (1972, p.163)

Punctuation is thus essential to all interaction, and in any interaction all parts (agents) punctuate. To identify one agent as actor and the other as observer, as I did above, is already to punctuate the sequence, give it a certain order and accord different roles to the participants. In punctuation we turn streams of events or experiences into ordered sequences that are often linear, with beginnings and middles and endings. We identify something as cause and another thing as effect, or as stimulus, response and reinforcement, thereby ordering them temporally and causally and making sense of what is happening. Traditionally, I submit, educationalists (practitioners and researchers alike) take the teacher's perspective and punctuate actions, sequences or events as originating with the teacher and call them instructions or assignments (if they originate with students, we might call them disruptions instead). This kind of punctuation gives rise to descriptions such as giving lectures, helping, encouraging, demonstrating, etc. The personalized conception of practice relies on punctuating events such that the teacher becomes the cause and the student the effect.

Punctuation is one of the basic terms of communication theory. Different punctuation yields competing descriptions and interpretations, and disagreements about how to punctuate streams of events lie behind countless relationship struggles, Paul Watzlawick, Janet Bavelas and Don Johnson argue in their communication theory classic (1967). Our default position, they claim, is to see ourselves as reacting to other people: *my* behavior is a response to *your* behavior. Their example, albeit fictive, has also become classic. A husband and a wife are locked in marital fights; he withdraws passively and she nags:

> In explaining their frustrations, the husband will state that the withdrawal is his only *defense against* her nagging, while she will label this explanation a

> gross and willful distortion of what "really" happens in their marriage; namely, that she is critical of him *because of* his passivity.
>
> (1967, p.56, emphasis in original)

A couple of observations are in order. First, we should not wonder that our punctuation mirrors our own first-person perspective. As suggested above, this is also a very convenient form of punctuation: it frees us from blame since, as every child learns at a very young age, the blame lies with the instigator. Second, in the marital fight example we see how the couple punctuate differently, each from their own perspective. Paradoxically, they also do exactly the same thing: they punctuate according to the same assumption, that their behavior is a response to the other's antecedent actions or utterances. Third, in this example neither of the interlocutors are able to lift their gaze and look at the *pattern* of their interaction. Neither of them see how their own behavior reinforces the other's behavior and in turn becomes stimulus for the other, thus perpetuating their nagging-withdrawing pattern. They create their own interactional pattern together, and neither of them see it or understand their own contribution to it.

In educational contexts, this form of punctuation, common as it may be, runs counter to the discipline's understanding of itself as intentional or goal-directed. In so far as teachers punctuate practice in such a way that they themselves become the provider of stimuli and the students become the respondents, it is easy to understand why such phrases as "my practice" or "in your experience from your practice as counselor..." are so widespread and make so much sense to us. What both ways of punctuating have in common is their individualistic orientation and concomitant focus on persons. Our language seems to reinforce the individualized punctuation; teachers might say "I taught Pythagoras to fifth-graders last week", or more generally, "I did X to bring about Y". And if practice is "mine", I can improve it by thinking and acting differently. Traditional punctuation deals in things and persons. System theoretical punctuation deals in patterns, relationships and form – phenomena that are often invisible to the naked eye and have no location. For that reason, they often understandably fall off our radar screen.

Dormitive mistakes

How do we shift from seeing individuals to seeing relationships, patterns and systems that individuals create together? That is to say, how do we punctuate relations rather than individuals? This is a deep epistemological shift, Bateson argues; it is difficult to achieve because we are so accustomed to the traditional way of punctuating. Shifting focus requires effort, but is by no means impossible. Minimally it requires double descriptions.

"Double description" simply denotes the descriptions of how all involved participants in the activity or interaction punctuate the interaction. In the interest of simplicity, let us stay with two. This allows us to study the pattern that plays out between them; the system they together have created. The Cecilie example can illustrate how this might work. In order to find out what is going on in the scene with Cecilie and the kids, the researcher will have to look at the punctuations and descriptions made by both parties. The identity of Cecilie's action no longer relies solely on her intentions and judgments, but also on those of the other party. And here arises the possibility of a dormitive mistake:

> If double descriptions of relationships are dissected and each part held to be something localized inside a person, a "dormitive principle" is created. To see a nagging husband without considering a withdrawing wife may lead to treating a "nagger" rather than treating a nagging/withdrawing relationship.
> (Keeney, 1983, pp.37–38)

Bradford Keeney got the roles of husband and wife from the original example wrong, but that is of no concern. Of great concern, on the other hand, is the dormitive mistake: to treat attributes that are relational as if they are personal. Bateson takes the term "dormitive mistake" from the play *The Hypochondriac* by Molière (*Le Malade Imaginaire*, 1673). In this play we meet a medical student who, when asked to explain why opium causes sleep, responds that it must be because opium contains a "dormitive principle", a *virtus dormitiva*. After Molière, this has come to name a kind of explanation that in reality explains nothing; the student explains that opium makes people fall asleep because it is its nature to make people fall asleep. More precisely, the mistake consists in shifting from the interpersonal field to postulate instead some inner tendency, instinct or attribute which is made responsible for the result, action or observation in question. Such a way of thinking represents a reification of the inner tendency, by treating it as a fixed entity with causal powers (Bateson, 1980). This is for Bateson a big epistemological sin – I venture to say he thinks there is no forgiveness for it. But all the words we use to describe personality traits, Bateson says, "have their roots in what happens between people, not in something-or-other inside a person" (1980, p.146). The wife nags because she is a nagger, kids make noise because they are noise-makers, boys act aggressively because they are aggressive, Cecilie teaches acceptable behavior because she is a good, responsible preschool teacher (to be). Such explanations, Bateson claims, are plain nonsense (1980, p.146).

According to Bradford Keeney (1983), in all forms of professional practice, attempts at defining attributes or characteristics of the *good practitioner* is tantamount to looking at only half of the relationship and ignoring the other half. Descriptions of personality traits actually consist of descriptions of extracted halves of larger relationships. It makes no sense to think of somebody as being "friendly", "a good teacher", "nagging" or "passive" outside a relationship that involves at least two parts. Personality descriptions generally consist of such halves, Keeney thinks. When we attribute properties to people, we cut out a chunk from a larger sequence of experiences and events and turn it into a dormitive principle, which we then reify into a fixed inner tendency that can be used to explain behavior, attribute culpability, etc. Thus, we ignore the other half of the relationship and are guilty of committing a dormitive mistake: we look at a single person rather than looking at how traits emerge and are maintained in the interactional pattern.

If you wish to understand what is going on in an interactional sequence or in a classroom, it will not do to interview just one of the involved parties – that will give you only half the story. On Bateson's view, to explain people's behavior you do not resort to inner tendencies or supposed personal traits, you reconstruct the contexts the individual is a part of. And in order to explain why people exhibit the traits that they exhibit, you map the concrete contexts or relationships that could conceivably bring about such traits. Traits, Bateson says, "are to be reduced or expanded to derive their definitions from patterns of interchange, i.e., from combinations of double descriptions" (1980, p.147). Thus, on this view, teachers cannot explain students' disruptive behavior by lack of motivation or aggressiveness. On the systemic way of thinking, relationships are primary and the relata are secondary. Only by holding on tight to the primacy of relationship can we avoid dormitive mistakes, Bateson thinks. This is an unusual and difficult way of thinking which takes some getting used to. Dormitive thinking is a way of punctuating that is learned and constantly reinforced by regular language use – I, my, you, they. Circumventing it is quite a challenge.

Summing up

Understanding educational practice as a systemic concept is more adequate than understanding it as a personalized concept, I submit, for the simple reason that without students (patients, clients) the point of the practitioner's activity vanishes. Teachers do not act in isolation; their actions presuppose the presence of another group of actors. A systemic understanding is possibly oriented toward the here and now; a feature it shares with the personalized view. In that regard MacIntyre's concept of practice stands out because it explicitly accommodates tradition and historically established standards and goods. There is no doubt that educational practice has long traditions, even if the standards are unclear and disagreements over what constitutes quality in teaching abound. It would be of great interest if the systemic conception of practice could be expanded to accommodate the long traditions of practice. This is not the place for a serious inquiry into that topic, but I wish to suggest a couple of things I think might be important in such an expansion.

First, there is the notion of a *context marker*, which might provide an inroad into the kind of temporality I am after. Context markers are a source of information about what kind of context we find ourselves being part of (Bateson, 1972). They are signals that help us classify the context. In many cases they are invisible and subtle. If a preschool teacher asks a five-year-old if she needs help to tie her shoes, the meaning is clear enough. But at the same time a relationship is signaled in which the teacher takes the role of the helper and the child the role of the helped. You not only learn to tie your shoes; you also learn something about your own role. It might be very easy for teachers to define roles like this, because they learned to punctuate the activity called "teaching" in a certain way when they were students. We learn, Bateson says, definitions of the contexts in which we participate, and we learn what our own role is expected to be. Schools, of course, also have very clear context markers. Lecture halls are structured such that one cannot mistake the roles of lecturer and audience. Context markers have long histories and both teachers and students perceive them and act accordingly. On occasion it might be difficult to know whether a student who begins an activity does so as response to a stimulus provided by the teacher, an entire context or a context marker. If we react in certain ways because something in a situation reminds us of something else, chances are we are picking up on a context marker.

Second, there is the question of standards. MacIntyre tells us that practices (*praxis*) have established internal standards that demand obedience of the participants in the sense that they must submit their performance to be judged by those standards. Now, it may well be that a systemic conception of practice will imply more dynamics in the standards than MacIntyre's view allows for. If teachers and students create practice together, they also contribute to creating the standards together and we cannot speak of submission to standards any more (at least not wholesale submission). A systemic view might yield a better understanding of how standards are established and changed than the internal goods view does. At the outset there are no particular internal goods or standards built into systemic views – if we want them, we have to add them ourselves. Neither "good" nor "bad" practice is immediately explainable in the systemic perspective, so if we want that, we have to build into it normative presuppositions concerning the aims and the ethical conduct of the activity.

Desiderata for a concept of educational practice?

Let me bring back Wilfred Carr's lament about the concept of practice: it has a plethora of meanings and the search for a unified definition is futile (Carr, 1995). I certainly agree with Carr about the plethora of meanings – like most broad terms "practice" does indeed cover a multitude of meanings and education stakeholders might draw on different ones on different occasions to suit their own discursive purposes. I have in this chapter not attempted to provide a definition, if by definition is meant a listing of necessary and sufficient conditions for some entity to count as an educational practice. I have instead looked at three broad approaches to practice – a personalized approach, an internal goods approach, and a systemic approach – and I have looked at their uses and limitations. A personalized understanding of practice does not accommodate such constructions as "departmental practice", nor does it capture the implicitly present students. On the other hand, it is attractive because it focuses on concrete individuals, what they think and do. "My" practice, "your" practice and "improvement" of practice become understandable entities. If we employ MacIntyre's definition, "improvement" is harder to understand, because practice becomes a much larger phenomenon. The same holds for the systemic view – what do you improve there, when you improve practice? The systemic view precludes talk of "your" and "my" practice. I have constructed my account of practice precisely to overcome that particular limitation of the personalized view – any concept of educational practice ought to include the students, and be talked of accordingly. "Ours", not "mine". Practice is constituted by the parts, through their interactions and relationships, presence and perception of context markers, and so on. There is nothing inherent in MacIntyre's conception to preclude the incorporation of other actor groups, although as we have seen, there is a tendency to focus on the practitioners. Were teaching to count as a practice, would also the students have access to internal goods, or are they only for the teacher? MacIntyre himself declares that teaching is not a practice, so the question would have to go to the educationists who have adopted his concept of practice. MacIntyre's conception has built into it a sense of temporality and continuity that I take to be important in education. It is unclear to me whether the other two conceptions easily could accommodate this feature, although I have hinted as much.

So what should we do? It is not an uncommon strategy in such cases as this to suggest that all three initial views be merged into one; or, alternatively, that the central elements from each view are picked and put together into a fourth view, which then supposedly combines all insights. I can understand the allure of such a strategy: taking what one judges is best from each view and putting it together in a new view. On the other hand, what is distinctive about each view may be lost if blurred in an assembled view, and the fact that each view explains some of the uses of the term "practice". More importantly, the personalized view and the systemic view are incompatible. The personalized view locates practice in one actor (or one category of actors), whereas punctuation and dormitive mistakes are features of the systemic view that explain why this is untenable. At the outset, therefore, we might be just as well served by retaining all three conceptions of practice, but each employed with recognition of their limitations and a glance toward the other two.

All the same, I cannot resist the temptation to suggest some tentative desiderata for educational practice. There is, however, a couple of caveats to mention. First, practice is not identical to the entire field of education. Practice makes up one part of the field, and perhaps a large one at that, but there are parts of the field of education which have different foci and topics (see Chapter 2). Second, like Wilfred Carr, I have refrained from trying to present a *definition* of practice. Carr does not specify what kind of possible definition he had in mind, but he might have assumed that a definition should be detailed and cover all uses of the term; conversely, all uses of the term should have a common core – which Carr doubts. If I had to go for a definition of practice, I would go for one that is general and minimal. It should be general to avoid restrictions to a particular context and concomitant worries about the range of application of the term. It should be minimal for much the same reason: definitions that are minimal in their attributes are broad in their phenomenal range, whereas detailed maximal definitions necessarily encompass fewer phenomena. Thus, my proposed minimal attributes are possible desiderata, not a bid for a definition. Third, we may want to add to the mix a continuum of typicality or representativeness, such that some activities are considered typical of educational practice (working in the classroom with fifth-graders on the nature of lightning and thunder) while others are considered atypical (organizing peer-grading on a learning platform). What is considered typical changes with time and context.

As my discussions in this chapter make clear, I am partial to the systemic view because it offers the possibility of including students (clients more generally) in a concept of educational practice. To explicitly include students in the concept is a desideratum, I claim, because one cannot think of educational practice without them. Teachers' grading of student assignments, which they may do at their own kitchen table in the evening, may be considered an atypical practice; we may think of the students as present in the form of their assignments; we may consider it to lie in the outskirts of practice, since it caters to core activity practice, or we may decide to use the term "activity" or "habit". Practice and habits are not the same thing. The systemic view brings with it a number of unusual concepts and ideas; with its focus on form, patterns, organizational complexity, wholes, etc. it directs our attention to things we normally pay little attention to. But it does not in itself provide any content – the systemic view is a skeleton that needs to be filled in. And here is my second desideratum: teleology. A concept of educational practice should encompass a purpose, a direction. There is no need why this should be taken to preclude activities done for their own sake. On occasion activities could even be performed solely for their own sake, but that would be a form of practice that should be the exception rather than the rule. The purpose itself, of course, should regularly be the object of scrutiny by all manner of stakeholders. Third, practice should encompass history, standards, knowledge, skills, understandings, responsibilities, communication – but none of them should be set in stone. The minimalist approach leaves such details open for contextual variation and change over time. These desiderata make up the bare essentials, or at least some of them. It is a formal framework, to be filled with changeable contextual content. On this understanding it becomes very difficult to say what it means to *improve* practice, but I suppose we cannot have our cake and eat it too.

Does it matter?

Does it matter which conception of practice we adopt, or whether we mix them together according to our own liking? Yes, I would say, it does matter. It certainly mattered much to some educationalists to categorize teaching as an internal goods kind of practice. I think it is vitally important that a conception of educational practice be holistic and abstract. That will serve to remind us that educational practice has a long history and that it is complex and highly variegated. Thus, a holistic and abstract conception can serve as an inoculation against narrow focuses on parts of the activity being taken for the whole enterprise. So yes, our conception of practice does matter.

9 Theory and practice

I would like to begin this chapter with a small anecdote. In the 1980s I trained as an elementary school teacher. One of the aims of teacher education back in those days was that our practice as teachers eventually should be "theory-governed". We all agreed that that sounded both impressive and desirable. Nevertheless, during practicum, the first thing we discovered was that the theories did not "work". The problem was twofold. On the one hand, the theories did not seem to fit the reality we met in schools. We read Piaget, for example, but found that a good many of the particular fourth-graders we met did not quite conform to the description of the stages. We read about school types, and found that the school we visited did not fall under any of the types. When theory and observation conflict, people tend to trust the observation (we tend to be empiricists in that sense). On the other hand, there was a problem concerning what kind of theory could conceivably "govern" practice, which, as I recall from my teacher training years, consisted of a hurly-burly of children, colleagues, parents, curricula, textbooks, shortage of time, diffuse demands, conflicting viewpoints, expectations to self and others, and more or less half-baked ideas. No single one theory can govern all of that. But neither can you have one theory for each entity, problem or issue you meet in practice; that would be unwieldy and unmanageable. So what could a poor student teacher do? None of us knew what theory was besides being what you read in education textbooks; something that supposedly told you what the world was like, how children learn, how to plan lessons, etc., often only to discover that it did not turn out as you wanted or expected. Many student teachers across the globe have no doubt concluded that what you need is not theory, but practical experience. After graduating from teacher training college, I went on to university, with an increasing interest in *theory* and eventually in *meta-theory*.

I intend this anecdote to serve as background to the following two convictions I formed during teacher training: first, that practice simply cannot be theory-governed. At that time, I had no principled philosophical reason to think so; it was rather for the sheer impracticality of it. And second, more obscurely, I also came away with the viewpoint that practical experience alone is insufficient to make a good teacher. Theory, in some form or other, is necessary, I came to believe. I still hold both convictions, but it is the latter one that carries philosophical weight. Substantiation of it is deferred to Chapter 10, where I aim to provide a response to the challenge laid down by Gary Thomas concerning the uselessness of theory (Thomas, 1997).

This chapter is about the theory–practice relationship and how it could be conceived. No doubt the problem of the relation between theory and practice can be addressed at different levels and from different perspectives. After a small survey concerning what meaning can attached to the term "theory", Robert Dearden (1984) concludes that "…the distinction between theory and practice is not just one distinction but a shifting set of contrasts made to serve different, although possibly equally valid, purposes" (p.6). I shall inquire into a select few and by no means do I think I have exhausted the possibilities. Ultimately, I shall argue, the relationship is best understood as a "gap".

The relationship of theory and practice

The traditional view of the nature of educational theory, as normative and practice-oriented, is closely tied to the theory–practice relation – the two issues are usually treated as different aspects of the same problem. To invoke Ewald Terhart's "map" of the field of education once more (cf. Chapter 2), the nature of educational theory is traditionally treated as if the entire field consisted of the corner where Terhart places the qualification of pedagogical practitioners (Terhart, 2016).

Discussions of the relationship between theory and practice tend to take place at high levels of abstraction and involve large, undifferentiated conceptions of both theory and practice; presumably exemplifying the kind of vague understanding of theory that Thomas criticizes. I would like to introduce here a distinction concerning the use of the term theory that is reminiscent of Bromberger's (1963) distinction between "theory" as denoting an entire domain or field, as in "educational theory", and "theory" as treating *of* some specified phenomenon, as in Piaget's theory of cognitive development (cf. Chapter 3). The distinction I now have in mind is a distinction between "strong" and "weak" notions of theory and of the theoretical. A strong notion of theory is akin to Bromberger's well-articulated theory that deals with some delineated aspect of the world. The "weak" sense of theory and the theoretical captures much of what Thomas talks about: claims, views and beliefs that go well beyond the observational, both concerning terms and assumptions, but which may fall short of explicit articulation and be too "loose" to qualify as a theory both on the Semantic Conception and on the Received View. Thomas is surely right that "theory" is often used in this loose or weak sense. But instead of dismissing it outright, let us see what we can do with it. Thus, in this section we are going to look at the big theory–practice picture, paint with broad strokes, and use "theory" and "practice" alike as large, undifferentiated terms, encompassing both strong and weak notions. "Theory" is roughly what we think, and practice is roughly what we do. An array of different possible relationships emerges.

Theory and practice as a dichotomy

I pick up here on an end left loose in Chapter 8: Erich Weniger's description of the theory–practice relationship. Or more correctly, what he saw as a common understanding of it: neatly divided, all theory grey (and dull, I infer), all practice teeming with life and real people (Weniger, 1990). The dichotomous view implies an understanding of theory as the opposite of practice, as mentioned by Thomas (1997, p.82). Theory then becomes everything that practice is not, and vice versa: theory is general and abstract, practice is particular and concrete. Weniger finds this view puzzling, if not paradoxical. Writing in the 1920s, he attributed the origin of the dichotomy to the institutionalization of teacher education and the professionalization of teachers. The teachers themselves were among the first to claim that professionalization was dependent upon theory. The paradox Weniger wrestles with consists of two incompatible assumptions: on the one hand, the assumption that the *raison d'être* of educational theory is its usefulness or even necessity for practice and its improvement; on the other hand, the assumption that theory and practice are "reinlich geschieden", neatly divided.

Weniger's essay was originally published in 1929, but his identified "allgemeine Auffassung" might still hold sway in certain quarters. Theory and practice are very different entities: practice contains emotions, experiences, actions, communication, actual individuals, etc., whereas theory contains symbols, calculi and abstractions that may not even be recognizable in practice. Yet it may be an exaggeration to call the divide a dichotomy. Weniger does not discuss in any detail what he actually takes the divide to be besides neat and clean-cut, but to treat two entities as being in a dichotomous relationship is serious business. A dichotomy is an exclusive disjunction, an either-or constellation with no middle, no intermediary steps and no third alternatives. Applied to the theory–practice relation it becomes the view that whatever would fall into the domain covered by theory and practice is *either* theory *or* practice: one or the other, never both at the same time. They mutually rule each other out. One must agree with Weniger that if this is what "reinlich geschieden" means, it definitely does not bode well for the professionalization of teachers. Theory and practice are effectively cut off from one another.

The theory–practice relation as a gap

If you conceive of the theory–practice relation as a dichotomy, but still want theory to play a role for practice and vice versa, the solution is to give up the dichotomy. Instead, you can perceive the relation as a gap. This will, at least at the outset, preserve the idea that theory and practice are different things, while at the same time incorporating a possibility of connection between the two. The metaphor of a "gap" inevitably invokes the metaphor of a "bridge". So the theory–practice problem becomes one of building suitable bridges between the two, and you want to bridge the gap because you think that theory and practice should somehow hang together, perform certain functions for each other. What kind of bridge you might want to build obviously depends on what kind of gap you diagnose, and whether you think the gap ought to be bridged. If you are a theoretician, pursuing theory for its own sake, you probably would not see a theory–practice problem at all.

Gaps can be variously described as "distance", "difference" or "mismatch" between theory and practice. One way to bridge it that immediately springs to mind, and which we have touched upon before, is the is-ought relation. Theory represents what *is*; practice deals in what *ought* to be and what *ought* to be done. Leo Friedrich, briefly mentioned in Chapter 2, holds that since the process of education broadly conceived invariably contains normative elements, this should be reflected in our theorizing about education. He depicts educational theories as being situated on an axis between factual and normative considerations, moving back and forth along this axis and mediating between the factual and the normative (Friedrich, 1987). It is hard to imagine what kind of entity this would make educational theory, but we will leave that particular problem aside. It is more important here to note that Friedrich apparently has no problem with putting *is* and *ought* together. But if you, like Paul Hirst (1966), hold the view that normative implications can never be derived from factual premises alone, the gap between theory and practice becomes logically unbridgeable – unless of course you add a normative element to the factual premises, or you make it the job of the educational theory to translate factual premises into normative ones. That would make educational theory secondary and dependent and render its scientific status dubious indeed. Or one could adopt a laxer and more pragmatic stance to the is-ought problem, and derive *ought* from *is* in the manner we do every day (being read to stimulates interest in literature, so parents ought to read bedtime stories to their children every night), without worrying about the inference supposedly being logically insurmountable.

At this point it is pertinent to introduce theory in the weak or "loose" sense. Theory in this sense is vitally important to the theory–practice debate. When Wilfred Carr (1995) claims that educational practice is fundamentally theory-laden, his claim relies on the weak sense of theory. Carr's view here is analogous to Norwood Russell Hanson's famous thesis that all observation is theory-laden (Hanson, 1958). There is no such thing as theory-free observation, Hanson argues. Observation is essentially *seeing that* and as such it is an epistemic achievement (not a perceptual one); all observation is shaped by the purposes and prior knowledge of the observer. It is not unreasonable to construe the theory–practice relationship along the lines of the theory–observation relationship. And that seems to be what Carr is doing: educational practice, he says, is full of more or less implicit assumptions concerning unobservable entities and connections of various kinds – in other words, theory in the weak sense.

If Carr is right and practice is infused with (the weak kind of) theory, then there is no gap between theory and practice. The theory will always fit the practice, simply because it is the way in which practice is understood and described. So if we still want to speak of a gap, we have to rethink it. We could, for example, diagnose a gap between strong and weak theory. We could envision building a bridge between them to allow mutual interchange; we may want to revise the strong theory to make it fit the weak theory; or we may want to argue that the theory with which practice is laden is inadequate. In that case, there is a gap between theory and practice in the sense that the theory which *does* inform practice is not the theory we *want* to inform practice. We may thus wish to revise, transform or replace the old weak theory, old ways of seeing and understanding, with new allegedly better or more adequate theory.

I presume that practice can be laden with theory both in the strong and in the weak sense. Some parts of practice may be informed by carefully evidenced theories, for instance concerning reading instruction. Practice, as we have seen, is multifaceted and multilayered and it is unreasonable to expect strong theories to cover every nook and cranny of it. It is far more likely that there will always be theory in the weak sense, in the form of preconceptions, prior knowledge, (mis) understandings, prejudices and unarticulated assumptions that shape what we perceive, see and do. Theory in the strong sense, I submit, cannot hope to replace all weak theory in a theory-laden practice. As my experience as a student teacher taught me: too many theories of the strong kind to handle at the same time would be unmanageable.

The theory–practice relation as an equilibrium

What could be an alternative to a gap between theory and practice? One possibility is to view them as reciprocal or as maintaining some form of equilibrium (see Kvernbekk, 2012, for an in-depth discussion). A good many educationists, John Dewey among them, favor a reciprocal relationship between theory and practice. They tend to emphasize the exchange between theory and practice, such that both are continually revised in light of each other.

Such continual revision, I shall argue, amounts to keeping a kind of equilibrium between theory and practice. It may take slightly different forms and it may also involve an additional layer of complexity to our understanding of theory (in its broad undifferentiated meaning), which I will come to below. A dynamic relationship between theory and practice that allows both to develop is an attractive picture, and furthermore provides a response to the problem of the gap (if one thinks that a gap is a problem). So suppose you have diagnosed a gap between theory and practice, and you want to close the gap by bringing them in line, rather than by building a bridge: which would you change? The theory or the practice? That depends on the status you accord to the theory.

To get a handle on this question I shall briefly invoke Roger Wertheimer's useful distinction between what he terms systems of actuality and systems of ideality (Wertheimer, 1972). By "system" Wertheimer means a "more or less well organized and integrated system of laws … concerning some more or less well-defined sets of properties of some more or less well-defined set of objects" (p.88). A scientific theory is a paradigm case of a system of actuality; a moral code is a paradigmatic case of a system of ideality. Both types, he says, entertain the same form of laws; the difference lies in what is *done* with them. I should interject here that the formulation of a law that Wertheimer has in mind is clearly reminiscent of the Received View and Hempel's rendering of it (see Chapter 3), but that need not concern us here. What concerns us here is the potential use of the two systems. Within systems of ideality, Wertheimer states, authors or speakers do *not* intend to describe regularities in actual behavior. Rather, a system of ideality describes what people do when they act in conformity with this system. If people do not act accordingly, we do not judge the system of ideality and its laws to be wrong; instead, we judge the actors to be wrong in doing what they do – we use the law to evaluate their behavior. Hence, we demand that practice changes, to conform to the theory.

In systems of actuality, on the other hand, the law is judged to be wrong if cases of deviation are discovered. That is to say, instances and counter-instances are used to assess the law. And in cases of mismatch, we revise the law so that it becomes in line with the observations – or we revise the theory to line up with practice. Now, to repeat the question: if you find a gap between theory and practice in education, which should or would you revise, the theory or the practice?

In some cases, this seems fairly straightforward. Evaluation theory (cf. Chapter 5) concerns assessment and ranking of various performances in accordance with a given set of criteria. Performances that do not measure up might fail – it is clearly the performance, the practice, that has to change, not the theory. It is the same with standards of professional conduct, for example as discussed by MacIntyre (cf. Chapter 8): the standards inherent in his conception of practice demand obedience. If your performance is not up to the current standards, you strive to change your performance. That is to say, if we fail to live up to norms, regulations or standards, it is *we* who are to be blamed, not the norms, regulations or standards. In mismatches between theory and practice in systems of ideality, the *practice* changes. Unless, of course, we judge that the norms, regulations and standards are unduly strict or downright unrealistic so that nobody *can* live up to them. Neither norms nor criteria nor regulations nor standards are hewn in stone.

But what about other kinds of educational theory? Is a normative goal-directed theory best viewed as a system of actuality or a system of ideality? I have insisted, both in Chapter 4 and in Chapter 7, that normative goal-directed theories do make empirical claims, namely about the movement of some teleological entity toward a more or less well-defined goal state. It is an empirical question whether such movement takes place or not, and in this respect a goal-directed theory is a system of actuality. If the theory does not bring the results it is supposed to bring, we judge that the theory is in need of revision. On the other hand, and this is an intriguing possibility: could it be that such theories exert normative pressure on practice, so that if practice fails to live up to the goal states depicted by the theory, we judge that practice is deficient and in need of revision? If so, we treat normative goal-directed theories as systems of ideality. Maybe the question of which kind of system normative goal-directed theories belong to must be determined contextually, according to which feature one wishes to accentuate.

Before getting to Dewey, I would like to very briefly bring back Reidar Myhre's view (Myhre, 1980), touched upon in Chapter 8. At the outset, Myhre seems to have a sequential view, claiming that practice (e.g. of upbringing) existed long before any articulated educational theory did – although, one might think that theory in the weak sense existed in this practice. But once theory in the strong sense came into existence, it had to enter into some form of relationship with practice, and Myhre perceives the job of (strong) theory as analyzing and organizing practice. Parts of practice, I infer, may be reorganized as a result, but some parts may remain unchanged after analysis, and practice as a whole, Myhre says, is large enough to maintain its own dignity and relative independence of theory. There is thus no need for practice to change to conform to theory. There might be a need for theory to change to conform to practice: if the job of the theory is to analyze practice and clarify practical issues, but otherwise leave practice untouched, it may need to be revised to be able to do its job properly. On this view practice takes precedence and guides theory.

Let us back up a bit and look at how a reciprocal relationship might come into being in the first place. John Dewey (1991) is a good place to start. Here is how he explains the relationship between habits of thought (practice) and rules of thought (theory):

> Any habit is a way or manner of action, not a particular act or deed. When it is formulated, it becomes, as far as it is accepted, a rule, or more generally, a principle or "law" of action. It can hardly be denied that there are habits of inference and that they may be formulated as rules or principles.
>
> (p.21)

Hence, habits of inference begin by being simply habits, ways of doing it, but develop into rules. Some rules, Dewey says, may be necessary to every successful inferential inquiry. "Successful" means that the inquiry in the long run yields the results that are either confirmed in further inquiry, or corrected by the use of the same procedures. Thus, the reciprocity of theory and practice is close-knit indeed, albeit with a bias in favor of practice. Rules (theory) arise out of practice, become crystalized and articulated, then feed back into practice in a way that modifies practice, making it more effective or adequate. As Israel Scheffler (1973) comments in his insightful and incisive explication of Dewey's position, the function of theory and thought is to reconstruct practice by deliberately solving problems as they occur, more efficiently than stereotypical repetition and random variation could (p.151).

As I said, one can well understand the allure of this picture. Theory and practice are very much in line with one another and exist in a dynamic equilibrium, both being useful for one another. We should not wonder that this view has attracted a number of followers in many domains. But let us take a closer look. The equilibrium picture leaves us with theory that never gets out of practice. Its justification depends on its practical, instrumental merits, to what degree it yields the required results. We should not think that the only function of theory is to transform practice. As Scheffler points out, ideas, thoughts and theory come in all kinds, and "only certain simple types can be analyzed as instruments for transforming the world" (p.154). Scheffler thus thinks that Dewey's conception of the function of theory is unduly narrow. I tentatively conclude at this point that while some theories within a field or domain, such as education, might well be thought of as arising from practice and passing back into practice, it would be a mistake to demand this of *all* theories (in the strong version of theory). It would amount to imposing an unnecessary constraint on theories. In any given domain, theories may serve different functions, and besides, we should not *a priori* reject theory as an academic pursuit for its own sake.

One more perspective remains to be discussed in this section: Nelson Goodman's take on the equilibrium issue (Goodman, 1983). He provides a different way of bringing theory and practice into line – in this case it is not a question of reciprocity or mutual exchange, but of balance. Goodman specifically writes about justification, but I shall generalize his views to cover theory and practice. Then basic idea, then, is that theory and practice mutually justify each other when brought into an equilibrium. A lengthy quote from Goodman makes clear how he thinks about this:

> How do we justify a *de*duction? Plainly, by showing that it conforms to the general rule of deductive inference. An argument that so conforms is justified or valid, even if its conclusion happens to be false. ... Yet, of course, the rules themselves must eventually be justified. The validity of a deduction depends not upon conformity to any purely arbitrary rules we may contrive, but upon conformity to valid rules. ... But how is the validity of rules to be determined? ... Principles of deductive inference are justified by their conformity with accepted deductive practice. Their validity depends upon accordance with the particular deductive inferences we actually make and sanction.
>
> (p.63)

This form of justification looks blatantly circular. Inferences (practice) are justified if they conform to the rules of inference (theory), and the rules (theory) are justified if they conform to accepted practice. Goodman freely admits that his argument is circular, but denies that it poses a problem. The circle is not a vicious one, but rather a virtuous one, he argues:

> The point is that rules and particular inferences alike are being brought into agreement with each other. ... The process of justification is a delicate one of making mutual adjustments between rules and accepted inferences, and in the agreement achieved lies the only justification needed to either.
>
> (p.64)

Clearly there is no gap between theory and practice on such a view. This is not the continuous transformation Dewey envisions; this rather hints at a more static picture. One can perhaps understand the allure of this picture, too: theory and practice in perfect balance, mutually justifying each other. Fine for practitioners seeking justification for their activities; fine for educational researchers seeking justification for their practically oriented theories.

On the other hand, this way of understanding the theory–practice relation would be grist to Thomas' mill, in particular his critique of theory as a force of conservatism (1997, p.76). And rightfully so! It is all too easy to imagine that if theory and practice are kept in check by one another and mutually justify each other, they also mutually reinforce each other. But the blame does not lie exclusively with theory; it lies equally as much with practice. For even practice can be a force of conservatism, serving to reinforce and conserve existing sets of concepts, rules and ways of thinking. Interestingly, I think Thomas' conservatism critique applies to Myhre, but inversely, so to speak. For Myhre, practice as a whole is an entity unto itself and maintains its own dignity by precisely not being impinged by theory. It may thus serve to reinforce the status quo.

But mutual conservatism is not the only problem with Goodman's view. If rules are valid because they accord with established practice, then invalid rules must be thought of as failing to accord with established practice. Invalid rules should be dropped, Goodman says (p.64). But there are obvious counterexamples here. We may all agree that jumping to conclusions is an invalid inferential principle. Yet many people, including myself on various occasions, make inferences in accordance with it. And what about *modus ponens*, an inferential rule that is thought to be valid? It fails to codify inferential practice because people often do not reason in accordance with it, and so should be deemed invalid and dropped. Harvey Siegel (1992), in his discussion of Goodman's equilibrium, concludes that accordance with established practice is neither necessary nor sufficient for the justification and validity of inferential rules.

Furthermore, just as Myhre's and Dewey's views discussed above seemed to have a certain bias in favor of practice, so does Goodman's equilibrium. As Hilary Putnam puts it, in his foreword to Goodman's book, "What he [i.e. Goodman] insists upon, and all that he insists upon in this connection, is that *any* proposed solution be judged by its ability to systematize what we actually do" (1983, p. xiii). But why should we regard systematization of practice as central to the justification of theory? The answer, Siegel argues, is that we should not think so. It is rather the case, he says, that "practice affords no justification to principles which fit it. The reason it does not is simple: inferential practice itself stands in need of justification" (1992, p.36). This is eminently generalizable to educational practice. As a matter of principle, all practice is open to critique and challenge. We ought to be very careful, then, what role we give to practice in the justification of our theories – a topic that latches on to the evaluation of theories discussed in Chapter 7. I generally have in mind here evaluations that in different ways involve practice, such as usefulness, relevance, effectiveness; and I especially have in mind Hirst's claim that educational theory must pass the test of practice (Hirst, 1993). There is no telling exactly what this test is and how we judge whether a given theory has passed it or not.

I conclude that while Deweyan reciprocity and Goodmanian equilibrium no doubt overcome the gap between theory and practice and thus serve to bring theory and practice in line, they also make theory dependent on practice for its existence, its application and its justification. And with no distance between theory and practice, theory is robbed of its potential to provide new perspectives, new ways of seeing, or indeed new critiques of existing practice. Instead, it has all opportunities to become the force of conservatism that Thomas takes it to be.

Personal theory

The term "personal theory" denotes the idea that practitioners, or perhaps educationists in general, should develop their own "theory" to guide their activities, to use in reflecting upon the same activities, etc. Gary Thomas is deeply skeptical of such theories, and I would tend to agree with him. The knowledge and skills practitioners of all stripes possess are surely of different kinds and cover different issues: learning theory, didactics, planning skills, rules of thumb, assumptions, prejudices, etc. It is hard to imagine how such divergent entities could be amalgamated into one single coherent theory. However, we cannot deny that practitioners have a big stock of knowledge and beliefs, some in the form of strong theory and some in the form of weak theory, and some in the form of unarticulated preconceptions and misconceptions. Thomas, drawing on Foucault, again sees the threat of conservatism as the main point of criticism:

> Looking at student essays and academic articles in education, one of the dangers of this structured reflection (as it represents theory in education) is in its conformity to the archive, its desire not to be anarchic or radical, but rather to cleave to the structure of established and respectable methodologies, literatures, rules and procedures. ... It is the placement of personal educational theory within the archive that surely makes it so often anodyne.
>
> (1997, p.87)

Thomas favors fragmented, local and specific knowledge, refusal of and resistance to established modes of thought. "This is in contrast to the often anodyne reflections that pass as theorizing in education", he says (p.87). My worries about personal theory are akin to Thomas', but on a much smaller scale. Thomas moves at the political level; I move at the level of practice. Thus, again I think that the problem of personal theory is that it might serve to reinforce and justify one's own practice, parallel to the Goodmanian equilibrium I discussed above.

Let me bring Weniger and his conception of an educational theory, briefly discussed in Chapter 2, back into the picture. It will be remembered that he distinguishes between three degrees of theory, which must be understood to make up one theory; the degrees representing different levels or aspects. The first is an ethical *a priori*, often wholly implicit outlook on the world. The second is the practitioner's articulable collection of knowledge and beliefs; quite divergent in character, consisting of doctrines, rules of thumb, experiences, etc. The third is a theory whose job it is to monitor the consistency between the practitioner's theories of the first and second degree. Any discrepancy between the two, between what you do and what you say you do, will result in false, insincere practice, Weniger says. They thus have to be kept in line with each other. Or brought in line, if the third theory detects an imbalance.

Theories of the third degree are *theoretical*, Weniger insists. But like the other two, the third one never gets out of practice. We can easily envision a theory of the first degree growing organically out of practice or out of social life in general, becoming less implicit and more articulated by way of a theory of the second degree, but even the third-degree theory is meant to return to practice and make practice more systematic, more rational and less random (Weniger, 1990, p.42). It will be recalled that all three degrees of theories are personal. They belong to the practitioner. It stands to reason that if a practitioner uses all three theories and finds that as a result of this his or her practice has become more systematic and rational, he or she will regard the theory as justified. Theory and practice mutually reinforce each other. At play here, of course, is the personalized understanding of practice (cf. Chapter 8). One should not be surprised that a personalized understanding of practice is intimately connected to personal theory.

The Norwegian philosopher of education Lars Løvlie once launched a view of three levels of *practice* that are strikingly similar to Weniger's three levels of theory (Løvlie, 1974). Practice-level P1 represents concrete actions, such as the ones we find in Roar Pettersen's examples of practice in Chapter 8. Level P2 is concerned with planning, designing activities, and of justification of activity and actions. Level P3 concerns ethical reflections on the other two levels, perhaps specifically on P1 – is what I do morally right, professionally responsible, etc. All of this is practice, and it is a personalized understanding of practice. This is "my" practice; I plan, I think, I execute and I reflect. It is also an example of theory-laden practice: the knowledge, beliefs and assumptions I employ when I plan, think, execute and reflect. The parallel between this conception of practice and Weniger's conception of theory is striking. It is hard to say where theory ends and practice begins, and vice versa. I conclude that when our focus is on the individual practitioner, theory and practice are intimately tied together. This intimate connection does not necessarily lead to unfortunate circles of mutual reinforcement of the two, but it can. The biggest problem, as I see it, it that theories of this kind do not transcend practice. They afford no eagle-eye view from which to evaluate practice – for that, we need a gap between practice and some theory in the strong sense.

Experience rather than theory?

It is possible to adopt the view that practice is self-sufficient; that practitioners learn everything they need to know in practice and from practice. In that case, we obviously do not speak of a relationship between theory and practice anymore, since theory is taken out of the equation. The self-sufficiency argument goes something like this: practice, understood as performance of certain activities, implies knowing both *what* to do and *how* to do it. Theory is neither necessary nor sufficient for performing these activities. It is not sufficient since knowing the theory does not tell you how to act in practice, and it is not necessary since one can learn to perform these actions without recourse to theory at all. Practice, in other words, is theory-free and sufficient unto itself.

It might have been something like this that I and my student teacher fellows had in mind upon making the discovery that the theories we learned in college neither fit reality in schools nor worked as expected. If you have no need of theory, what can you have instead? Experience, we thought. Experience is a difficult term to handle, and proper treatment of it falls outside the scope of this book. I shall content myself with a couple of observations. First, while practice and experience might be declared theory-free if we have strong theory in mind, it might be harder to do so if we have weak theory in mind. Let me invoke Weniger (1990) again. Any whiff of a dichotomy between theory and practice, he says, reflects a fundamental misconception of the theory–practice relation. He argues extensively and passionately against practitioners who reject theory and instead claim that practical experience is sufficient – sufficient for good, responsible practice, that is. For what is meant by practical experience? How is it gained? Weniger's position is that "Erfahrung ist in Wahrheit immer das Ergebnis einer Fragestellung, also einer – wenn auch nicht ausdrüchlichen – Theorie" [In truth, experience is always the result of a question, that is, a theory – even if the theory is not explicit] (p.33). Every practice is theory-laden, Weniger states. This theory may be undifferentiated and in the form of assumptions and more or less connected beliefs; it belongs to the practitioners and is expressed in the way they interpret situations and in how they act in them. And more to the point: without this theory, practitioners can have no practical experiences because they will be unable to ask questions of the situation. Weniger makes it quite clear that references to practical experience, "die Erfahrung lehrt es so" [experience shows it] (p.37), frequently serves to justify sloppy or inadequate practice. If Weniger is right, then, theory – at least in the weak form – is heavily embroiled in the very making of practical experience. Different theoretical assumptions give rise to different questions, which in turn give rise to different practical experiences. It is of vital importance for Weniger that the theory of the practitioner provides a fundamental openness to practice, even if, as I have argued, the theory never gets out of practice. I have long since adopted Weniger's attitude toward experience: "...es darf keine Tyrannis der 'praktischen Erfahrung' gegenüber dem jeweils Neuen der erzieherischen Aufgabe geben", he declares (p.40). There must never be a tyranny of practical experience toward the always *new* of the educational situation.

Second, also harking back to the theory–practice dichotomy, people who espouse such views frequently couch the problem in terms of generality versus particularity. Practice is inevitably particular: students are particular; teachers are particular; objects, events and situations are particular. Generalized knowledge, for example in the form of theories, does not fit or does not work. And so, one might conclude, what you need is particular, local knowledge. As an example, let me briefly inquire into an article by teacher educators Jos Kessels and Fred Korthagen (1996). They have refined their views since then, and I am not targeting their views in particular. The 1996 article is simply a good, clear example of this kind of view. Discussing what kind of knowledge a student teacher needs to become a teacher, Kessels and Korthagen adopt an Aristotelian perspective: "...what we need ... is not scientific understanding (episteme) but practical wisdom (phronesis)", they say (p.19), and furthermore, that "the point of phronesis is that the knowledge a student needs is *perceptual* rather than *conceptual*" (p.21, my emphasis). Episteme is viewed as research-based, generalized knowledge applicable to a wide range of cases. Perceptual knowledge is practical, it is about concrete particulars, and it is acquired through experience. Such knowledge, they argue,

> ...is the basis for a proper judgment of the situation and for an appropriate choice of behavior. ... Given such perception, no further proof or theoretical justification is needed.
>
> (p.20)

I find this to be a striking formulation of the idea that practice is self-sufficient. This seems to mean that a problem, a diagnosis, a situation, etc. can be known just by observing what is there to be observed, namely O-entities, without making any inferences and without the need for any theoretical justification. T-entities are not observable and therefore cannot be perceived in this way; they require T-terms for their potential identification and use in situational understanding. But the job of the teacher educator, Kessels and Korthagen claimed, is to help the students *see*, not to teach them a number of concepts: "For the 'matter of the practical' is not helped very much by such conceptual knowledge" (p.21). The contrast to Weniger could not be more dramatic. I shall return to their and similar views in a subsequent section.

I would like to bring back in Charles Clark (1976), whose views about education I briefly touched in Chapter 2. Clark's views are experience-oriented in that he argues that education can only be observed from *within* the practice. Practice can only be described by reference to the principle that is being practiced, he says (p.15). That is, not from any perspective external to practice. It stands to reason that you also must be a practitioner to identify the principle. Educational theory (principles) becomes a matter that is exclusive to practitioners: formed from within practice and recognized from within practice. Moreover, Clark states, to be able to observe *education* you have to embrace the values and principles constitutive of the concept (p.15). This is a radical view indeed – to recognize and identify an educational practice you not only need to know the principle it embodies; you must be *committed* to this principle. Mutual reinforcement of principle and practice becomes an even greater danger – if you have internalized the principle which informs and shapes your practice, made it yours and are emotionally committed to it, you are not likely to want to change it. Besides, Clark's requirements combined rule out most, let alone all, researchers as legitimate observers of education.

My own business in this section is to argue that experience may share more likenesses with theory than advocates of the self-sufficiency view might think. Theory, it will be recalled, is general and abstract in character. It is true that practice is particular. But *experience*, as when people explain what they have learned from many years of practice, is *general* in character. Experiential learning and knowledge surely draw on linguistic sources and make use of abstract terms and theoretical terms. Teachers may thus learn from their experience that students' motivation increases when they receive feedback on their written assignments – a piece of knowledge as general as any theory. They may learn that certain methods of reading instruction work better than others – a general piece of knowledge whose construction also involves comparison. The construction of experiential knowledge, I submit, surely proceeds along at least some of the same lines as theory construction: a selection of salient features (which means that many details about each student and situation are selected away), use of unobservables (such as references to student beliefs, understandings, motivation, intelligence, etc.) and induction (generalization across individuals or situations, often expressed in terms of *most, often, many, usually, most places*, etc.). What generalizations we make and what we therefore think we learn from our experience depends crucially on which features we choose to pay attention to, which form the basis for our inductions.

Summary

The relationship of theory and practice is a much-discussed topic in education and a perennial problem in all professions. To bring out the various possible relationships as clearly as possible I have looked at theory and practice as large undifferentiated entities – with one important qualification: a distinction between "strong" and "weak" theory. People who diagnose a gap between theory and practice (and subsequently want to bridge it) tend to think that the gap is between practice and theory in the strong sense, that is, well-articulated theory dealing with some carefully delineated aspect of the world. There will always be weak theory in practice, in the form of prior beliefs, preconceptions, (mis)understandings, etc.

I opt for a form of gap between practice and theory in the strong sense, for the following reasons. First, we should keep the relationship flexible. The forms of theory and practice being in line that I have discussed (Dewey and Goodman) both depict theory as entering into *one* kind of relationship with practice. I have no objections to *some* theory being in line with practice, but I do not think that we should demand this of *all* theory. Surely we can envision many different functions for theory and different forms of theory–practice relationship, and it is important to keep this open. Second, we must leave room for theory for theory's own sake. Some "strong" theory could very well be developed specifically for practice, but theory is also a worthwhile academic pursuit in itself. Some theory should be left at a distance from practice or free of practice altogether. From this distance, theory could provide new ways of seeing, surprising angles, incisive critique or mind-boggling perspectives – all of which I think theory should do. Thus, as a matter of principle I settle for a version of the gap as the default theory–practice relationship.

10 Theory applications and other uses

In this chapter I propose to inquire into the various uses that theories can be put to. I by no means presume that my inquiry is exhaustive. To set the stage, recall the challenge that Gary Thomas' (1997) views on theory in education (cf. Chapter 3) poses to anybody who is fond of theory, including me. His main thesis is that a lack of definition has led "theory" to come to loosely denote intellectual endeavors, nothing more. He cites Fred Kerlinger's definition of theory (p.78): theory as a set of interrelated constructs and propositions – a definition that can now be recognized as the calculus of the Received View (RV). He cites George Mouly's definition, which says that theory is a convenience for organizing facts and constructs into manageable form – the toolshed view, as Thomas calls it (p.78). The name is apt, since this definition can now be recognized as being antirealist in spirit: theories do not represent the phenomenon but are tools for use. These definitions are completely different, Thomas argues, as different "as chalk and cheese". However, they may not be quite as different as they appear at first glance; both are antirealist, and the facts and constructs of Mouly's definition can be organized into the calculus of Kerlinger's definition. However, Thomas argues that "theory" cannot have two or more meanings so widely disparate if it is to be used seriously. Theory is not useful in education, he claims; it is a force of conservatism that reinforces existing sets of practices and methods (pp.75–76). He runs through a number of examples and concludes that theory in education is antagonistic to pluralism in ideas: fertility is sacrificed to orderliness (p.101). My initial response is threefold: theory is more dynamic than Thomas assumes; it might be wise to separate between a theory and its use, and the theory itself can hardly be blamed for sloppy or tradition-conserving uses of it. The first response should be gleaned from earlier chapters: neither parameters nor postulates are hewn in stone, but objects of debate and evaluation. Much ground needs to be covered before I can justify the wisdom of separating a theory from the method of its use; that is the topic of the following section. The third response is simply a general conviction that theory use requires thought.

Inroads to application based on the Semantic Conception of theories

This section picks directly up from the meta-theoretical discussion in Chapter 3. I would like to set the stage by taking up again Giere's map metaphor. I am very fond of this metaphor and I have referred to it in both Chapter 3 and 7, but in this chapter we shall look at it from another angle, namely application. A map is a highly versatile form of representation. According to the mapmaker's intentions, maps can be made to represent features of landscapes such as roads, rivers and mountains; they can represent temperatures, or they can represent global distribution of wealth. Whichever parameters are selected, simplification is necessary if a map is to be useful. As Mein Herr from Lewis Carroll's story argues, a map on the scale of the landscape itself is useless (cf. Chapter 7). Maps have to be manageable to be useful. We shrink them to manageable size, and we simplify the landscape to be mapped. And then what happens when we use them?

Suppose you are hiking in the mountains. You have a map to help you get safely from a to b. The map will tell you about relative locations of roads, villages, relative distances, trails, streams, bogs, shelters, how steep the mountain side is, and so on. But will it tell you absolutely everything you need to know to get from a to b? No, I suggest. It will tell you much of what you need to know. But it will not tell you that a recent flooding destroyed the bridge across the stream; it will not tell you to wear rubber boots (Wellingtons) rather than leather hiking boots; it will not tell you that the rocks are slippery; it will not tell you whether you will meet other people along the way; it will not tell you that there have recently been ten bear sightings in the area; and it will not tell you that two fir trees were uprooted in a storm and are now blocking the trail. All of these things are contextual and you will have to negotiate them along the way. The map provides direction and overview; the landscape provides details and particulars. And the particulars will vary – next time you hike along the same trail, there is a new bridge in place. There may even be changes to the route, such that the map is no longer accurate. Landscape navigation requires a combination of abstract information, represented by a map, and contextual information concerning the particulars of the landscape. Now, I am going to suggest, much the same is the case with application of theory.

Now we are back to theory in the strong sense, theories of the kind I have analyzed in Chapters 4, 5 and 6 – neither theory in the weak sense nor theory as domain or field. The Semantic Conception (SC) provides a perspective on the application of theories; roughly parallel to the use of maps I sketched above, but with a greater level of technical details. Let me reiterate: on SC, a scientific theory

> ...does not deal with phenomena in all of their complexity; rather, it is concerned with certain kinds of phenomena only insofar as their behavior is determined by, or characteristic of, a small number of parameters abstracted from those phenomena.
>
> (Suppe, 1989, p.65)

On this view, then, theories are concerned with characterizing the behavior of models or abstract systems and not phenomena. All theories, Suppe says, involve an *as if* – they describe what phenomena *would have* been *if* no other parameters exerted any influence on them. All theories are *abstract* in this sense; many factors, attributes, causes and relations characteristic of the phenomenon will fall outside the scope of the theory. I trust the analyses in Chapters 4, 5 and 6 have borne out this feature in educational theories. Theories are *idealized* if they contain parameters which for some reason cannot take on the allowable values of the parameters (e.g. human black boxes). This means that only when the idealized conditions are met can the theory directly predict what will happen. Typically, however, idealized conditions are not met. Like all scientific theories, educational theories concern how phenomena will behave in idealized, isolated circumstances, not in concrete situations. That entails that educational theories cannot be directly applied to practice. This fact significantly changes the theory–practice ballgame and a thorough revision of our ideas of how theory is related to practice is needed. Wilfred Carr's views (Carr, 1986) provide an instructive contrast. Recall his description of educational theories as theories of theory and practice, and rival views of educational theory therefore incorporate rival views of how theory relates to practice. In crystallized form:

> …ideas about the nature of educational theory are always ideas about the nature of educational practice and always incorporate a latent conception of how, in practice, the theory should be used.
>
> (Carr, 1986, p.177)

I am going to argue for the opposite conclusion: that we do much better to distinguish between a theory and the method of its application.

One-step and two-step relations between theory and practice

It is evident from Carr's description that he (at least in this 1986 article) thought that a theory is directly used in practice; that there is a one-step relation between theory and practice (or whichever phenomenon the theory treats of). This is an intuitive and understandable way of conceiving the theory–practice relation. It is also reminiscent of RV. This is by no means to suggest that people who understand the theory–practice relation as a one-step relation are positivists, far from it. It is rather to suggest that their assumptions concerning the direct application of theories to phenomena show some affinity to the role of correspondence rules in RV. In fact, the affinity is sufficiently large for the same criticisms to apply. Wilfred Carr's 1986 views will serve as an example.

On RV, the empirical meaning of the theory is provided by the correspondence rules. The correspondence rules, it will be remembered from Chapter 3, serve several functions in a theory. They define T-terms, they couple together T-terms and O-terms, and most importantly for present purposes – they specify admissible procedures for applying theory to the phenomenon and tell us how a law (law here in the positivist sense, as a universal empirical generalization) manifests itself directly in the behavior of the phenomenon. Since the correspondence rules themselves are considered part of the theory, it follows that the theory determines its own use. It is for this reason that the behavior of actual phenomena can be deduced from the theoretical statements; in other words, the interpreted formal system describes the *actual* behavior of entities in the world. Behavior deduced from the theoretical statements can be a prediction about what will happen in some specified circumstances, or an explanation of what actually did happen in some specified circumstances.

Now, Carr's claim that educational theories incorporate a latent conception of how they should be used in practice offers an obvious parallel to the notion of correspondence rules. On RV, the correspondence rules specify how the theory is to be applied in much the same manner as Carr claimed to be the case for educational theories. The set of correspondence rules is thought to be finite; a feature that entails that the ways in which a theory can be applied are limited in number. Furthermore, since the set is an integral part of the theory, any change in it will result in a new theory, not in new ways of applying the same theory. Carr, not unsurprisingly, painted in broad strokes and provided no concrete examples of how an educational theory could determine its own use – such examples would indeed be hard to come by. Yet, it seems reasonable to at least to suggest that the set of application procedures is finite, since he spoke of *rival* conceptions of how a theory relates to practice. The procedures incorporated in one conception are surely not incorporated in a rival conception.

While RV embodies a one-step relation between theory and phenomenon, SC embodies a two-step relation. It stands to reason that if what a theory tells you is what the phenomenon *would have* been *if* the selected parameters were the only ones to influence it, the theory cannot really be expected to also tell you how the *actual* phenomenon will behave. At least not by itself. On SC, selected parameters and theoretical postulates make up a model of the phenomenon, an abstract and idealized replica of the phenomenon. The theory is directly about this model; for example, there are theoretical laws stating how the model will develop through a more or less defined state space. What we have is a two-step relation – one step between phenomenon and model, and another step between model and theory. The relation between theory and phenomenon is, therefore, a two-step relation, and the theory only *indirectly* characterizes the actual phenomenon and its equally actual behavior. It is this indirect, two-step relation which allows us to separate the theory from its method of application. As paradoxical as it may sound, I shall argue that this separation is a good thing, but also something of a double-edged sword. Most importantly, it provides great flexibility in theory application. The theory does not itself decide how it should be used: that is up to the *user*. I shall explore the implications of the two-step relation in some detail in subsequent sub-sections. But first let me wrap up the meta-theoretical points touched on so far. RV embodies the O/T distinction (see Chapter 3), SC does not. The reliance on the O/T distinction forces RV's account of correspondence rules to lump together a variety of different aspects of scientific theorizing and thereby obscure a number of epistemologically important features, most notably concerning application of theories. The idea that the correspondence rules specify how the laws of the theory manifest themselves in the behavior of the directly observable phenomenon may be clear and intuitively understandable, but it is far too rigid to be satisfactory for theories in a field such as education. SC, however, does not require the O/T distinction in the analysis of scientific theories, simply because theories are not applied directly to phenomena but rather to the intermediary model. This provides us with more adequate tools to grasp what is involved in application of theories and in the theory–practice relation. Use of theories, as we shall see, is no straightforward, simple process, but rather requires overview, knowledge, and skills of the user.

A brief note on theory testing

I am no methodologist and I have no particular interest in the testing of theories, but in this context a step-motherly note is warranted, for two reasons. First, just like the theory–practice relation, testing is concerned with the relationship between theory and phenomenon, albeit in a different way. And second, testing serves to bring out the complexities of the relationship between a theory and the phenomenon within its scope. While the account below takes the natural sciences as its assumed context – the founding fathers of SC get their examples from the natural sciences – there is no reason to think that things are any easier in fields such as education.

As we have seen, one of the functions of correspondence rules is to specify the experimental procedures for applying a theory to observable phenomena. It is this particular feature of RV that Patrick Suppes (1967) referred to, when he described it as "far too simple". He makes the point that,

> ...the story is much more complicated than the familiar remarks about co-ordinating definitions [i.e. correspondence rules] and empirical interpretations of theories would indicate. The kind of co-ordinating definitions often described by philosophers have their place in popular philosophical expositions of theories, but in the actual practice of testing scientific theories a more elaborate and more sophisticated formal machinery for relating a theory to data is required.
>
> (1967, p.62)

Suppes then goes on to outline a hierarchy of theories that intercedes between the scientific theory and the phenomenon. This hierarchy, he states, arises from the methodology of experimentation. This methodology is theoretical in nature and serves to develop the elaborate theories of experimentation which constitute the hierarchy. There is no simple procedure for giving correspondence rules for a theory, Suppes concludes (p.63).

Suppes has himself provided a fairly detailed account of the hierarchy of theories (Suppes, 1962). The discussion pertains to the experimental testing of theories with measurable parameters, notably physical theory, but would apply equally to non-experimental theories since they also require design and data. At the top of the hierarchy is the scientific theory itself. The connection of experimental data with the scientific theory requires a determination of the various data that are compatible with the theory. This is commonly called the *theory of the experiment*;

its purpose is to say which of the models described by the theory represents the phenomenon. The carrying out of the experiment requires a *theory of experimental design*, which is comprised of the setup, the instrumentation, the data-gathering procedures, and so on. This theory does not explicitly state all design principles, Suppes says: it tacitly assumes some conditions – usually designated the *ceteris paribus* conditions. The data obtained in the experiment will be "raw data", which must be transformed into data representing the model before the two sets of data can be compared. This transformation requires a *theory of the data*, which determines how raw data can be converted into hard data; that is, data about the model.

This leaves us with the following daunting picture of the "hook-up" between experiment and theory: it consists of *ceteris paribus* conditions, theory of experimental design, theory of data, theory of experiment. This should make it abundantly clear that RV's treatment of correspondence rules amounts to an oversimplification which obscures a number of important features concerning the relation of a theory to its phenomena. Frederick Suppe (1977) in addition suggested that the hierarchy shows that it is a mistake to view correspondence rules as integral components of theories. The possible (legitimate) ways of applying a theory to a phenomenon are in principle unlimited, and the number of correspondence rules should thus be unlimited. On RV, however, the number of correspondence rules is finite. Accordingly, there is no telling whether all the possible ways of applying a theory to a phenomenon can ever be specified in any set of correspondence rules. Thus, Suppe argues, it seems implausible to view the correspondence rules as components of the theory.

Prescription

It is high time to bring Paul Hirst and his conception of educational theory back into the picture. I quoted him at length in Chapter 2, and the crux of the quote merits repetition:

> The function of the theory is to determine precisely what shall and what shall not be done, say in education.
>
> (Hirst, 1966, p.40)

I am not after Hirst in particular, but I will use this formulation as an example of all thoughts to the effect that an educational theory in reality is a form of a recipe for action. The immediate context of this formulation is Hirst's well-known debate with O'Connor over the nature of educational theory. O'Connor – probably unbeknownst to himself – used RV as the yardstick for theories, and concluded that "theory" in education is mostly a courtesy title. Hirst, in response, developed his view that educational theories are different both in kind and function from scientific theories. Scientific theories are the end product of inquiry and represent what *is*; educational theories are constructed to determine and guide activity and they contain an *ought*. Hirst makes much of the is-ought distinction, and I hinted in Chapter 4 that I think he makes too much of it. Nevertheless, the *ought* plays an undeniable role in guiding and prescribing action. In passing, there is nothing absolute about *ought*. In everyday language use *ought* is associated with recommendations or advice – which one may choose to follow or not. Hirst's use of the stronger modal auxiliary *shall*, along with *determine precisely*, makes his conception of theory look more like a recipe for action.

At the outset it seems natural to endow goal-directed theories with an element of prescription; they do, after all, aim to tell us how to achieve a certain goal. This in itself is not a problem, and I shall come back to it subsequently. The questions for Hirst are rather how precise the determination of what shall be done should be, and who to blame when things do not go as expected (or praise when things do go as expected).

Hirst has, as far as I am aware, not provided any examples of what a theory might look like if it is to function as a recipe. I take the "what shall be done" to refer to the teacher, the practitioner, and not to the students. The educational theory determines what the teacher shall do; it is a recipe for the teacher. But at which level of abstraction should we determine what shall be done? Recall again Pettersen's examples of educational practice, discussed in Chapter 8: to give a lecture, to demonstrate the Pythagorean principle, and so on. Would "give" and "demonstrate" be precise enough, or do we need something more specific, such as "draw a triangle of the following proportion, then point to the hypotenuse and say '….'"? I cannot imagine what an educational theory would look like if the latter level of specificity is required. But it would be a recipe, much like MacIntyre's recipes from Chapter 8, where each act is individually described (1996, p.209). That may be useful in cookery, but not in educational practice – the prescription for teaching Pythagoras alone would be a small book. "Precisely" cannot mean too high a level of specificity, then; that would make for an unwieldy and rigid theory. If we use "demonstrate" as our preferred level, then the teacher will be granted some leeway. "Demonstration" can manifest itself in different ways. And would we then need one detailed theory for the teaching of Pythagoras, another equally detailed theory for the teaching of evolutionary theory? One recipe for each goal stated in the curriculum? In the absence of any concrete examples, it is hard to say what Hirst envisioned for his proposed theory.

Hirst's view of an educational theory shares two significant traits with Carr's view of educational theories as theories of theory and practice: there is a one-step, direct relationship between theory and practice, and the theory specifies its own implementation. It is the job of the theory to determine what shall be done; it is not the job of the practitioner. A theory which can determine precisely what shall be done in a given situation surely is meant to perform this job irrespective of the practitioner. If the recipe is specific enough, it might even be the case that all practitioners follow it in the same way, making practice in the relevant classes highly similar (if it were possible). (In passing, it is worth noting here that this particular problem has a parallel in evidence-based practice, where it goes by the name of fidelity: whether interventions aimed at some specific goal should be implemented exactly as prescribed by the intervention developers, or exactly as where it first was implemented – else the desired effect cannot be expected/promised/guaranteed.) If the theory determines, then whose *ought* is at play? Whose beliefs and value judgments will be operative? Those of the theoretician, whoever he or she is? If practice is successful, does the credit then lie with the theory? And if the goal is not obtained, does blame lie with the theory, such that we judge that the theory was wrong? Or does blame lie with the practitioner, whose implementation perhaps was unfaithful?

The idea that the theory determines its own implementation is, as discussed above, reminiscent of the notion of correspondence rules. Just like these rules determine how the laws of the theory manifest themselves in the phenomenon, so Hirst's theory decides its own implementation – by what feature Hirst's theory does this is not clear, of course. There is no reason to think that an educational theory on Hirst's view contains anything like correspondence rules. This has a lovely ironic quality about it – Hirst is sharp in his criticism of O'Connor's views of educational theory. O'Connor adheres, probably unknowingly, to RV: theories as logically connected sets of axioms and hypotheses, verifiable by observation. Hirst is strongly critical of this theory conception, yet his own conception is endowed with a function akin to that performed by RV's correspondence rules.

A radically different view of the function of educational theory is voiced by Erich Weniger (1990, p.32),

> ...daß es ein grundsätzliches Mißverständnis der Funktion der Theorie durch den Praktiker ist, wenn er glaubt, die Theorie könne und wolle ihm die Entscheidung in dem konkreten Fall vorschreiben oder abnehmen [the practitioner fundamentally misunderstands the function of theory if he thinks it can prescribe what he should do in concrete cases, or make decisions for him].

Thus, while Hirst locates the responsibility in the theory, Weniger locates it in the practitioner. Weniger's conception of educational theory is individualized in the sense that the practitioner "owns" his or her theory, and yet, he says, your theory should never become a recipe for you. It is vitally important for Weniger that practitioners remain fundamentally open to practice: there will always be something new present; some changes will always happen that will require different responses. No tyranny of experience, and no tyranny of theory. Now, I am not going to accuse Hirst of endorsing the tyranny of theory, but his conception of an educational theory does involve a tyranny: the theory itself decides how it should be used; it decides what should be done, surely irrespective of practitioner and irrespective of the diversity of practice. It is a clear weakness in his conception of theory that it allows no room for the diversity of practice.

Auxiliary hypotheses

Like all scientific theories, educational theories concern how phenomena will behave in idealized, isolated circumstances, not in concrete situations. Remember the *as if* – it entails that educational theories cannot be directly applied to practice, and therefore cannot provide any direct and definite prescriptions concerning which course of action to choose. We thus need to reconstruct our notion of the prescriptive function of goal-directed theories. What follows is not a version of the theory–practice dichotomy, which would effectively preclude any communication between theory and practice. Rather, what follows is an argument for the separation of a theory and its method of application. To make a theory function in non-isolated circumstances we also need a body of auxiliary hypotheses to be used in conjunction with the theory. Here is Nancy Cartwright on the effect of abstraction:

> [Abstraction] means that there is never any recipe for how to get from the abstract theory to any of the concrete systems it is supposed to treat. We have only the trivial advice, 'Add back all the causes that have been left out and calculate the total effect by combining the capacities'.
>
> (1989, p.185)

Cartwright wonders if this is the best that can be done. I take her to mean that even if there are no recipes, theory application does not have to be a completely arbitrary process. Patrick Suppes argued that theory testing, which is a form of application, requires a sophisticated apparatus involving a hierarchy of theories. Here I am going to call such hierarchies *auxiliary hypotheses*, and I should make it clear that I think that in most cases they look different from and are not nearly as carefully worked out as Suppes's hierarchy. A few comments before we look at some examples are in order. Both Suppe (1989) and Thompson (1989) speak of auxiliary *theories* to be employed in the application of a given theory. Suppe also uses the term auxiliary *hypotheses*, which is the term I shall adopt. The term *auxiliary theory* would seem to lead to unnecessary complexities; if we think such a theory possesses the same properties as an "ordinary" theory, then it, too, would need another auxiliary theory for its application, and so on and so on. If, on the other hand, an auxiliary theory differs significantly from a theory, we had better reflect that conceptually to avoid confusion. When I was working on my doctoral dissertation all those years ago, this is the question that caused me the greatest consternation: how to link a generalized description, a theory, to a concrete phenomenon, case or situation. My struggles to conceptualize auxiliary hypotheses as something other than a new theory came from my initial picture of the problem as a continuum between general and particular. To get to the particular end of the continuum we needed to fill it with knowledge that became gradually less general and more particular – or so I thought at the time. I did not resolve the issue to my own satisfaction back then. I will lay out my current understanding of it subsequently; for the moment let me just say that my attitude to this specific issue is considerably laxer now. On the other hand, my conviction in the wisdom of separating theories from their method of application has, if anything, grown stronger. RV completely obscures the role played by auxiliary hypotheses in theory application by agglomerating all the various aspects holding between theory and practice into one transition. On SC, the model of the theory is highly abstract and far removed from the (empirical) phenomenon. It may sound paradoxical, but this feature of theories ensures great flexibility in their application, precisely because it opens them up for the use of auxiliary hypotheses. The use of auxiliary hypotheses means that one and the same theory can be applied in different ways, in different situations, by different practitioners. This flexibility is of prime importance if the concrete phenomenon is characterized by great complexity, diversity and flux, and that is the case with educational phenomena – practice included.

Application of educational technology

Educational technology (ET) was briefly introduced in Chapter 3 as an example of a goal-directed theory; or rather, as an ideal-type example of a family of similar theories. Possibly nobody holds this kind of theory anymore, but it makes an excellent example. Note that "technology" in this context refers to systematics in teaching, not to the use of digital equipment. In its simplest form ET says that in order for students to learn certain knowledge (the goal), the teacher should present this knowledge in small pieces, give immediate feedback on students' responses or solutions, and not let the students pass on to the next level until the current level is mastered (environmental organization). This is a goal-directed, prescriptive theory and it provides a description of how the teleological entity, an idealized student, *ought to* behave; the influence of other parameters is assumed to be negligible. In behavioral terms, the parameters might be described as specified goal state, stimulus, sequencing of small steps, overt response and reinforcement. The theory concerns how the teleological system will behave in isolated, idealized circumstances; it describes an idealized student interacting with an environment that must be characterized as radically stripped-down and focused. But the theory does not thereby tell you how particular, concrete students will behave under such circumstances. ET, we should note, comes through as a recipe to be used by the teacher. The goal concerns the students and describes a change that is considered desirable. The theory does provide a general prescription of how to maximize the probability for attaining not just one specific goal, but goals of a certain type: knowledge or skills that can be organized in the manner described by the theory. However, it does not determine precisely what the teacher should do. A classroom is a non-isolated situation and, consequently, the influence of other parameters must be considered when applying the theory. So how does that work?

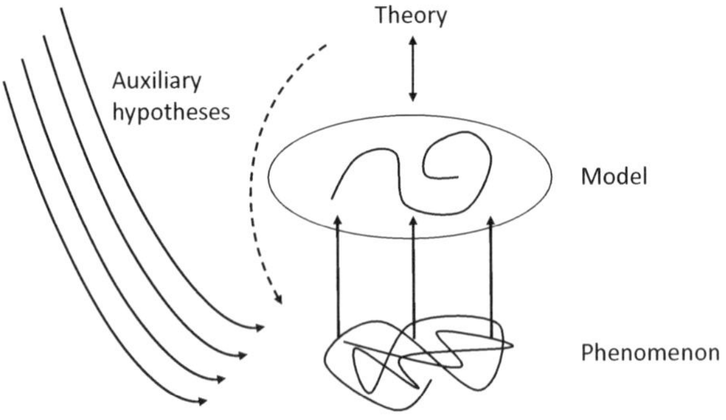

Figure 10.1 Theory application: Theory in conjunction with (contextual) auxiliary hypotheses

The first thing to do when applying a theory is to make sure that one knows the theory. In this case, the theory is clearly formulated – evidently many opinions can be voiced about it, but the theory itself is clear, and we know what it says about the phenomenon it treats. People who construct theories, educational researchers and others, must formulate their theories as clearly as they can – you cannot use a theory if you do not know what it says. The next thing to do is to identify factors omitted by the theory. Which are they? Cartwright, as we have seen, suggests that one thing we can do in moving from abstract/general to concrete/particular is to add back in all the causes that have been left out. Selection of parameters for a model implies selecting away a number of factors, not only causes, but properties and relations, not only of the students but also of the environment. It is not difficult to identify possible parameters regarding the teleological entity, since the student in this theory is something of a black box. Examples such as interests, motivation, other ways of learning, and the impact of social surroundings easily spring to mind. When we apply ET in non-isolated situations, we must consider the possible influence of these parameters. Thus, third, we map out how the concrete, non-isolated situation deviates from the isolated situation presumed by the theory; and finally, we form auxiliary hypotheses about which factors we would do well to consider in application of ET. That is to say, we use the theory in conjunction with a set of auxiliary hypotheses, and we infer from that how best to adjust the theory to the situational conditions when applying it. For instance, knowledge can be partitioned into pieces in many different ways; feedback can be given in many different ways: encouragingly, discouragingly, verbally and non-verbally; and mastery of level is (also) a matter of judgment. A teacher who knows his/her students might tailor both knowledge bits and feedback forms according to what his/her students might accomplish and thrive on, rather than being faithful to the textbook and instructions for the teacher. The teacher thus needs to know the theory, he/she needs to know which parameters are not treated by the theory, he/she must assess the relative significance of those parameters, and he/she must judge how they should influence his/her adjustment and use of the theory in practice. If it is a theory the teacher employs often, perhaps a set of useful auxiliary hypotheses can be developed. On the other hand, situations vary, students vary, classrooms and schools vary – hence, the set of auxiliary hypotheses can vary. ET can be used in different ways by different people precisely because it is abstract and general, and the variability of practice is accommodated.

Summing up: first, it should be noted that we do not add back in *all* the factors that were left out. We add back in the ones we judge to be *relevant* to the task at hand. There is obviously much more to say about a given student than pertains to his or her school life, and different practitioners may make different judgments. Second, auxiliary hypotheses may also be general, if they arise from repeated experience. This is the point that caused me such consternation when I wrote my dissertation: how general theory and general auxiliary hypotheses together could result in concrete decisions. But once I gave up the image of an abstract-concrete continuum, a simple solution presented itself: a practitioner puts together general theory, generalized beliefs extrapolated from experience, along with particular knowledge of students and situations, and from this nexus he or she makes an *inference* about how to adjust the theory and how to manifest the theory's prescriptions in concrete action. In a sense it is a leap, rather than a gradual transition from general to particular. Third, it is not the theory itself that determines what should be done; it is the *user* of the theory. Even theories that are obviously prescriptive, such as ET, do not tell the practitioner precisely what to do. Theory application is, and should be, flexible. Finally, a couple of remarks concerning ET. It may be both easy and difficult to use this theory, and for much the same reason. Easy, because the absence of parameters concerning the teleological entity offers great flexibility in use; difficult, because the same flexibility makes it hard to know where to begin or which auxiliary hypotheses to form – ET is oversimplified. Moreover, despite the central role of the teacher, he or she is not explicitly a part of the theory. ET, as it is expressed, is a recipe for the teacher to use. As such it offers no resources for the teacher to take himself or herself into account as part of the environment with which the student interacts. But if we take the student's point of view, we see that the environment largely consists of the teacher, who provides knowledge bits and feedback. Quite conceivably, a teacher employing ET would need to fashion a set of auxiliary hypotheses concerning himself or herself as part of the students' environment.

Application of Rosalind Driver's science education theory

Driver's theory contains all the elements that SC suggests should be present in a goal-directed theory; albeit in varying numbers and to varying degrees of accuracy. I am again going to draw on Norris' and my analysis (1997). Depending on how you see it, the theory has a threefold goal state, seven categories (with sub-categories) of parameters describing the teleological entity, and six categories (again with sub-categories) of parameters describing the environment. The very complexity and degree of detail of this theory suggest that it is difficult to apply. Keeping track of the (changing) values of all these parameters, their relations and possible implications for one another, all at once, is by no means a trivial task. So what does a teacher do who wishes to apply Driver's theory in her science education classes? Which auxiliary hypotheses can be formulated in the application of Driver's theory? What is the role of the teacher? Since auxiliary hypotheses intercede between abstract model and concrete phenomenon, they are usually but not necessarily formed on the basis of knowledge about the concrete phenomenon, whether the teleological entity or the situation. The following examples from Driver's theory do not look at what the teacher should *do* in the classroom, but auxiliary hypotheses a teacher may have to formulate and use in making judgments about whether or to what degree students have attained the goal in question. The discussion below is thus a continuation of the analyses in Chapter 5.

Part of the goal state of Driver's theory refers to conventional or current scientific beliefs about different natural phenomena. How is a teacher to judge whether student A's utterances – which may be only a sentence or two – count as a formulation of the content-specific goal? Possibly we need auxiliary hypotheses concerning student A's intended meaning, which may need to be interpreted; what kind of scientific insight we can reasonably expect from student A; the accuracy of textbook descriptions of natural phenomena; the accuracy demanded by the teacher or the test, etc. Driver (1989) describes an example where four students, aged 13, try to explain the properties of water, ice and vapor. They discuss the idea of a connection ("bonding") between molecules, and think aloud that it may be like a magnetic or electric force. When water boils, the bonding is broken, one of the students suggests. But then what is happening when vapor cools down? The discussion continues as follows:

P2: Yeah, but the point is, how do we get the bonding back?
P4: Slow down the vibrating...
P2: Slow down the vibrations...
P4: I suppose it's ever present there but ... yeah, it hasn't got a chance to, like, grip them, you know, and keep them together. Well, where it slows down, you know, it might get to grips with the...
P3: A bit easier to keep slower things together.

(Driver, 1989, p.92)

Driver claims that this discussion represents movement toward the goal state. Which auxiliary hypotheses could be involved in her claim, regardless of whether it is true or not? First, the teacher needs to formulate a hypothesis about which students, P2, P3 or P4, have moved toward the goal state. Each student contributes different parts of the story. So is there *one* story here that all the students have acquired and understood? Second, *uttering* something, in the sense of trying out an idea, is not the same as changing one's beliefs. The teacher therefore needs a hypothesis that the linguistic utterances of the students indicate that their beliefs have changed from "getting the bonding back" (the original problem) to an understanding that the force which creates the bonding is always present. Third, the teacher needs a hypothesis which renders the students' imprecise language in terms of the language used in conventional science (force, momentum, kinetic energy, etc.). Whether explicitly or implicitly, the teacher must judge what the students have learned, and what she herself is to do. Neither judgment can be made solely on Driver's theory – the particularities of the situation must also be considered.

Here is another example, in which the most relevant parts of the goal state are coherence of ideas, the ability to compare old and new ideas and test them against experience. Driver (1989) concludes that the students show progress in their thinking. The students have been given materials of the same size and form, but of markedly different weight. The task is to describe and explain their observations. Here is an excerpt of the discussion:

DARREN: Yeah, they *could* be [both plastic], but they look like different materials.
DANIEL: But it wouldn't make any difference if they were the same material, say like paper, paper might be all spread out, all the particles in it might be spread but in wood they're all bunched together.

DARREN: Yeah, and when they make...
DANIEL: They make paper from pulp and wood and that.
DARREN: And they might be – it becomes lighter, obviously.
DANIEL: Oh yeah. 'Cos all t' particles are spreading out. So that's what I think's happening.

(Driver, 1989, p.87)

If now Driver's theory is true (cf. Chapter 7), it should, when coupled with a suitable set of auxiliary hypotheses, tell us whether this interaction represents progress toward the goal state. What is the basis for Driver's claim that it does? Most likely – Driver does not spell this out – it is the change in the values of the content parameters; more specifically, the scientific explanation of density. The students' explanation seems to assume that things made of the same material (paper and wood) can differ in density. They share ideas and test them against experience, as the theory says they should. But it is not obvious that their ideas become more coherent. They compare wood and paper and seem to conclude that paper has less density: "it becomes lighter". The use of the word "lighter" might raise suspicion that they confuse weight and density. In order to conclude that this represents progress and movement toward the goal, the teacher must accept auxiliary hypotheses to the effect that students think that particles are "objects" too small to be observed; that they know the difference between weight and density; that they just forgot to look at the significance of volume, etc. A teacher must know her students well to make such judgments. But then, teachers may also be wrong.

Hopefully these examples illustrate that auxiliary hypotheses often are based on situational appraisals, including teachers' knowledge of their students. Hopefully they also illustrate that auxiliary hypotheses are necessary in theory application, also when the theory is as detailed as Driver's and in that respect quite the opposite of ET. Conceivably, the most important set of auxiliary hypotheses that teachers using Driver's theory need concerns the transformation of student discussions to data that show their knowledge (and beliefs) about various natural phenomena. The teacher must also simply assume that the students take the discussions seriously and do not try to hide their beliefs (for whatever reason). No set of correspondence rules could ever house all the auxiliary hypotheses that are necessary in the application of a complex theory such as Driver's. Theory use is by no means simple or straightforward.

Inclusion of normative and metaphysical considerations in theory

I argued in Chapter 4 that I think goal-directed theories have an empirical core, but I elected nonetheless to analyze such theories as *also* containing a normative component in the shape of a desirable goal. However, SC opens up for a different way of viewing this issue; and it merits a brief discussion anyway because it is one of the themes on which Hirst and O'Connor strongly disagreed. Hirst wants to import value components into the theory itself:

> ...it is a fundamental task of the theory to determine the ends and goals to be pursued as much as the means to be employed. ... [E]ducational theory in large measure depends on the making of value judgments about what exactly is to be aimed at in education.
>
> (1966, p.52)

O'Connor (1973, pp.56–57) makes the following comment to Hirst's claim:

> Suppose ... that value judgments could appear in a theory of education side by side with empirical statements. What would be the relations between them? ... But then they serve exactly the same purpose (namely, guiding actions) as they would serve if they were extrinsic to the theory. So by constructing such a logical hybrid we gain no advantage that we would not gain by leaving our value premises outside the theory.

On this issue I tend to side with O'Connor, albeit with a caveat. It is actually possible to imagine goal-directed theories as wholly empirical, with the goal state being, as it were, outside the theory, and the theory simply telling us how we should attain it (the *ought*). If we keep the goal as an integral part of the theory, we get the logical hybrid that O'Connor speaks about, which RV cannot handle but which SC can handle. But there is a second set of normative considerations here; those that enter into the *ought* – it must be these kinds of value judgments O'Connor had in mind, since he describes their purpose as "guiding actions". That is, on the assumption that goals themselves do not guide actions. I have analyzed this part of goal-directed theories as empirical. And I agree with O'Connor that this second kind of normative considerations are better left outside the theory, but for different reasons. O'Connor worries about the justification of value judgments, should we import them into the theory, and perhaps also about *whose* values they then are. But O'Connor did not have SC at his disposal, and SC offers a role for this kind of consideration: they impact how the theory is applied. Circumstances external to the theory invariably influence the application of the theory, and there is no reason to suppose that all practitioners hold the same values. Thus, I suggest, normative considerations concerning implementation could be construed as parts of the auxiliary hypotheses employed in theory application. For example, how reinforcement (feedback) should be administered: should this particular student be praised in front of the whole class? Especially encouragingly, since this particular student is mentally fragile? Should all students be made to read their answers aloud? Besides, we can of course deliberate whether we should apply a given theory at all. We may know how to maximize the probability of obtaining a certain result, but ethical considerations may count against it. In such cases, too, the normative considerations are extrinsic to the theory.

The question concerning metaphysical considerations is the same: should they be incorporated as parts of the theory, or are they better viewed as extrinsic? Again, unsurprisingly, Hirst and O'Connor disagree. Hirst finds O'Connor's treatment of metaphysical beliefs and moral values far too dismissive: "And when it comes to characterizing educational theory, the significance of these elements in it is crucial", Hirst says (1966, p.38). But it is time now to bring other voices into the discussion. The metaphysical considerations I have in mind primarily concern views of human nature: the constitution of human beings, their possibilities, rights, capacities, variation in and distribution of abilities and aptitudes; all with religious, evolutionary, sociological and other overtones. The German philosopher Otto Friedrich Bollnow (1975) claims that it is the view of human nature that keeps the various components of educational theory together in a coherent whole. To understand the place and role of the components you therefore need a firm grasp of the view of human nature – it comprises the ultimate justification of the principles and categories of the educational theory. The other components of an educational theory are aims, content and process – essentially, a goal-directed theory but explicitly furnished with metaphysical presuppositions. Interestingly, the same view is propounded by Ernest Nagel (1969), who comes from a completely different tradition (cf. Chapter 2): he holds a view of human nature as one of the components of an educational theory (p.12). This seems to echo Bollnow, and also Reidar Myhre, Norwegian philosopher of education who formed my early views of educational theory. Myhre (1980) thinks like Bollnow: the view of human nature is the foundation of the educational theory, and from this foundation we derive aims, content and process (the main didactical categories). But how advisable is it to incorporate a view of human nature into the educational theory itself? It may very well be that any goal-directed theory presupposes a certain view of human nature but they are better understood as extrinsic to the theory, simply as background assumptions. That would yield a much-needed flexibility in the relation between a theory and its presuppositions. People may share a view of human nature and yet differ widely as to what educational aims, content and processes they think are appropriate.

Summary

The application of theory is not a problem that can be solved once and for all. It requires knowledge, skills and judgment of the practitioner – in fact, I think of theory application largely as a skill, a skill, moreover, that can be learned and honed in practice, by doing it. This conclusion in itself – that theory application requires judgment – should be no big surprise. One of the virtues of SC is that it explains why this is so. On SC, there exists a separation of the theory and the method of its application, necessitated by the two-step relation between theory and phenomenon. What is needed to get from the abstract theory to the concrete phenomenon is a suitable set of auxiliary hypotheses. These concern the identification of relevant contextual factors omitted by the theory, and thus how the concrete, non-isolated situation in practice deviates from the isolated, idealized situation characterized by the theory. Such sets will no doubt vary with context, although if practice is stable and predictable, surely the auxiliary hypotheses will reflect this and also be stable and enduring. Any such set, I surmise, will need to comprise situational appraisals and knowledge of the particular individuals, students or clients involved (or else generalized knowledge of them will have to suffice). Auxiliary hypotheses fundamentally belong to the relation between theory and phenomenon and do not comprise just any experience or piece of practical knowledge or rule of thumb that practitioners might devise. On the other hand, I submit, the experts on theory application are those who actually apply the theory, not those who construct it. Application requires contextual information.

Context is vitally important in education, since it accounts for so much of what students learn and come away with in education. The variability in contexts is great, and should be allowed to be so. The two-step relation between theory and phenomenon accommodates this great variability. The construction of auxiliary hypotheses makes it possible for the same theory to be used in different ways by different practitioners, or differently by the same practitioner on different occasions – all in order to make justified and good decisions about how to adjust the theory to the problem at hand. The practitioner needs to put all the information together, theory and auxiliary hypotheses, including ethical considerations, and infer from all that his or her best course of action. Not just *one* course of action is possible; this is not a matter of deduction. The two-step relation could perhaps be described as a double-edged sword: it entails that there is no recipe for getting from abstract to concrete, but the very same distance also entails needed flexibility in theory application.

I have devoted much space to possible prescriptive uses of theory in this section. That is because this is the classical topic in the discussions of educational theory. Educational theories are traditionally thought of as goal-directed theories, and it does seem natural to endow goal-directed theories with an element of prescription; they do, after all, aim to tell us how to achieve a certain goal. But how does this prescriptive function pan out? No theory, I have argued, can tell the practitioners precisely what to do. Theories are not and cannot be prescriptive in a strict sense – they do not provide recipes that one can follow. But they can be weakly prescriptive, and of course frequently are used as such, when applied in conjunction with auxiliary hypotheses and ethical considerations. Theory application is far from being a simple or straightforward process; to the contrary, it requires both judgment and skill. My analysis points to the irreducible role of the practitioner, as well as to need of avoiding both the "tyranny of experience" that Weniger warns against, and the "tyranny of theory" represented by theories that decide their own implementation.

Other uses and misuses of theory

Theories are used for a variety of purposes. Among their standard uses, listed in all textbooks on philosophy of science, are description, explanation and prediction of phenomena. Educational theories, as we have seen, are standardly used to modify some phenomenon. One can also employ theory to justify one's own beliefs and decisions, to evaluate decisions and courses of action retrospectively, to make diagnoses, or to understand what is going on more generally. It is simply not the case that use is dependent on theory type; all types of theory can be used for different purposes (with smaller or greater success, of course). Nor is it the case that forms of theory use are restricted to domain. When I was a student of education, the textbooks I read would typically hold that the job of theories in the natural sciences is to describe, predict and explain; whereas the job of educational theories is to modify the phenomenon in some desirable way (e.g. Myhre, 1980, Skjervheim, 1992 – however, this is not a Norwegian phenomenon; as we have seen the distinction between scientific and educational theory is widespread). Hence, the natural sciences had "theoretical theories" with an epistemic aim, practical sciences such as medicine and education had "practical theories" with desirable modification as their aim. Domain, theory type and theory use were assumed to belong intimately together, to form exclusive units. It is one of my main claims in this book that the divide between scientific theories and educational theories cannot be upheld, and SC is my chief tool and central to my argument for this claim. Moreover, theories, or any piece of research for that matter, can be used for purposes not devised or even condoned by the producer of the theory – use is up to the user. Theory uses are not mutually exclusive, so one and the same theory can be used for a multitude of purposes. Driver's theory, for example, can easily be used to describe the phenomenon, explain results, guide action, justify decisions in retrospect, and quite possibly other uses as well.

Largely in keeping with the discussions concerning educational theory in the field of education, this chapter has so far centered on the application of theory to practice. If you think of educational theories as goal-directed, practice-oriented and action-guiding, it is natural for the theory–practice relationship to take precedence, and for educational research to be judged relevant if it in some way contributes to practice. Usually this contribution translates as student achievement, or improvement of student achievement. This is fine; I of course have no objection to this use of theory, with all the caveats concerning implementation that I have rehearsed in the previous section. But this is only one form of theory use, and, I shall argue in this section, perhaps not the most important one. Theory can be put to other equally or more important forms of use, and there are other forms of usefulness besides effectiveness. To respond adequately to the challenge posed by Gary Thomas (1997) – "What is the use of theory?" – we need to look at other possible uses of theory as well. The following discussions are independent of any particular meta-theory, but deeply involve realist and antirealist approaches.

To set the stage, let us look again at the notions of relevance and usefulness and expand on them somewhat. In Chapter 7 usefulness was discussed in terms of goals, aims and intentions – we deem theories useful to the degree they contribute to fulfilling our intentions. But if usefulness is couched exclusively in terms of practical relevance and effectiveness, we seriously narrow our field of vision and miss out on a number of (potentially) important issues. Having said that, I am also going to expand somewhat on the very idea of using theory. The previous section dealt with application of theories as a *whole*. Now it is important to say that we can also employ parts of a theory, one or two parameters (concepts) of a theory, and even more than one theory at the same time (although that is exceedingly complicated). Even single concepts can be useful, because they help you identify features, aspects or attributes of phenomena, serve to integrate disparate views, or bring clarity and insight because they facilitate recognition of phenomena. All of which, I would say, is *useful.* Not because it facilitates or improves the bringing about of learning outcomes, but because it aids our thinking. I shall explore this in some detail.

Differently put, theories and their elements can be relevant in many different ways, and we cannot know beforehand how this will play out. As David Labaree (2008) observes, "Relevance is a tricky quality to define because it is easier to recognize in retrospect than in prospect, and efforts to make research more relevant can make it useless or misleading" (p.421). That is to say, we cannot decide in advance that some pieces of research simply are (practically) relevant while others are not. Different people, theoreticians and practitioners alike, find different concepts and theories relevant for different purposes for different reasons. As I argued in the previous section, since practice is so contextualized, auxiliary hypotheses will have to be context sensitive and people will make different judgments as to what the most important contextual features are. These broad notions of usefulness and relevance will serve as the backdrop for the discussion in this section.

Description

Philosophers of science tend to call a theory *successful* especially when it can *explain* occurrences, effects, changes, features or aspects of phenomena (e.g. Ladyman, 2002, Rosenberg, 2012). But we begin with description. You do not, of course, need a theory to describe a phenomenon. All languages have many words, and a great many of those are for things that are manifest to the unaided senses: objects, attributes, movements. I think description is vastly underrated: as I said in Chapter 8, descriptions might come at different levels of abstraction and involve references to both observables and unobservables. As far as descriptions include the latter, they become more theoretical in character, more given to interpretation. It is time to bring Jos Kessels and Fred Korthagen (1996) back into the picture. I touched upon their views in Chapter 9, where the topic was the (alleged) self-sufficiency of practice. Here the topic is description. It will be recalled that they claim that practitioners do not need scientific understanding (episteme), but rather phronesis, which they cast as a perceptual form of knowledge, in contrast to a conceptual form of knowledge. Perceptual knowledge is about concrete particulars and is necessarily acquired in practice, through experience. Student teachers should learn to *see.* Their conclusion merits repetition: "For the 'matter of the practical' is not helped very much by such conceptual knowledge" (p.21).

It is hard to know what to make of such a divorce of perception and concepts. What kind of concepts are we dealing with here? What sort of educational "things" can we see that would give us perceptual but not conceptual knowledge? Only things that are manifest to our unaided eyesight? This will include objects (books, individuals) and properties of objects (color, shape); but also events (a person entering a foyer), states of affairs (the person's being in the foyer) and facts (*that* the person is in the foyer). The same process of perception evidently need not be involved in all these cases of seeing. Knowing what things look like is not the same as knowing what they are called, and thus constitutes a piece of knowledge that is perceptual but not conceptual. You can know what a book looks like, but if you do not have the word you cannot communicate your observation to anybody. Thus, I infer, Kessels and Korthagen do not rule out the use of descriptive, observational terms. But can you, for example, *see* that something, say an achievement, has improved? This would be tricky if no conceptual knowledge is to be involved. Improvement judgments require comparison of achievements over time, a set of criteria, and principles for valuation, such that you can accord $achievement_1$ a higher value than $achievement_2$. I doubt that Kessels and Korthagen would be willing to rule out such judgments, despite their conceptual nature. So what kind of conceptual knowledge do they have in mind that is thought not to help practical matters? One thing they do have in mind is the general character of conceptual knowledge. One might respond to this that knowledge about the looks of things is also general – knowledge of the looks of a class of objects, such as books, allow us to identify new specimens we come across as members of the class of books. However, here we have other fish to fry.

Suppose we are practitioners after Weniger's heart. In order to learn from experience, Weniger says, we ask questions of the situation. But what sort of questions could we ask, if all we are interested in is perceptual knowledge? If we only deal in observables? Would we not be restricted to describing the appearance of things? Description *is* important, but descriptions that deal in observables only will not take us very far. The interesting educational entities are T-entities: learning, Bildung, motivation, aims, self-understanding, and so on. Let us assume, then, that the conceptual knowledge Kessels and Korthagen have in mind is *theoretical* in character. That is to say, concepts that (1) refer to entities, properties, states of affairs and facts that do *not* manifest themselves to the unaided senses, but which instead denote unobservables; and (2) refer to underlying processes, causal connections, mechanisms, dispositions or capacities and serve to explain that which manifests itself to our unaided senses.

At this point a brief detour is required: the concept of (scientific) observation. Norwood Russell Hanson (1958) argues that observation is essentially *seeing-that*. Not simply seeing, but seeing-that. This expression signals the vitally important fact that seeing is an epistemic achievement, shaped by the knowledge and intentions of the observer. There is a sense, Hanson admits, in which we are visually aware of the same thing, but observation and visual experience are not the same. The *ways* in which perceivers are visually aware are profoundly different, and the reason is that they bring different knowledge, experience and theory to the seeing. Hanson says, famously: "...the physicist sees an X-ray tube, the child a complicated lamp bulb; the microscopist sees a coelenterate mesoglea, his new student sees only a formless, gooey stuff" (p.17). A teacher can see that a student is exhibiting a high degree of social competence; the student teacher sees a student asking another student to collaborate on an assignment. Teaching the student teacher to see social competence does not amount to showing him/her a thing he/she has not seen before. It amounts to teaching him/her a new concept, embedded in theoretical knowledge, *and* to teach him/her the possible manifestations of the concept in practice so that he/she can *recognize* the phenomenon. This latter point is important: educational (and other) phenomena, such as social competence, do not come with labels on them – again we meet the perennial problem of linking T-terms to O-terms. Then the student teacher can organize his/her visual experience in a different way and thereby see new things and have new experiences. Experience, on Hanson's view, as an *à propos* of a subsection in Chapter 9, is heavily theory-laden.

Seeing-that is a tool for expressing the relationship between seeing and knowing. And, most significantly, it opens up for seeing other things than objects and properties of objects, and thereby for making complex and sophisticated descriptions. Above all, seeing-that enables us to see facts, such as seeing *that* there is a person in the foyer or *that* a first-grader is (highly) socially competent. Recognizing a first-grader *as* socially competent means that our student teacher, upon seeing the behavior of the first-grader, comes to know that this first-grader is socially competent. To get a further grip on theory-infused descriptions I am going to employ Fred Dretske's concepts of direct and indirect fact perception (Dretske, 1990). This pair of concepts is immensely useful; a number of important and interesting issues fall into place here (see also Kvernbekk, 2000, for an in-depth discussion of forms of *seeing* in practice). Direct fact perception we have already met; for example, *that* a student is writing or *that* two students are whispering together. The fact that is seen is expressed by the sentential clause – according to Hanson, seeing-that necessarily has a linguistic component, a sentential clause, without which nothing we ever observed could have relevance to our knowledge. Indirect fact perception is what happens when we say, for example, that we see that student A is in deep thought, that student B's motivation for mathematics is low, or that student C's social competence is growing. None of these facts are directly observable, so how can we say that we see them? We regularly do say that we see such things, both in our daily lives and in our professional lives. Such observations are indirect and mediated in some way. Typically, Dretske says, we see that x is y *by* seeing that c is d. Properly speaking, we make an inference; we see that c is d, and on the basis of that we infer that x is y. In everyday language we often report that something has been seen to be the case (x is y), even though our seeing is indirect. We see that somebody is bored *by* seeing that they yawn, sigh and drum their fingers on the table, but we report it as direct: I see that you are bored. As MacIntyre argues (see Chapter 8), some descriptions of people's actions may characterize the intention – an indirect fact perception. I venture to say that this kind of indirect seeing is pervasive in everyday life, and that conceptual knowledge will enable you to see more, to make more sophisticated observations.

Descriptions come onto the stage in two places here. First, evidently, reports of indirect fact perceptions make for complex descriptions. Second, the first step in this process should not be missed. It is easy enough to take an indirect fact perception for a direct fact perception, so that what is actually an inference comes through as a forthright apprehension of some phenomenon. Many of our everyday observations run on commonsense and generalizations and simply skip c, d and jump directly to x, y, which then is reported as a direct perception. But while the observation of c, d may be right, the inference may be wrong. An innocent example: many years ago, a colleague described me as being deep in thought while I was having lunch in the canteen. I am occasionally deep in thought, but (usually) not while having lunch. To this day I have no idea what my colleague *saw* (c, d) that made him jump directly to x, y, but I am as certain as I can be that he was wrong. A description of c and d would slow down the inferential process sufficiently for the observer to make a judgment about the connection between c, d on the one hand, and x, y on the other. A description of c and d would prevent us from jumping too quickly to interpretation. Moreover, conflating the direct and the indirect is an epistemological sin with possible ethical ramifications. Is it really the case that c, d are manifestations of x, y? If not, we risk attributing to people intentions, motives, attributes or dispositions they do not have. Why would we think they are connected in the first place? Because we have assumptions concerning this relationship; assumptions that are theoretical in nature because they concern the relation between some unobservable and its observable manifestations. C, d and x, y provide different levels of abstraction in our descriptions and are therefore essential for capturing what I in Chapter 8 called the identity of actions. Thus, the perceptual and the conceptual are intimately intertwined. Dretske's concepts of direct and indirect fact perception clarify a number of things – but also have the effect that the boundary between description and interpretation becomes blurred.

Explanation

Explanations are generally answers to *how* or *why* questions. How did we come to be in this situation? Why did we get $result_2$ and not $result_1$ as we expected? There is a big literature on what exactly would constitute scientifically acceptable answers to such questions (e.g. Hempel, 1965), and nowadays there seems to be agreement among philosophers of science that the capacity to explain is a sign of scientific success. Theories, Alex Rosenberg says, explain by making a set of claims about invisible, unobservable, undetectable components and their unobservable properties (2012, p.125). We have identified something observable, an event, a result, a state of affairs, and the explanation of how or why this came to be crucially appeals to T-entities. This is *use* of theory. Maybe not of an entire theory, but certainly of some of its T-terms. Suppose we apply Driver's theory in our science education class and consistently fail to achieve the results we (think we) are supposed to achieve. The results are observable in the sense that they show up in formal or informal tests. How can this be, we ask ourselves? What might an explanation look like? Obviously, such a question will have several competing answers. One explanation may utilize parameters describing the teleological entity; for example, initial understanding of phenomenon, openness to new ideas, disposition to engage – all of these are unobservable, and they may contribute to an explanation of poor results if the teacher judges the values of these parameters to be lower than expected. A competing explanation based on the same theory might involve appeal to parameters describing the environment, or the interaction between students and environment, such as friendship among students, classroom atmosphere, quality of student dialogues, and so on. Just for the record, other explanations can be had that do not involve Driver's theory at all, but perhaps invoke staff conflicts, lack of resources or general school culture. Also just for the record, everyday explanations follow the same pattern – they may not involve strong T-terms, but they will involve weak T-terms, T-terms which refer to unobservables of kinds that abound in everyday parlance and culturally assimilated commonsense (intention, understanding, laziness, intelligence, perseverance, satisfaction, expectation, personality, and so on).

Theories have other resources to offer besides parameters or T-entities more generally. Strong T-terms evidently do not stand alone; they are embedded in theoretical structures. If I explain a student's behavior as being due to intermittent reinforcement, I am not only using a single T-term; I am invoking the whole theory of operant behaviorism (Skinner, 1938), and I can further infer a history of irregular and unpredictable reinforcement in this student's learning of behavior. First and foremost, that means that I can make use of the *postulates* of the theory. Postulates, it will be recalled from Chapter 3, concern the relation between parameters; they indicate how the parameters (or T-entities) hang together. Thus, I will *understand* how this student came to exhibit a certain behavioral pattern, and how other people have contributed to this pattern by providing an irregular mixture of positive and negative feedback on actions and achievements. More generally, postulates are of course vitally important in explanations; usually we do want to know why something happened or went the way it did, and that requires that we can put T-entities in relation to one another, look at their influence, and link that to how things have manifested themselves in the phenomenon, event or state of affairs we wish to explain. If you use a suitably elaborate theory in your explanation, it will furnish you with postulates to aid your explanation. If not, your explanation risks becoming hostage to commonsense, stereotypes or prejudices – but not necessarily; to be sure common sense is sometimes good enough. If the theory you happen to use is false, your explanation becomes hostage to false beliefs and the resulting understanding will be a misunderstanding. Most adequate explanations will, I surmise, contain postulates or perhaps even presuppose a theoretical law. Many such postulates in educational theories concern causation, I have argued, and if the theory is suitably elaborate it will help you distinguish between causal necessity, causal sufficiency, probabilistic causation and INUS conditions – these will yield different explanations of the same event and are important to keep apart.

Thus, I conclude, theories provide explanations by appealing to unobservables, helping you connect these unobservables to the observable phenomenon you want to explain, and by offering postulates which help you connect these unobservables. Hopefully that will give you a deeper understanding of how things hang together. This is an important use of theory, much more important than prescription.

A few things should be said to connect explanation with the broader field of philosophy of science: most notably, realist and antirealist perspectives. Theories, as we have seen, provide explanations by invoking unobservables. So do commonsense explanations; just think how often we explain actions or behavior by referring to abilities and dispositions, intentions, understandings, disorders, intelligence, expectations, personality, etc. Antirealists downplay explanation, due to their disquiet about T-entities (Ladyman, 2002). Realists are allowed to think that T-entities exist (but should not commit themselves willy-nilly). If an unobservable exists, it can be used to explain observable events, results or states of affairs, and the theory can identify the mechanism or process by which the observable event is brought about. We meet here with deep philosophical problems. The provision of explanations, Rosenberg argues, is one of the most important functions of science (Rosenberg, 2012). I have realist inclinations and so would tend to agree with him; especially since I have connected explanations in education to understanding of the phenomena. But how, Rosenberg asks, can we understand the fundamental indispensability of terms that identify unobservable entities (T-terms and T-entities) when research practice so clearly signals the primacy of observation and experience? There is no direct evidence for the existence of T-entities and yet science cannot discharge its explanatory functions without unobservables (p.158). Scientific practice is generally empiricist, both Ladyman and Rosenberg think, since we all share and act on the idea that knowledge is justified by experience. Rosenberg, for his part, clearly has realist inclinations and his viewpoint is definitely worth citing:

> How to reconcile the demands of empiricism with the demands of explanation is the hardest problem for the philosophy of science, indeed for philosophy as a whole. For if we cannot reconcile explanation and empiricism, it is pretty clear that it is empiricism that must be given up.
>
> (2012, p.147)

If you do not think that T-entities exist, then nor do you, evidently, think that T-terms refer to them, since there is nothing to refer to. T-terms are thus viewed as summaries of observations, a kind of derived, shorthand talk. But the explanatory power of theories hinges on the T-terms not being shorthand – if they are shorthand, they only summarize occurrences, results or events and do not explain them. If a complete translation of T into O is demanded (T=O), then all explanatory potential is lost because the T-term becomes only summary. Hence, antirealists downplay explanation. Educationists will have to decide for themselves whether they hold explanation important, and which attitude they accordingly will have to assume toward the T-entities they engage.

Prediction

A prediction is a foretelling, a specification of future occurrences, events or results, whether we claim that the events *will* happen or only that they *might* happen. Predictions come in different sizes and shapes, as it were. We can predict the existence of yet undetected entities, we can predict highly specific individual outcomes, we can predict aggregate results, or we can identify ranges or intervals for our predictions. Predictions borne out by subsequent observation are taken as powerful indicators of the success of science (leaving aside all intricacies of theory testing and interpretation of ambiguous results), and are viewed as reasons to accept the theory or hypothesis in question. Prediction is, arguably, more important to antirealists than to realists. As discussed in Chapter 7, realists and antirealists interpret predictive successes differently. If you are an antirealist, you are skeptical about the existence of T-entities, you treat T-terms as summaries of O-terms, and you think of theories or knowledge more generally as tools, not as representations capable of truth or falsity (in the correspondence sense). What you want from theories is dependable performance – that is, the prediction should regularly bear out, at least often enough to be judged of interest. If you are a realist, you can accept theories without such predictive tests. For example, socialization theory would hardly be testable by predictions, especially on an individual level, but it does provide *explanations* (or contribute to explain) for how or why people or groups change the way they do, and is for that reason acceptable.

Prescriptive educational theories must clearly possess predictive power to function. To apply such a theory is in essence to predict that certain outcomes will be brought about. Educationists will have to decide for themselves whether they think this is enough. Antirealist educationists can make do with an input-output logic, where what you need is the correlation between input and output, like Watson's S-R theory. On this theory you can predict the occurrence of R given S (with the caveats mentioned in Chapter 7). However, the theory does not and cannot *explain* how R came about, because it omits any postulates pertaining to the relation between S and R. Correlations by themselves explain nothing – but see here Hempel's accounts of explanation, which picture explanations as deductive arguments where one of the premises is a universal empirical law, which is in fact a correlation (Hempel, 1965). Interestingly, Ignaz Semmelweis also really only had a *correlation*, between hand washing in chlorine lime and a subsequent reduction in death rate in the maternity ward. But he wanted a theory to *explain* the observed effect and postulated the existence of cadaverous matter as a causal agent. Bacteria, unobservable at the time – but with eminent explanatory power!

I end this sub-section with Patrick Suppes (1974), who in his Presidential Address to the American Educational Research Association (AERA) among other things argues that it should be a primary thrust of theory in educational research to seek mechanisms or processes that answer *why* questions. In other words, that provide explanations. This, Suppes points out, is not Deweyan problem-solving. Theories cannot be replaced by problem-solving, he argues: that would neglect and slight the intellectually important history of theory (p.5).

Summary

This section has been devoted to uses of theory other than action-guiding: the classical educational idea about theory use. Theories are used for a multitude of purposes; for example, description, explanation, prediction, understanding, modification of some aspect of the world, guiding of action (more or less strictly circumscribed), justification of action and decisions, and quite possibly more.

The philosophy of science traditionally highlights three kinds of theory use: description, explanation and prediction. Of these, description is hardly ever discussed; it is probably considered to be easy, straightforward and not much of an indication of scientific success. I have devoted space to description for several interrelated reasons. I think description is underrated and deserving of much more space in educational research projects than usually accorded. Observability comes in degrees, and phenomena can be described at various levels of abstraction. Which words to employ, for example, when describing actions? Which level of abstraction is appropriate? The boundary between description and interpretation is not clear-cut, but rather fuzzy and admitting of ambiguous cases. I leaned on Fred Dretske's concepts of direct and indirect fact perception to make the point that descriptions (largely) are dependent on theory, at least those we might classify as indirect fact perceptions. A T-term that catches a number of disparate observations might yield recognition and understanding of a phenomenon: "Oh, so *that's* what's going on!" If theory and theoretical concepts guide what you see and how you understand a situation, the quality of the theory naturally becomes an urgent concern. Dretske's twin conceptions have the further advantage that while inspiring (at least) two layers of description, they also inspire us to slow down our inferential processes and check on the assumed connection between c, d and x, y. If we conflate direct and indirect perceptions, we may unjustifiably believe in the correctness of our own description. There might exist a theory that can justify this connection, or it might be simply habitual reasoning. Description is useful, and it requires T-terms – not for guiding action, but for understanding what is going on.

Explanation is also useful. Theories provide postulates to inform you how things can or do hang together, and thus yield a deeper understanding of phenomena. I discussed this in some detail to provide at least a partial response to Gary Thomas' lament about the use of theory. If you are a realist, you may hold that T-terms, e.g. motivation, creativity and intelligence, can be used both to describe and explain behavior. If you are an antirealist, you may use such T-terms to describe behavior, the terms being summaries of observed behaviors, but you cannot use them to explain behavior. Prediction is generally hailed as a major indicator of scientific success. It is interesting in educational contexts because it latches itself more easily on to effectiveness considerations, which by many are considered to be of prime usefulness in education. Myself I settle for description and explanation as the most important uses of theory. More important, in fact, than action-guidance.

Possible side effects of theory use

Gary Thomas' challenge concerning the alleged uselessness of theory in education (Thomas, 1997) has loomed large in this chapter, and it is finally time to face it head on. He claims, among other things, that a lack of definition has led the term "theory" to loosely denote intellectual endeavor. Theory is simply not useful in education; at least, the domains in which theory is valuable are very limited.

Theory is a force for conservatism, an instrument of reinforcing existing sets of practices and methods; far from being the emancipating force some writers imagine, theory discourages diversity in thought.

These are serious allegations. Thomas is right, of course, that there are many meanings and uses of the term "theory", many of them decidedly vague and unsatisfactory, and some may have come about because people have to have a name for the bodies of knowledge they employ and talk about. But as I have argued in previous chapters, definitions of "theory" do exist; and, more importantly, carefully worked out meta-theories do exist. Definitions by themselves tend to be skimpy and uninformative (witness the definitions of theory in Chapter 3); meta-theories serve to flesh out the details and identify examples. Moreover, I have in this chapter discussed different uses of theory, some standard and some specifically tailored to goal-directed theories. None of these uses, I judge, are actually touched by Thomas' critical analysis. It seems to me that his discussion is more about the potential negative side effects of using theory – not the use of the theory itself, which may be to furnish an explanation of an observed result, but the side effects of using it. And here Thomas touches an issue that clearly deserves more attention. His allegations against theory in education merit a lengthy quote:

> Theory's acquired potency for bestowing academic legitimacy is troublesome, for it means that particular kinds of endeavor in educational inquiry are reinforced and promulgated, while the legitimacy of atheoretical kinds is questioned or belittled. Educational inquiry is thus distorted; within education research, strange interstices are created by the hegemony of theory. I argue that theory of any kind is thus a force for conservatism, for stabilizing the status quo through the circumscription of thought within a hermetic set of rules, procedures, and methods. Seen in this way, theory – far from being emancipatory as some have claimed (e.g., Carr, 1995) or a vehicle for "thinking otherwise" (Ball, 1995) – is in fact an instrument for reinforcing an existing set of practices and methods in education.
>
> (p.76)

Furthermore, he says, theory in education pays too much heed to that which is already established (p.88); we compact, trim and force the worlds we deal with into theoretical molds and thereby risk distorting and misperceiving them (p.98); and finally, theory in education petrifies thought and is downright antagonistic to pluralism in ideas (p.101). His solution, inspired by Foucault and Feyerabend, is to call for "ad hocery" rather than theory; on the assumption that progress is not the fruit of theory but of anarchy in thought (p.77).

Thomas singles out some theories (including Piaget's theory and grand theories) for special attention, but his conclusions are sweeping statements concerning all educational theory, at an aggregate level. This is not about theory being useful to some specific person in some specific way; this concerns all theories and the entire research community. Thomas is not the only person to worry about side effects of theory use. A concrete example comes from Les Tickle, more low-key, but serious enough. In the early 1990s, Tickle did an inquiry with newly educated teachers (Tickle, 1993). These teachers participated in a program based on Donald Schön's well-known concept of "reflection in action". The program naturally aimed at developing reflective practitioners. The basic idea was one of mutual exchange of theory and practice: the teachers should develop their ability to use theoretical knowledge to understand and identify problems in practice, connect theory with experience-based ingenuity and problem-solving, and thus keep theory and practice in a fruitful, mutual movement. But what happened? Tickle's formulation of his main finding is striking: "The outcome of reflection was non-reflection" (p.xii). I love this formulation! It is precise, paradoxical, truly mind-boggling and sends one's thoughts racing. And most certainly it does not express what teacher educators would deem a sensible, reasonable use of theory.

So what is going on? Tickle's explanation makes use of a number of unobservables: most (if not all) of them concern attributes, expectations or strategies employed by the teachers. They do, Tickle hypothesizes, experience "informational overload" and are not in possession of appropriate strategies to handle complex everyday transactions. Practice exhibits an overwhelming multitude of factors, individuals, beliefs, mutual relations and interactions, all of them with more or less variation, and it is not possible to keep all these factors firmly in your grasp at all times. At the same time, they experience a (subjective) need for confidence, to know that one can handle the job, to be on top of things, to feel mastery of the work. This is a perfectly legitimate need and one can well understand the teachers. Thus, Tickle says, the novice teachers used theory to de-problematize teaching, to stabilize the unstable, to simplify the complex, and to make the unpredictable predictable. The search and need for mastery and control led them to fixate features in practice; that is, hold them stable and unchangeable, and thereby become able to see them as typical and repetitive and amenable to inductive experiential learning. The new, the different and the randomly present, so vitally important to Weniger, are pushed out. Tickle's program might have satisfied internal scientific evaluation criteria, such as consistency, conceptual clarity, explanatory power, etc., and yet its results deviated so much from the expectations.

All theory use can have unintended and unwanted consequences of this kind. Thomas argues as if all the consequences theory use has are negative and detrimental to thought. But the claim is not only sweeping; it is also empirical and needs to be substantiated in the old familiar way: by observation and experience. That might be a tough task! On the other hand, Tickle's story provides evidence that theory use *can* have negative side effects. I round off this section with a couple of comments. First, to the extent that theory use has negative side effects, is the theory itself to blame? I have throughout this chapter argued that use of theory is up the user, so I would find it hard to blame the theory for any detrimental effects it may have on the individual educationist or the community. We can say of the theory that it is false, or inadequate, or oversimplified; but that concerns the quality of the theory and not the attitudes adopted by the user following use of the theory. Second, I think there is room for nuance here: it may well be that some kinds of theories are more prone to the kind of effect that Tickle describes. I have in mind here prescriptive theories, because they at the outset emphasize practice as stable and predictable, with features one can identify as typical, recurring, permanent. Hirst's educational theory is a case in point: if a theory can prescribe precisely what shall be done for a large number of practice situations, it must be presupposed that a large number of features and factors are stable, invariant, predictable. Third, theory use *can* have negative side effects. It *need* not, and as I said above it is an empirical question whether it actually *does*. But it *can*. So how big is the risk? If we judge that the risk is small, even negligible, we keep learning and using theory, and maybe on occasion there are detrimental effects such as the one described by Tickle. I should interject here that I do not know what further happened to these teachers, but it is not inconceivable that once they got on top of their game they could "let up" and begin reflecting again. If we, on the other hand, judge that the risk of negative side effects is a near certainty, we may judge that the best we can do is to forgo theory altogether and aim for, for example, ad hocery, as Thomas does. Given the manifest utility of theory, I opt for the first strategy. Theory is worth the risk.

Summary

I have in this chapter discussed two broad topics within the immensely large, overarching topic of *theory use*: application as based on SC and standard uses of theory commonly discussed in philosophical literature. Since much of my argumentation has been cast as a response to Gary Thomas' challenge concerning the usefulness of theory in education, I have also included a short discussion of possible detrimental side effects of using theory. I have discussed theory use from different perspectives and in much detail, and I hope I have responded adequately to the challenge. I think theory is necessary. Moreover, I think it is unavoidable. And if it is unavoidable, we had better worry about its quality. False and inadequate theories can cause misunderstandings, false beliefs and unjustified courses of action – but can also be effective. Falsity and effectiveness do not rule one another out.

The section on the understanding of theory application that emanates from SC is, of course, an important section. It lays out in some detail the implications of the nature of theory for application. On SC, there is a two-step relation between (abstract) theory and (concrete) phenomenon. Theories are simplifications, and we should not wonder that they do not match the phenomenon. SC entails a separation of the theory and the method of its application. To apply a theory, you need the aid of a suitable set of auxiliary hypotheses, and in many cases the user of the theory will have to furnish this set himself or herself. Taken together, the two-step relation and the set of auxiliary hypotheses between them ensure great flexibility in theory use. The theory can be adjusted to the particular situation at hand, and be used in different ways, by different people, in different situations, at different times. This flexibility comes at a cost: theory application is by no means a simple straightforward process. To apply a theory, you must know the theory; you must identify which parameters are not treated by the theory and assess the relative significance of those parameters; you must identify how the theory deviates from the non-isolated situation; and you must judge how the contextual parameters should influence your adjustment and implementation of the theory in practice. None of this is easy. Since contexts vary and change, the set of auxiliary hypotheses should not be hewn in stone. I stayed with goal-directed theories as examples, mainly since prescription is the traditional educational use of theory. To be sure, theories can guide action, but they cannot prescribe it in detail. There are possible qualities of recipes for action that I have not discussed, such as immediate comprehensibility and ease of application. But I have concluded that educational theory is *least* suited to its traditional practice-guiding, prescriptive function. The ideal of a theory-governed practice is unfeasible – and should not be an ideal at all. The same applies to research-governed practice, which seems to be much in vogue these days. It should not and cannot be an ideal, for the same reasons that theory-governed practice cannot be an ideal: it ignores the context and the great variability of educational practice. Application of theory requires judgment, and SC explains why this is so.

I have argued, and hope to have demonstrated, that the uses of theory are many and highly variegated. Theories are useful in many ways, and that includes uses of parts of them, for example, specific T-terms and postulates, to explain outcomes, observations, effects and lack of effects. Unobservables, designated by T-terms, are indispensable to both description and explanation. Description, I have argued, is vastly underrated, both in terms of importance and in terms of difficulty. As for explanation, even everyday explanations make excessive use of T-terms, such as motivation, presuppositions, intentions and diligence. (As we saw in Chapter 8, Bateson would not approve; he would have us explain behavior in terms of the contingency patterns of contexts – also unobservable.) I have come to think that this use of theory is the most important one, since deeper understanding of various phenomena and their intricate interrelations might follow in train – does not *have to* follow in train, but *can*. Descriptions and explanations may be false, predictions may be disconfirmed, understandings may be shallow and misunderstandings may happen.

Using theory might have unintended consequences; Tickle's study shows that it can. It can also have unintended effects that are positive, such as people overthrowing prejudices and false beliefs and adopting a well-supported theory instead. Practitioners should definitely have more than one theory in their repertory, to have accessible to them a reservoir of terms, parameters and postulates, and thus several possibilities for description, explanation, understanding and guiding action *and* for counteracting dogmatism.

11 Conclusion

After many discussions and analyses of various topics pertaining to educational theorizing, what can and should we now say about educational theories, their nature and possible uses? It is not in the nature of philosophy to provide last and final words about its topics, and I do not presume that the last word has been said about the nature of educational theories with this book. All the same, I have some conclusions to offer. It is time now to take stock and to point to possible areas for further investigations. Just let me state as a fact if anybody ever doubted it: the domain of education does have proper theories.

Not only does the domain of education have proper theories; it has theories of different *types*. I have identified and exemplified three such types: goal-directed, equivalence and interlevel theories. As suggested, the last word on this issue is likely not said yet – other types of theories (theories with different structures) might be identified as well. I leave that question open. Different kinds of phenomena require different kinds of theories for their representation, and complex phenomena require complex theoretical structures. We should not assume that theories of instruction have the same structure as theories weighing criteria for grading, or as theories involving transformations between aggregate levels. It is important to pick an appropriate form of representation for any given phenomenon, or else we risk misrepresenting it. Education is a diverse and large domain and it stands to reason that it should have more than one type of theory.

Much of the literature on the alleged special nature of educational theories runs on a presumed contrast between educational and scientific theories. First, that educational theories aim at practical results whereas scientific theories do not. Second, that the role of value judgments is thought to be prominent in educational theorizing but absent in scientific theorizing. The distinction between educational theories and scientific theories has kept recurring throughout the chapters. It cannot and should not be upheld. Several considerations all converge on this conclusion. First and foremost, the Semantic Conception of theories (SC), the meta-theory I have enlisted, tells us that no theories, regardless of domain and (original) purpose, attempt to characterize the phenomena they take as their objects in all their complexity. There is invariably a selection of parameters. All theories are simplifications – a fact which in its turn causes trouble for the application of a theory, but which also allows great flexibility in its application. Furthermore, it is SC that provides the tools for the identification of different types of educational theories. Concerning practical results, some educational theories evidently do aim at practical results, if by that we mean the bringing about of a desired change of some sort. This is not unique to education, since we would want to say that research in biotechnology or agriculture also aims at some practical result, perhaps even more palpably practical than the results of education. Finally, a brief comment on the role of value judgments. Yes, educational theorizing is shot through with value judgments. But so is all scientific theorizing, concerning choice of topic, appropriateness of method, ethical concerns in data collection and in the reporting of results, proposed use of results, and so on. Research is on the whole a deeply normative enterprise.

The distinction between educational and scientific theories is generally thought to be co-extensive with a distinction between practical and theoretical or pure theories. Many philosophers of education, representing both the Anglo-American and the Nordic-Continental traditions (e.g. Chambers, Hirst, Myhre, Skjervheim), make it. I think we can identify two more assumptions here. First, there is an underlying assumption concerning the nature of domains and the nature of theories, such that a domain assumed to be practical must have practice-oriented theories and *only* that. This, I have argued in Chapter 2, is a misrepresentation of the domain of education. Yes, a substantial part of it is oriented toward professional and practical issues, but a substantial part of it is oriented toward other forms of questions and phenomena – philosophy, history and sociology of education, for example. Besides that, as a matter of principle I see no reason why we should demand such uniformity between the nature of a given domain and the nature of the theories in it. That is not only overly rigid; it would force the same theoretical structure on all the phenomena of theoretical interest in that domain. Conversely, a number of interesting phenomena might fall outside the scope of the domain because they do not conform to the decreed form of the theories in it. Second, there seems to be an underlying assumption concerning the uses or functions of theories, such that any given theory has only one form of use. This, too, I find unduly rigid. There is no reason to think that a theory should have only one use. On a very general level, there is a two-way relation between theories and the phenomenon they strive to capture and applied field in which they occur. On the one hand, we have (possible) implications flowing from the theory to the applied field, hypotheses to be tested, and so on. On the other hand, there are questions arising from the applied field that can be asked *of* the theories, for example concerning what a given theory can tell us about aspects of the phenomena of interest. When we, using SC, separate a theory from its method of application, it becomes abundantly clear that decisions concerning use lie with the user, not with the theory. Thus, we get a much more flexible and intuitive picture in which one and the same theory can perform different functions, in accordance with the purposes of the user. Educational theories, like theories generally, are representational devices that enable us to understand, describe and explain phenomena, and when desired, to change them. All theories cannot perform all kinds of tasks, but, I venture to claim, most if not all theories can perform more than one task. Describing and providing understanding could easily be combined with action-guiding and the justifying of decisions, for example. The quality of the various uses is, of course, another matter. There are good and bad ways of using theory.

The adequacy of meta-theories

Two of my main conclusions rely on SC. I have employed SC as my main analytical tool, and as a lens through which to look at the domain of education. My first main conclusion, concerning the existence of different types of theories, comes about because SC offers a rich set of elements, factors and relations to work with, including parameters, theoretical postulates and theoretical laws. Concerning the identification of types of theory, the concept of a theoretical law has proved to be a powerful tool indeed. It served a major role in alleviating my early unsatisfying struggles with the nature of educational theory (see Chapter 1). It implies that there are several possible theoretical structures, so why should education settle for only one? The concept of a theoretical law thus substantiated my observations that educational theorists and researchers *do* develop theories that do not conform to the traditional conception of an educational theory as practical and action-guiding. SC is a rich conception that accommodates an array of different theories and allows us a pluralistic view of the nature of educational theories. By the same token, it deprives educationalists of the idea that educational theories are of a special kind.

My second main conclusion also derives directly from employment of SC: the often-proposed distinction between scientific and educational, theoretical and practical theories, cannot be upheld. All theories are composed of the same building blocks.

It may be that the same conclusions could have been reached by other pathways as well. There are other meta-theories besides the two examined in this book. But since my meta-theory of choice undoubtedly has played an important role, a bird's eye view of it is worthwhile. We construct theories to do something for us: describe, predict and explain phenomena and observations, justify decisions, modify some aspect of the world, and so on. I suggested in Chapter 2 that a meta-theory should help us get a better understanding of *how* theories do their jobs, what they actually *say* about the phenomena they represent and *how* they say it. I suggested the following desiderata for a meta-theory:

- It should tell us what sort of entities we find when we unpack a theory
- It should tell us how these entities are connected
- It should tell us how the theory is related to the phenomena within its scope

As we have seen, the Received View (RV) and the Semantic Conception (SC) give different answers to all these questions. RV tells us that (1) theories consist of a logical calculus and correspondence rules; (2) the relations between the axioms and theorems of the logical calculus are deductive; (3) there is a one-step relation between theory and phenomenon, and (4) that the correspondence rules determine how the theory manifests itself in the phenomenon. SC tells us that (1) theories consist of parameters, theoretical laws and theoretical postulates; (2) the connections between the parameters are described by the theoretical postulates; (3) there is a two-step relation between theories and phenomena, and (4) that there is a separation between a theory and its method of application such that application is not decided by the theory itself. I have throughout all the chapters compared the two meta-theories and indicated that I find in favor of SC and why. I will not repeat all of that here but confine myself to one comment especially concerning (3) and (4): the view entailed by SC explains why a theory cannot be thought of as a recipe to be followed. Application of a theory is not determined by the theory itself, but by the user. No theory can therefore determine precisely what should be done in practice, but can, like other generalizations, provide general recommendations and guidance for actions. There can be no tyranny of theory. If it appears that there is, one must find the tyrant among its users, not within the theory itself.

Next, I would like to make some observations concerning what a meta-theory can do for the domain to which it is applied, in our case education. That is, I propose to look at their usefulness for the domain. First, let me say that I am largely sympathetic to O'Connor's approach to the problem of the nature of educational theories. O'Connor took a meta-theoretical approach, as I have done, with the significant difference that we employ different conceptions of theory structure. I am also sympathetic to his view that the construction of educational theories should be subject to the same standards as other scientific theories. But when identifying this "standard", O'Connor employs the RV. He establishes that educational theory does not satisfy the axiomatic-deductive structure demanded by this view, and hence, his assertion that in the domain of education, "theory" is but a courtesy title. That is to say, O'Connor used RV as a lens, and when he found nothing in the domain of education that satisfied the demands of RV, he concluded that the domain was at fault and not the lens.

O'Connor must have viewed RV as a crystal-clear conception of theory, in the sense that either something qualifies as a theory or it does not. I have used SC as a lens and found different types of theories. I have concluded that this is as it should be in a large and diversified domain. I am not arguing, however, that SC can serve as an absolute standard for judging whether something is a theory or not. It has indeed allowed me to identify different types of educational theories, but there are bodies of knowledge in the educational field that are such that it is hard to decide whether they count as theories or not. Didactic models, for example: theories or not? Interestingly, in a similar vein one might question whether S-R theory strictly speaking is a theory. Yes, it is commonly spoken of as a theory, and yes, Suppe uses it as one of his examples to show that SC is applicable outside the natural sciences. However, if we demand of theories that they should be able to explain occurrences and observations, S-R theory might not count as a theory. S does not *explain* R, and the theory offers no other explanatory resources, for example in the form of theoretical entities, causal connections or other underlying mechanisms that bring about R. Some would no doubt view S-R "theory" as an empirical generalization of the form "whenever S is present R is also present", and claim that it falls short of being a theory. There might thus be borderline cases in the employment of SC. It is not clear whether RV would have borderline cases like this. RV is much more tightly knit, with its axiomatic-deductive structure and correspondence rules which tie together the theoretical and the observational, and it might be clearer on what counts as a theory and what does not. Recall from Chapter 3, though, Suppes' claim that virtually no theories admit of reformulations according to the canons of RV – hardly any bodies of knowledge we call "theories" actually satisfy RV's requirements. Given that SC has borderline cases, is that a problem? I would argue not. Most concepts have borderline cases, and we should not wonder that a conception of theory, too, might have borderline cases. But, I claim, the most important issue is not whether a given body of knowledge qualifies as a theory or not. It is much more important that a conception of theories, such as SC, helps us identify, develop, refine and structure bodies of knowledge in the domain. That, in turn, could help us formulate deep-running theories in education. Theories, as Suppes (1974) so optimistically puts it, of the kind that "have driven alchemists out of chemistry and astrologers out of astronomy" (p. 6).

Identification, development, refinement and structuration of bodies of knowledge are things that any worthwhile meta-theory should provide. We can, for example, cash this out in terms of construction and application of theory. And here, I argue, SC really shows its usefulness. As already said, it helps us identify different types of theories, which is a great service to our domain. Let us look at theory construction in some more detail. SC aids our theory construction in different ways, I suggest.

First, SC alerts us to the question of the appropriateness of a given representational form. I am developing a method of reading instruction; what kind of theoretical structure is best suited to capture the relevant phenomena? Or if I am studying the behavioral patterns of suburban children in informal learning arenas, what kind of theoretical structure is best suited to capture the phenomena? Such decisions require prior knowledge of and various background assumptions concerning the phenomena. SC offers different theoretical structures to choose from and it is important to do justice to the phenomena and not force them into a representational form that does not fit.

Second, SC directs our attention to the selection of parameters. If I am studying behavioral patterns, which parameters do I need? How many should I opt for? How many unobservables can I reasonably employ? Are any of the parameters idealized? If so, how should I handle that? In a similar vein, if I know that I am working on a goal-directed theory, knowing what goal-directed theories normally contain will help me look for such "things" as my theory will need to be an adequate representation of the phenomena. I will need parameters concerning the teleological system, for example, but which and how many?

Third, SC directs our attention to theoretical postulates to provide connections between our chosen parameters. How should I understand these connections? As causally necessary? As causally sufficient? As probable? As a part/whole relationship?

Our choices here significantly influence how the theory represents the phenomena and hence, how we understand them.

Fourth, SC directs our attention to the more overall question of how we wish to portray the behavior of the abstract model in the state space. How narrow or wide do we take the state space to be? Is the model dynamic? Static? Is our theoretical law deterministic or indeterministic?

SC thus allows us to get a much clearer picture of what we are doing when we are constructing and revising theories. The theories may not yet be fully fledged, but SC has the potential to direct our search. It offers tools to help us identify, develop, refine and structure existing bodies of knowledge in the domain, budding theories and full-fledged theories alike. All of which is *useful*.

In a similar vein, SC offers a reasonable view of theory application. All theories, Suppe argues, run on an *as if* – they treat the phenomena as if their behavior is due to the selected parameters only, and that the influence of other factors can be safely ignored. All models are simplifications. This fact raises intricate issues of truth (discussed in Chapter 7) and of application (discussed in Chapter 10). The various versions of the nature of educational theory advocated by different philosophers of education seem to have (at least) one feature in common: the presupposition of a direct relationship between theory and phenomenon (practice). This is, I suppose, a quite natural and intuitive presupposition to make – I certainly made it myself when I was a teacher student, and I continued to do so until I discovered Frederick Suppe's writings on meta-theory. The one-step presupposition forces Hirst and Friedrich to incorporate norms or value judgments in the theory, and Carr argues that an educational theory incorporates notions of how it should be used in practice. O'Connor asks how empirical statements, metaphysical assumptions and value judgments could possibly be incorporated into one coherent theory, and answers that they cannot.

I have argued that a view of theory structure claiming that a theory has some integral component that determines its use is untenable. RV's account of correspondence rules embodies the notorious O/T distinction and obscures a number of epistemically significant features by lumping them into one step. This impairs our understanding of what is involved in theory application because the vital roles played by considerations extraneous to the theory itself are ignored. This includes ethical considerations, which I have argued are better kept outside the theory. Moreover, in the case of education, a theory that determines its own use is unable to take into account the variability of educational practice.

A conception of theory structure that separates the theory from its method of application may sound counterintuitive, but it makes good sense. It also makes theory application a good deal more complex. As Cartwright says, there is no precise recipe for how to get from abstract theory to concrete phenomenon, let alone practice. Such a separation is supported, first, by the fact that theories do not treat phenomena in all their complexity; and second, it is in all likelihood more faithful to the *actual* practice of theory application which, as seasoned practitioners might describe it, requires "adaptation" of the theory to the concrete situation. SC explains why such adaptation is necessary and what it consists in, and thus greatly refines our views on theory use or application. The application of theories, given their nature, requires the use of auxiliary hypotheses to estimate how the concrete situations deviate from the idealized situations described by the theories. This allows great flexibility in theory application, for it means that the same theory can be used in conjunction with differing sets of auxiliary hypotheses, but it requires much thought from the user of the theory. The user, after all, knows both theory and concrete situation and is the one who has to put all the information together and make defensible and informed decisions about what to do. The two-step relation between theory and phenomena (most notably practice) is something of a double-edged sword. It makes theory application a challenging process that requires sound judgment in the practitioner, but it also makes it flexible. The variability of practice can thus be taken into account and accommodated. SC thus provides a much clearer picture of what is involved in theory application. That is *useful*.

Prospects for future investigation

There are many things to investigate in the field of education; many new pathways to explore and no doubt many ways to reshuffle existing ideas to combine into new insights. For the particular topic that I have explored in this book – theories and meta-theories – a couple of issues suggest themselves for future investigations.

First, types of theory: how many are there? I have identified three, but I would be surprised if that exhausts the possibilities. Education is a manifold field and educational phenomena tend to grow more diverse and more complex. Second, the twin issues of individuation and revision or development of theories: when we speak of theory development, we often mean that changes and adjustments are made to the theory. So suppose you revise a theory by adding an extra parameter or two and by changing a theoretical postulate from causal sufficiency to probability. How many (and which) changes do you have to make before the theory counts as a *new* theory? How should we handle the idea that the same theory can exist in different versions? Third, the formulation of deep-running theories in education. It would be of great interest to unpack already existing deep-running theories (to the extent that we have them) to ascertain their structure, the role of unobservables, and so on. It would also be of great interest to look at what kind of reorganization, reshuffling and theoretical integration is required for the formulation of such theories.

Finally, I would suggest *possibility* as a worthwhile avenue to explore. I have touched on it here and there, but not engaged with it. But surely assumptions concerning possibility lie as unstated premises and constraints under many theoretical postulates, ideas about state spaces and understandings of how things might develop. In the educational world we encounter what is actual and not what is merely possible. But possibilities matter greatly in education. Some of them we call risks and try to guard against or prevent, some of them we wish to bring to realization. Possibilities, whether explicitly or implicitly, make up a large chunk of our understanding of actions, judgments of plans and evaluation of results, and are of utmost interest to theoreticians and practitioners alike.

References

Aristotle (1987). *The Nicomachean Ethics.* New York: Prometheus Books. Trans. J. E. C. Welldon.

Ashby, W. R. (1984). *An Introduction to Cybernetics.* London: Methuen.

Audi, R. (1991). *Practical Reasoning.* London: Routledge.

Austin, J. (1950). *How to do Things with Words.* Oxford: Oxford University Press.

Bateson, G. (1972). *Steps to an Ecology of Mind.* New York: Ballantine.

Bateson, G. (1980). *Mind and Nature: A Necessary Unity.* Glasgow: Fontana/Collins.

Beatty, J. (1981). Optimal design models and the strategy of model building in evolutionary biology. *Philosophy of Science*, 47, 532–561.

Bertalanffy, L. von (1968). *General System Theory. Revised Edition.* New York: George Baziller.

Beth, E. (1949). Towards an up-to-date philosophy of the natural sciences. *Methodos*, 1, 178–185.

Biesta, G. (2007). Why "what works" won't work: Evidence-based practice and the democratic deficit in educational research. *Educational Theory*, 57, 1, 1–22.

Biesta, G. (2011). Disciplines and theory in the academic study of education: A comparative analysis of the Anglo-American and Continental construction of the field. *Pedagogy, Culture & Society*, 19, 2, 175–192.

Bloom, B. S. (Ed.) (1956). *Taxonomy of Educational Objectives.* New York: Longmans.

Bollnow, O. F. (1975). *Die antropologische Betrachtungsweise in der Pädagogik* [*The Anthropological Perspective in Education*]. Essen: Neue deutsche Schule Verlagsgesellschaft.

Braithwaite, R. (1968). *Scientific Explanation.* Cambridge: Cambridge University Press.

Brezinka, W. (1978). *Metatheorie der Erziehung* [*Meta-theory of Upbringing*]. Munich: Ernst Reinhard.

Bridges, D. (2006). The disciplines and discipline of educational research. *Journal of Philosophy of Education*, 40, 2, 259–272.

Bromberger, S. (1963). A theory about the theory of theory and about the theory of theories. In B. Baumrin (Ed.), *Philosophy of Science: The Delaware Seminar, Vol. II* (79–106). New York: Interscience.

Bronfenbrenner, U. (1979). *The Ecology of Human Development.* Cambridge, MA: Harvard University Press.

Bruner, J. (1986). *Actual Minds, Possible Worlds.* Cambridge, MA: Harvard University Press.

Capps, J. (2019). The pragmatic theory of truth. In E. Zalta (Ed.), *Stanford Encyclopedia of Philosophy.* https://plato.stanford.edu/entries/truth-pragmatic/. Retrieved May 17, 2020.

Carnap, R. (1936). Testability and meaning. *Philosophy of Science*, 3, 420–468.

Carnap, R. (1956). The methodological character of theoretical concepts. In H. Feigl & M. Scriven (Eds.), *Minnesota Studies in the Philosophy of Science, Vol.* I (33–76). Minneapolis, MN: University of Minneapolis Press.

Carr, D. (2003). Rival conceptions of practice in education and teaching. *Journal of Philosophy of Education*, 37, 2, 253–266.

Carr, W. (1980). The gap between theory and practice. *Journal of Further and Higher Education*, 4, 1, 60–69.

Carr, W. (1986). Theories of theory and practice. *Journal of Philosophy of Education*, 20, 2, 177–186.

Carr, W. (1995). *For Education: Towards Critical Educational Enquiry.* Buckingham: Open University Press.

Carr, W. (2006). Education without theory. *British Journal of Educational Studies*, 54, 2, 136–159.

Carroll, L. (1988). *The Complete Works of Lewis Carroll.* Harmondsworth, UK: Penguin.

Cartwright, N. (1989). *Nature's Capacities and their Measurement.* Oxford: Clarendon Press.

Cartwright, N. (1999). Models and the limits of theory: Quantum Hamiltonians and the BCS models of superconductivity. In M. Morgan & M. Morrison (Eds.), *Models as Mediators: Perspectives on Natural and Social Science* (241–281). Cambridge: Cambridge University Press.

Castle, D. G. A. (2001). A semantic view of ecological theories. *Dialectics*, 55, 1, 51–65.

Chakravartty, A. (2001). The semantic or model-theoretic view of theories and scientific realism. *Synthese*, 127, 3, 325–345.

Chambers, J. H. (1992). *Empiricist Research on Teaching: A Philosophical and Practical Critique of its Scientific Pretensions.* Dordrecht: Kluwer Academic Publishers.

Clark, C. (1976). Education is not an academic discipline: A reply to Professor Peters. *Educational Studies*, 2, 1, 11–19.

Comte, A. (1968). *System of Positive Polity. Second Volume: Containing Social Statistics, or the Abstract Theory of Human Order.* New York: Burt Franklin. First published in French 1881–1854.

Craver, C. F. (2002). Structures of scientific theories. In P. Machamer & M. Silberstein (Eds.), *The Blackwell Guide to the Philosophy of Science* (55–79). Oxford/Malden, MA: Blackwell Publishers.

David, M. (2004). Theories of truth. In I. Niiniluoto, M. Sintonen & J. Wolenski (Eds.), *Handbook of Epistemology* (331–414). Dordrecht: Kluwer Academic Publishers.

Dearden, R. F. (1984). *Theory and Practice in Education.* London: Routledge & Kegan Paul.

Dewey, J. (1976). *Experience and Education.* London: Collier Macmillan.

Dewey, J. (1991). *Logic: The Theory of Inquiry.* J. A. Boydston (Ed.), *John Dewey, the Later works, 1925–1953, Vol. 12.* Carbondale, IL: Southern Illinois University Press. First published 1938.

Dretske, F. (1990). *An Invitation to Cognitive Science, Vol. 2: Visual Cognition and Action.* Cambridge, MA: MIT Press.

Driver, R. (1989). The construction of scientific knowledge in classrooms. In R. Millar (Ed.), *Doing Science: Images of Science in Science Education* (83–106). Bristol, PA: Taylor & Francis.

Driver, R. (1995). Constructivist approaches to science teaching. In L. R. Steffe & J. E. Gale (Eds.), *Constructivism in Education* (385–400). Hillsdale, NJ: Earlbaum.

Driver, R. & Oldman, V. (1986). A constructivist approach to curriculum development in science. *Studies in Science Education*, 13, 105–122.

Duhem, P. (1954). *The Aim and Structure of Physical Theory*. New York: Atheneum. First published in French 1906.
Dunne, J. (2003). Arguing for teaching as a practice: A reply to Alasdair MacIntyre. *Journal of Philosophy of Education*, 37, 2, 353–370.
Ennis, R. H. (1987). A taxonomy of critical thinking dispositions and abilities. In J. B. Baron & R. J. Sternberg (Eds.), *Teaching Thinking Skills: Theory and Practice* (9–26). New York: W. H. Freeman.
Ennis, R. H. (1996). Critical thinking dispositions: Their nature and assessability. *Informal Logic*, 18, 2 & 3, 165–182.
Feigl, H. (1970). The "orthodox" view of theories: Remarks in defense as well as critique. In M. Radner & S. Winokur (Eds.), *Minnesota Studies in the Philosophy of Science, Vol. IV* (3–16). Minneapolis: University of Minnesota Press.
Fraassen, B. C. van (1970). On the extension of Beth's semantics of physical theories. *Philosophy of Science*, 37, 325–339.
Fraassen, B. C. van (1976). To save the phenomena. *The Journal of Philosophy*, LXXIII, 18, 623–632.
Fraassen, B. C. van (1980). *The Scientific Image*. Oxford: Clarendon Press.
Fraassen, B. C. van (1989). *Laws and Symmetry*. Oxford: Clarendon Press.
Friedrich, L. (1987). Pedagogikkfaget – mellom det empiriske og det normative [Education – between the empirical and the normative]. In O. Evenshaug, T. Harbo & U. Stålsett (Eds.), *Pedagogikk og lærerutdanning* [*Pedagogy and Teacher Education*] (29–43). Oslo: TANO.
Giere, R. N. (1979). *Understanding Scientific Reasoning*. New York: Holt, Rinehart and Winston.
Giere, R. N. (1988). *Explaining Science: A Cognitive Approach*. Chicago: University of Chicago Press.
Giere, R. N. (2004). How models are used to represent reality. *Philosophy of Science*, 71, 5, 742–752.
Giere, R. N. (2010). An agent-based conception of models and scientific representation. *Synthese*, 172, 2, 269–281.
Gieryn, T. F. (1983). Boundary-work and the demarcation of science from non-science: Strains and interests in professional ideologies of scientists. *American Sociological Review*, 48, 6, 781–795.
Glanzberg, M. (Ed.) (2018). *The Oxford Handbook of Truth*. Oxford: Oxford University Press.
Goodman, N. (1983). *Fact, Fiction, and Forecast*. Cambridge, MA: Harvard University Press.
Groothoff, H.-H. (1973). Theorie der Erziehung [Theory of upbringing]. In H.-H. Groothoff (Ed.), *Pädagogik Fischer Lexikon* (72–79). Frankfurt am Main: Fischer Taschenbuch Verlag.
Hacking, I. (1982). *Representing and Intervening*. Cambridge: Cambridge University Press.
Halvorson, H. (2016). Scientific theories. In P. Humphreys (Ed.), *The Oxford Handbook of Philosophy of Science* (585–608). Oxford: Oxford University Press.
Handal, G. & Lauvås, P. (1992). *På egne vilkår* [*On One's Own Terms*]. Oslo: Cappelen.
Hanson, N. R. (1958). *Patterns of Discovery*. Cambridge: Cambridge University Press.
Hempel, C. G. (1952). *Fundamentals of Concept Formation in Empirical Science*. Chicago: University of Chicago Press.
Hempel, C. G. (1958). The theoretician's dilemma. In H. Feigl, M. Scriven & G. Maxwell (Eds.), *Minnesota Studies in the Philosophy of Science, Vol. II* (37–98). Minneapolis, MN: University of Minnesota Press.
Hempel, C. G. (1965). *Aspects of Scientific Explanation and other Essays in the Philosophy of Science*. New York: The Free Press.

Hempel, C. G. (1966). *Philosophy of Natural Science*. Englewood Cliffs, NJ: Prentice-Hall.

Hempel, C. G. (1970). On the 'standard conception' of scientific theories. In M. Radner & S. Winokur (Eds.), *Minnesota Studies in the Philosophy of Science, Vol. IV* (142–163). Minneapolis, MN: University of Minnesota Press.

Hempel, C. G. (1977). Formulation and formalization of scientific theories. In F. Suppe (Ed.), *The Structure of Scientific Theories* (244–254). Urbana, IL: University of Illinois Press.

Higgins, C. (2003). MacIntyre's moral theory and the possibility of an aretaic ethics of teaching. *Journal of Philosophy of Education*, 37, 2, 279–292.

Higgs, P. (1995) (Ed.). *Metatheories in Philosophy of Education*. Johannesburg: Heinemann.

Hirst, P. H. (1966). Educational theory. In J. W. Tibble (Ed.), *The Study of Education* (29–58). London: Routledge & Kegan Paul.

Hirst, P. H. (1973). The nature and scope of educational theory (2). In G. Langford & D. J. O'Connor (Eds.), *New Essays in the Philosophy of Education* (66–75). London: Routledge & Kegan Paul.

Hirst, P. H. (1993). Educational theory. In M. Hammersley (Ed.), *Educational Research: Current Issues (Vol. 1)* (149–159). London: The Open University.

Hoëm, A. (1978). *Sosialisering. En teoretisk og empirisk modellutvikling* [*Socialization. Development of a Theoretical and Empirical Model*]. Oslo: Universitetsforlaget.

Hofstetter, R. (2012). Educational sciences: Evolutions of a pluridisciplinary discipline at the crossroads of other disciplinary and professional fields (20th century). *British Journal of Educational Studies*, 60, 4, 317–335.

Hogan, P. (2003). Teaching and learning as a way of life. *Journal of Philosophy of Education*, 37, 2, 207–224.

James, W. (1975). *Pragmatism: A New Name for Some Old Ways of Thinking*. Cambridge, MA: Harvard University Press. First published 1907.

Kahneman, D. & Miller, D. (1986). Norm theory: Comparing reality to its alternatives. *Psychological Review*, 93, 2, 136–153.

Kamii, C. (1979). Piaget's theory, behaviorism, and other theories in education. *The Journal of Education*, 161, 1, 13–33.

Kaplan, A. (1964). *The Conduct of Inquiry*. San Francisco: Chandler Publications.

Keeney, B. P. (1983). *Aesthetics of Change*. New York: The Guilford Press.

Keiner, E. (2002). Education between academic discipline and profession in Germany after World War II. *European Educational Research Journal*, 1, 1, 83–98.

Kessels, J. P. A. M. & Korthagen, F. A. J. (1996). The relationship between theory and practice: Back to the classics. *Educational Researcher*, 25, 3, 17–22.

Key, E. (1911). *Barnets århundrade* [*The Century of the Child*]. Stockholm: Bonnier.

Kincaid, H. (1990). Molecular biology and the unity of science. *Philosophy of Science*, 57, 4, 575–593.

Kirkham, R. (1997). *Theories of Truth*. Cambridge, MA: The MIT Press.

Kuhn, T. S. (1970). *The Structure of Scientific Revolutions (2nd enlarged Ed)*. Chicago: University of Chicago Press.

Kvernbekk, T. (1994). *In Search of the Nature of Educational Theories*. Oslo: University of Oslo. Unpublished doctoral dissertation.

Kvernbekk, T. (2000). Seeing in practice: A conceptual analysis. *Scandinavian Journal of Educational Research*, 44, 4, 357–370.

Kvernbekk, T. (2005). *Pedagogisk teoridannelse: Insidere, teoriformer og praksis* [*Educational Theorizing: Insiders, Forms of Theory, and Practice*]. Bergen: Fagbokforlaget.

Kvernbekk, T. (2012). Argumentation in theory and practice: Gap or equilibrium? *Informal Logic*, 32, 3, 288–305.

Kvernbekk, T. (2014). My practice, our practice. In J. Baldacchino, S. Galea & D. P. Mercieca (Eds.), *My Teaching, My Philosophy: Kenneth Wain and the Lifelong Engagement with Education* (186–199). New York: Peter Lang Publishing.

Labaree, D. (2008). The dysfunctional pursuit of relevance in education research. *Educational Researcher*, 37, 7, 421–423.

Ladyman, J. (2002). *Understanding Philosophy of Science*. London: Routledge.

Lagemann, E. C. (2000). *An Elusive Science: The Troubling History of Education Research*. Chicago: University of Chicago Press.

Laudan, L. (1981). A confutation of convergent realism. *Philosophy of Science*, 48, 1, 19–49.

Lawn, M. & Furlong, J. (2009). The disciplines of education in the UK: Between the ghost and the shadow. *Oxford Review of Education*, 35, 5, 541–552.

Laymon, R. (1998). Idealizations. *Routledge Encyclopedia of Philosophy*, https://rep.routledge.com/articles/thematic/idealizations/v-1. Retrieved October 16, 2018.

Lewontin, R. (1974). *The Genetic Basis of Evolutionary Change*. Columbia, OH: Columbia University Press.

Lutz, S. (2012). On a straw man in the philosophy of science: A defense of the Received View. *HOPOS: The Journal of the International Society for the History of Philosophy of Science*, 2, 1, 77–120.

Løvlie, L. (1974). Pedagogisk filosofi for praktiserende lærere [Philosophy of education for teachers]. *Pedagogen*, 22, 1, 19–36.

MacIntyre, A. C. (1996). *After Virtue: A Study in Moral Theory*. London: Duckworth. First published 1981.

MacIntyre, A. C. & Dunne, J. (2002). Alasdair MacIntyre on education: In dialogue with Joseph Dunne. *Journal of Philosophy of Education*, 36, 1, 1–19.

McLaughlin, T. H. (2003). Teaching as a practice and a community of practice: The limits of commonality and the demands of diversity. *Journal of Philosophy of Education*, 37, 2, 339–352.

Merton, R. (1996). *On Social Structure and Science*. Edited by Piotr Sztompka. Chicago: University of Chicago Press.

Messick, S. (1995). Standards of validity and the validity of standards in performance assessment. *Educational Measurement: Issues and Practice*, 14, 4, 5–8.

Miller, D. (1994). Virtues, practices, and justice. In J. Horton & S. Mendus (Eds.), *After MacIntyre: Critical Perspectives on the Work of Alasdair MacIntyre* (245–264). Cambridge: Polity Press.

Mills, C. W. (1959). *The Sociological Imagination*. Oxford: Oxford University Press.

Moore, P. (1981). Relations between theory and practice: A critique of Wilfred Carr's views. *Journal of Further and Higher Education*, 5, 2, 44–56.

Morrison, M. (2007). Where have all the theories gone? *Philosophy of Science*, 74, 2, 195–228.

Myhre, R. (1980). *Pedagogisk filosofi [Philosophy of Education]*. Oslo: Fabritius.

Nagel, E. (1961). *The Structure of Science: Problems in the Logic of Scientific Explanation*. Indianapolis, IN: Hackett Publishing Co.

Nagel, E. (1969). Philosophy of Science and Educational Theory. *Studies in Philosophy and Education*, 7, 1, 5–27.

Neurath, O. (1959). Protocol sentences. In A. J. Ayer (Ed.), *Logical Positivism* (199–208). New York: The Free Press.

Newton-Smith, W. H. (1981). *The Rationality of Science*. London: Routledge & Kegan Paul.

Noddings, N. (2003). Is teaching a practice? *Journal of Philosophy of Education*, 37, 2, 241–252.

Nordahl-Hansen, A. & Kvernbekk, T. (2020). Construct validity in scientific representation: A philosophical tour. *Nordic Journal of Pedagogy and Critique*, 6, 88–99.

Nordkvelle, Y. (2004). Technology and didactics: Historical mediations of a relation. *Journal of Curriculum Studies*, 36, 4, 427–444.

Norris, S. P. (1983). The inconsistencies at the foundation of construct validation theory. In E. R. House (Ed.), *Philosophy of Evaluation: New Directions for Program Evaluation, No. 19* (53–74). San Francisco: Jossey-Bass.

Norris, S. P. (1989). Can we test validly for critical thinking? *Educational Researcher*, 18, 9, 21–26.

Norris, S. P. & Kvernbekk, T. (1997). The application of science education theories. *Journal of Research in Science Teaching*, 34, 10, 977–1005.

O'Connor, D. J. (1957). *An Introduction to the Philosophy of Education*. London: Routledge & Kegan Paul.

O'Connor, D. J. (1973). The nature and scope of educational theory (1). In G. Langford & D. J. O'Connor (Eds.), *New Essays in the Philosophy of Education* (47–65). London: Routledge & Kegan Paul.

Oelkers, J. (1994). Influence and development: Two basic paradigms of education. *Studies in Philosophy and Education*, 13, 91–109.

Oelkers, J. (2001). *Einführung in die Theorie der Erziehung* [*Introduction to the Theory of Upbringing*]. Weinheim: Julius Beltz.

Percival, F. & Ellington, H. (1988). *A Handbook of Educational Technology*. London: Kogan Page.

Perkins, D. N., Jay, E. & Tishman, S. (1993). Beyond abilities: A dispositional theory of thinking. *Merrill-Palmer Quarterly*, 39, 1, 1–21.

Peters, R. S. (1972). Education and the educated man. In R. F. Dearden, P. H. Hirst & R. S. Peters (Eds.), *Education and the Development of Reason* (3–18). London: Routledge & Kegan Paul.

Pettersen, R. (1993). *Pedagogisk teori og praksis* [*Educational Theory and Practice*]. Fredrikstad: ØVH.

Phillips, D. C. (1990). *Philosophy, Science, and Social Inquiry*. Oxford: Pergamon Press.

Phillips, D. C. (2018). The many functions of evaluation in education. *Education Policy Analysis Archives*, 26, 46, 1–14.

Phillips, D. C. & Kelly, M. E. (1975). Hierarchical theories of development in education and psychology. *Harvard Educational Review*, 45, 5, 351–375.

Piaget, J. (1970). Piaget's theory. In P. H. Mussen (Ed.), *Manual of Child Psychology*, No. 1, 703–732.

Putnam, H. (1962). What theories are not. In E. Nagel, P. Suppes & A. Tarski (Eds.), *Logic, Methodology and Philosophy of Science: Proceedings of the 1960 International Congress* (240–251). Stanford, CA: Stanford University Press.

Putnam, H. (1975). What is mathematical truth? In H. Putnam, *Mathematics, Matter and Method. Philosophical Papers Vol. I* (60–78). Cambridge: Cambridge University Press.

Putnam, H. (2003). Foreword to the fourth edition. In N. Goodman (1983), *Fact, Fiction and Forecast* (vii–xvi). Cambridge, MA: Harvard University Press.

Reichenbach, H. (1962). *The Rise of Scientific Philosophy*. Berkeley, CA: University of California Press.

Research Council of Norway (2004). *Evaluering av norsk pedagogisk forskning* [*Evaluation of Education Research in Norway*]. Oslo: RCN.

Research Council of Norway (2006). *En nasjonal strategi for norsk pedagogisk forskning* [*Educational Research in Norway: A National Strategy*]. Oslo: RCN.

Romiszowski, A. J. (1984). *Producing Instructional Systems*. London: Kogan Page.

Rosenberg, A. (2012). *Philosophy of Science*. London: Routledge.

Rowntree, D. (1974). *Educational Technology in Curriculum Development*. London: Harper & Row.

Russell, B. (1971). *The Problems of Philosophy*. Oxford: Oxford University Press.

Sand, T. (Ed.) (2008). *Flerkulturell virkelighet i skole og samfunn* [*Multicultural Reality in School and Society*]. Oslo: Cappelen Akademisk Forlag.

Schaffner, K. F. (1980). Theory structure in the biomedical sciences. *The Journal of Medicine and Philosophy*, 5, 1, 57–97.

Scheffler, I. (1973). *Reason and Teaching*. Indianapolis, IN: Hackett Publishing Company.

Schleiermacher, F. (1994). *Ausgewählte pädagogische Schriften* [*Selected Educational Writings*]. Edited by E. Lichtenstein. Paderborn: F. Schöningh. First published 1826.

Schön, D. (1983). *The Reflective Practitioner: How Practitioners Think in Action*. New York: Basic Books.

Schulz, W. (1979). Unterrichtspraxis und Unterrichtswissenshaft [Practice of teaching and science of teaching]. In W. Klafki, G. Otto & W. Schulz (Eds.), *Didaktik und Praxis* [*Didactics and Practice*] (81–104). Weinheim: Julius Beltz.

Scriven, M. (2007). The logic of evaluation. *OSSA Conference Archive*. https://scholar.uwindsor.ca/ossaarchive/OSSA7/papersandcommentaries/138. Retrieved March 4, 2019.

Searle, J. (1995). *The Construction of Social Reality*. New York: The Free Press.

Siegel, H. (1992). Justification by balance. *Philosophy and Phenomenological Research*, 52, 1, 27–46.

Skinner, B. F. (1938). *The Behavior of Organisms: An Experimental Analysis*. New York: Appleton Century Co.

Skjervheim, H. (1992). Eit grunnproblem i pedagogisk filosofi [A fundamental problem in the philosophy of education]. In E. L. Dale (Ed.), *Pedagogisk filosofi* [*Philosophy of Education*] (65–78). Oslo: Gyldendal Ad Notam.

Smith, R. (2003). Thinking with each other: The peculiar practice of the university. *Journal of Philosophy of Education*, 37, 2, 309–324.

Sneed, J. (1971). *The Logical Structure of Mathematical Physics*. Dordrecht: D. Reidel.

Stegmüller, W. (1976). *The Structure and Dynamics of Theories*. Berlin: Springer-Verlag.

Stichweh, R. (1996). Science in the system of world society. *Social Science Information*, 35, 2, 327–340.

Strand, T. & Kvernbekk, T. (2009). Assessing the quality of educational research: The case of Norway. In T. Besley (Ed.), *Assessing the Quality of Educational Research in Higher Education: International Perspectives* (263–278). Rotterdam: Sense Publishers.

Straume, I. S. (2013). Danningens filosofihistorie: en innføring [Introduction to the philosophical history of Bildung]. In I. S. Straume (Ed.), *Danningens filosofihistorie* [*The Philosophical History of Bildung*] (15–54). Oslo: Gyldendal Akademisk.

Suppe, F. (1972). What's wrong with the Received View on the structure of theories? *Philosophy of Science*, 39, 1, 1–19.

Suppe, F. (1977). Criticism of the Received View. In F. Suppe (Ed.), *The Structure of Scientific Theories* (62–118). Urbana, IL: University of Illinois Press.

Suppe, F. (1989). *The Semantic Conception of Theories and Scientific Realism*. Urbana, IL: University of Illinois Press.

Suppe, F. (2000). Understanding scientific theories: An assessment of developments, 1969–1998. *Philosophy of Science*, 67, Supplement, S102–S115.

Suppes, P. (1957). *Introduction to Logic*. New York: Van Nostrand.

Suppes, P. (1962). Models of data. In E. Nagel, P. Suppes & A. Tarski (Eds.), *Logic, Methodology and Philosophy of Science: Proceedings of the 1960 International Congress* (252–261). Stanford, CA: Stanford University Press.

Suppes, P. (1967). What is a scientific theory? In S. Morgenbesser (Ed.), *Philosophy of Science Today* (55–67). New York: Basic Books.

Suppes, P. (1974). The place of theory in educational research. *Educational Researcher*, 3, 6, 3–10.

Tellings, A. (2001). Eclecticism and integration in educational theories: A metatheoretical analysis. *Educational Theory*, 51, 3, 277–292.

Terhart, E. (2016). Interdisciplinary research on education and its disciplines: Processes of change and lines of conflict in unstable academic expert cultures: Germany as an example. *European Educational Research Journal*, 16, 6, 921–936.

Thomas, G. (1997). What's the use of theory? *Harvard Educational Review*, 67, 1, 75–104.

Thompson, P. (1989). *The Structure of Biological Theories*. Albany, NY: State University of New York Press.

Thorén, H. & Persson, J. (2013). The philosophy of interdisciplinarity: sustainability science and problem-feeding. *Journal for General Philosophy of Science*, 44, 2, 337–355.

Tickle, L. (1993). Capital T teaching. In J. Elliott (Ed.), *Reconstructing Teacher Education: Teacher Development* (110–124). London: Falmer Press.

Trowler, P. (2014). Depicting and researching disciplines: Strong and moderate essentialist approaches. *Studies in Higher Education*, 39, 10, 1720–1731.

Turner, S. (2010). *Explaining the Normative*. Cambridge: Polity Press.

Tyler, R. W. (1949). *Basic Principles of Curriculum and Instruction*. Chicago: University of Chicago Press.

Uljens, M. (1998). *Allmän pedagogik* [*General Pedagogy*]. Lund: Studentlitteratur.

Wain, K. (2003). MacIntyre: Teaching, politics, and practice. *Journal of Philosophy of Education*, 37, 2, 225–240.

Watson, J. B. (1930). *Behaviorism (Revised Edition)*. Chicago: University of Chicago Press.

Watzlawick, P., Bavelas, J. & Johnson, D. (1967). *Pragmatics of Human Communication: A Study of Interactional Patterns, Pathologies, and Paradoxes*. New York: W. W. Norton.

Weniger, E. (1990). *Ausgewählte Schriften. Zur geisteswissenschaflichen Pädagogik* [*Selected Writings: For Humanist-scientific Education*]. Weinheim: Julius Beltz.

Wertheimer, R. (1972). *The Significance of Sense: Meaning, Modality and Morality*. Ithaca, NY: Cornell University Press.

Winther, R. G. (2015). The structure of scientific theories. In E. Zalta (Ed), *Stanford Encyclopedia of Philosophy*. https://plato.stanford.edu/entries/structure-scientific-theories/ Retrieved October 16, 2018.

Index

Made in the USA
Las Vegas, NV
29 October 2024

20d3eb8e-91c0-429f-9f54-63db26c36479R01